Cyprus
a country study

Federal Research Division
Library of Congress
Edited by
Eric Solsten
Research Completed
January 1991

On the cover: Cypriot vase from seventh century B.C.

Fourth Edition, First Printing, 1993.

Library of Congress Cataloging-in-Publication Data

Cyprus : a country study / Federal Research Division, Library of
Congress ; edited by Eric Solsten. — 4th ed.
     p.   cm. — (Area handbook series, ISSN 1057–5294) (DA
pam ; 550–22)
     "Supersedes the 1980 edition of Cyprus: a country study,
edited by Frederica M. Bunge."—T.p. verso.
     "Research completed January 1991."
     Includes bibliographical references (pp. 265–279) and index.
     ISBN 0-8444-0752-6
     1. Cyprus.   I. Solsten, Eric, 1943-   . II. Library of Congress.
Federal Research Division. III. Series. IV. Series: DA pam ;
550–22.
DS54.A3C955   1993   92–36090
956.45—dc20   CIP

Headquarters, Department of the Army
DA Pam 550-22

For sale by the Superintendent of Documents, U.S. Government Printing Office
Washington, D.C. 20402

Foreword

This volume is one in a continuing series of books prepared by the Federal Research Division of the Library of Congress under the Country Studies/Area Handbook Program sponsored by the Department of Army. The last page of this book lists the other published studies.

Most books in the series deal with a particular foreign country, describing and analyzing its political, economic, social, and national security systems and institutions, and examining the interrelationships of those systems and the ways they are shaped by cultural factors. Each study is written by a multidisciplinary team of social scientists. The authors seek to provide a basic understanding of the observed society, striving for a dynamic rather than a static portrayal. Particular attention is devoted to the people who make up the society, their origins, dominant beliefs and values, their common interests and the issues on which they are divided, the nature and extent of their involvement with national institutions, and their attitudes toward each other and toward their social system and political order.

The books represent the analysis of the authors and should not be construed as an expression of an official United States government position, policy, or decision. The authors have sought to adhere to accepted standards of scholarly objectivity. Corrections, additions, and suggestions for changes from readers will be welcomed for use in future editions.

Louis R. Mortimer
Chief
Federal Research Division
Library of Congress
Washington, D.C. 20540

Acknowledgments

The authors wish to acknowledge the contributions of the writers of the 1980 edition of *Cyprus: A Country Study,* edited by Frederica M. Bunge. Portions of their work were incorporated into this volume.

The authors are grateful to individuals in various United States government agencies and international, diplomatic, and private institutions who gave of their time, research materials, expertise, and photographs in the production of this book. Special thanks are owed to the Embassy of Cyprus and the Turkish Cypriot Office, both in Washington, D.C. Thanks are also due to Ralph K. Benesch, who oversees the area handbook program for the Department of the Army. The authors also wish to thank members of the Federal Research Division staff who contributed directly to the preparation of the manuscript. These people include Sandra W. Meditz, who reviewed all drafts and served as liaison with the sponsoring agency; and Marilyn L. Majeska, who managed editing and book production.

Also involved in preparing the text were editorial assistants Barbara Edgerton and Izella Watson; Duncan M. Brown, who edited chapters; Cissie Coy, who performed the prepublication editorial review; and Joan C. Cook, who compiled the index. Linda Peterson and Malinda B. Neale of the Library of Congress Composing Unit prepared the camera-ready copy under the supervision of Peggy Pixley.

Graphics were prepared by David P. Cabitto, who also designed the volume's cover. Gail Oring designed the illustrations on each chapter's title page. David P. Cabitto, Harriet R. Blood, and the firm of Greenhorne and O'Mara prepared the maps from Tim Merrill's drafts.

Contents

List of Figures

Preface

This edition of *Cyprus: A Country Study* replaces the previous edition published in 1980. Like its predecessor, the present book attempts to treat in a compact and objective manner the dominant historical, social, economic, political, and national security aspects of contemporary Cyprus. Sources of information included scholarly books, journals, and monographs; official reports and documents of governments and international organizations; and foreign and domestic newspapers and periodicals. Researchers of Cypriot affairs face both feast and famine. There is much information about the origins and development of the island's complex intercommunal problem, some of it of a high quality. But readers curious about less vital political issues, or searching for economic or social data, often will find information sparse or of dubious validity.

Chapter bibliographies appear at the end of the book; brief comments on some of the more valuable sources for further reading appear at the conclusion of each chapter. Measurements are given in the metric system; a conversion table is provided to assist those who are unfamiliar with the metric system (see table 1, Appendix).

The contemporary place-names used in this study are those approved by the United States Board on Geographic Names, as set forth in the official gazetteer published in 1953. The Turkish name of towns or geographic formations located in the Turkish Cypriot-administered area is provided in parentheses after the place-name's first appearance in a chapter. A list of place-names so identified is provided (see table 2, Appendix). Greek Cypriot names are transliterated as they commonly appear in English-language publications. Because the United States government does not recognize the Turkish Cypriot state created in November 1983, its name, the "Turkish Republic of Northern Cyprus" ("TRNC"), is placed within quotation marks.

The body of the text reflects information available as of January 1991. Certain other portions of the text, however, have been updated. The introduction discusses significant events that have occurred since completion of research; the Country Profile includes updated information as available; and the Bibliography lists recently published sources thought to be particularly helpful to the reader.

Country Profile

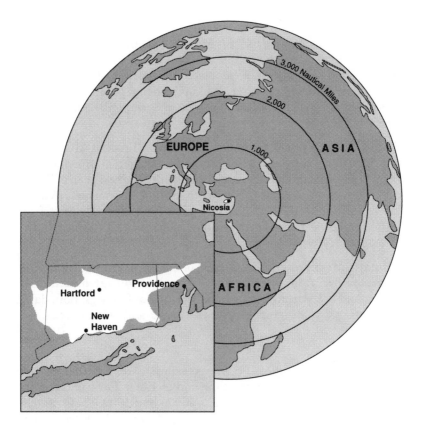

Country

Formal Name: Republic of Cyprus.

Short Form: Cyprus.

Term for Nationals: Cypriot(s).

Political Status: Former British colony. Achieved independence August 1960. Since mid-1974, northern 37 percent of island under separate Turkish Cypriot administration. "Turkish Republic of Northern Cyprus" ["TRNC"], proclaimed unilaterally

NOTE: The Country Profile contains updated information as available.

in November 1983, not recognized internationally except by Turkey as of early 1992.

Geography

Size: Third largest island in Mediterranean, after Sicily and Sardinia. 9,251 square kilometers, of which 1,733 square kilometers forested. Length, 225 kilometers; maximum breadth, 96.5 kilometers. Situated in eastern Mediterranean, about 386 kilometers north of Egypt, 97 kilometers west of Syria, and 64 kilometers south of Turkey.

Topography: Principal topographic features Troodos Mountains: dry limestone hills including Kyrenia Range; a broad inland plain—the Mesaoria; and narrow coastlands. Highest peak of Troodos Mountains, Mount Olympus, rises to 1,952 meters. Winter rivers starting in the Troodos flow rapidly in all directions. Two large salt lakes; many springs along the sides of Troodos Mountains and Kyrenia Range.

Climate: Mediterranean, with cycle of hot, dry summers from June to September, rainy winters from November to March, and brief spring and fall seasons between. Substantial differences, both daily and seasonally, in temperatures of coastal and inland areas.

Society

Population: Republic of Cyprus estimate of 575,000 in the government-controlled area at the end of 1990. Turkish Cypriots estimate their number at about 171,000 at mid-1990, about 40,000 higher than estimates by the Republic of Cyprus. Difference may stem in part from the tens of thousands of Turks who settled on the island after 1974. No de facto census since 1960.

Languages: Three principal languages: Greek, Turkish, and English. Knowledge and use of Greek and Turkish as second language, never common, declining further owing to de facto partition of the island; English the standard second language for Cypriots of both ethnic communities.

Religion: Virtually all Greek Cypriots Greek Orthodox Christians, adherents of the autocephalous Church of Cyprus, headed by a synod composed of bishops and an elected archbishop. The Armenian Apostolic Church—another of the eastern Christian religions that does not recognize the authority of the pope in Rome—has minor following. Also small numbers of members of churches in full communion with Rome—Maronites and Roman Catholics.

Turkish Cypriots are Muslims and form the second largest religious group.

Education and Literacy: Republic of Cyprus level of education high; literacy rate of 99 percent; illiteracy confined to the old. Free and compulsory education offered at preprimary, primary, and at secondary levels in academic and technical/vocational high schools. Higher education available at specialized schools and at one university opened in early 1990s. Many Greek Cypriots studied at foreign universities.

[Turkish Cypriots established parallel system and also had high literacy rate. Although several universities in operation by 1990, some Turkish Cypriots received higher education abroad.]

Health: Republic of Cyprus health care provided both through public heath service administered by Ministry of Health and private sector. Lower-income families entitled to free medical care and middle-income families to care at reduced rates. In 1990 six general hospitals and twenty-one rural health centers. Life expectancy 73.9 years for males and 77.8 years for females in 1990.

[Turkish Cypriots had extensive health care system administered by Ministry of Health and Social Welfare. In late 1980s, five state and four private hospitals and ten public health centers in addition to many clinics. Life expectancy 70 years for males and 72 years for females in 1979.]

Economy

Gross Domestic Product (GDP): US$5.3 billion in 1990; per capita gross national product (GNP) US$7,200 in 1988. GDP grew at an average annual rate of 8.4 percent between 1976 and 1986, with slight downturn in late 1980s.

[Turkish Cypriot GNP: US$425.4 million in 1989; per capita income US$2513. GDP grew at an average annual rate of 6.4 percent between 1977 and 1988; growth rate in 1989 was 7.1 percent.]

Agriculture: Made up 7.7 percent of GDP in 1988 and accounted for 15.8 percent of employment in 1987. Important irrigation projects and government subsidies guaranteed continued strength of sector. Crops accounted for most agricultural production; livestock about one-fifth; fishing and forestry negligible. Agricultural exports important; potatoes accounted for 10 percent of export earnings in some years; citrus and wine exports also noteworthy. Gradually evolving free-market trade with European Economic Community in 1990s could threaten branches of Cypriot agriculture.

[Turkish Cypriot agriculture accounted for about 9 percent of GDP in 1990 and provided employment for about 30 percent of work force. Citrus fruits most important export product. Shortage of year-round water an obstacle to sector's growth.]

Manufacturing: Accounted for about 16 percent of GDP and 20 percent of employment in late 1980s. Wide variety of light manufacturing, with clothing and foods the most important products. Clothing most important export. Dismantling of tariff protection and low Third World wages would challenge subsector in 1990s.

[Turkish Cypriot manufacturing accounted for about 12 percent of GDP and 11 percent of employment in 1989. Almost entirely light industry, with clothing and textiles most important products. Clothing accounted for 30 percent of exports in late 1980s.]

Services: Accounted for over half of GDP at end of 1980s. Tourism most important subsector, with over a million foreign visitors each year. Financial and business services also important.

[Turkish Cypriot service sector accounted for well over half of GDP and nearly half of employment at end of 1980s. Tourism most dynamic element, with about 300,000 foreign visitors by 1990.]

Balance of Payments: Persistent large negative trade balance. Large tourism earnings and positive capital account balances generally yielded positive balance of payments.

[Large negative Turkish Cypriot trade balance offset by earnings from tourism and import license fees.]

Exchange Rate: Average exchange rate in 1990, Cyprus pound (C£) 0.46 to US$1.

[Average exchange rate in 1990 for the currency used by Turkish Cypriots, the Turkish lira (TL), 2,608.6 to US$1.]

Transportation and Telecommunications

Railroads: None.

Roads: In 1989 roads in the government-controlled area amounted to 9,824 kilometers, of which 5,240 kilometers were asphalted or tarred and 4,584 kilometers were dirt or gravel. Some of the republic's roads were superhighways; more such roads under construction in the early 1990s.

[In the mid-1980s, the "TRNC" possessed 6,080 kilometers of roads, 800 kilometers of which unpaved. Major roads connected Nicosia with some other urban areas.]

Ports: Limassol, followed by Larnaca, important ports; Paphos and Vasilikos also received traffic.

[Famagusta (Gazimağusa) most important Turkish Cypriot port, equipped with modern facilities. Small ports at Kalecik and Kyrenia (Girne).]

Civil Airports: As of the early 1990s, Nicosia International Airport closed, a result of the Turkish invasion of 1974. Replaced by the international airports at Larnaca and Paphos. Also a number of smaller airports in the government-controlled area.

[Turkish Cypriots operated two international airports, Ercan and Geçitkale.]

Telecommunications: Excellent telecommunications facilities. More than 200,000 telephones, all with international direct dialing. Three submarine cables and three satellite ground stations connected to international systems guaranteed ready communication abroad. State television and radio network, in addition to private radio station.

[Turkish Cypriots had a modern telecommunications system, with connections abroad going via Turkey. All villages connected to fully automated exchange services. Government operated two television and radio stations.]

Government and Politics

Form of Government: Elected president for five-year term, appointed Council of Ministers, elected House of Representatives of fifty-six members for five-year term. Constitutional provision of Turkish Cypriot vice president, three members of Council of Ministers, and twenty-four members of House of Representatives in disuse for decades.

[Turkish Cypriots nonparticipants in governance of Republic of Cyprus. State resulting from unilateral declaration of independence in 1983, "Turkish Republic of Northern Cyprus," recognized only by Turkey. Elected president for five-year term, appointed Council of Ministers, elected Legislative Assembly of fifty members for five-year term.]

Legal System: Supreme Court final appellate court; district and assize courts with civil and criminal jurisdictions. Supreme Council of Judicature—composed of attorney general, members of the Supreme Court, and others—deals with appointment and promotion of judges.

[Turkish Cypriots employ a parallel system, with additional special courts for family matters.]

Politics: Resolving intercommunal crisis major political issue. Four political parties represented in House of Representatives accounted for over 95 percent of vote; several right- and left-wing splinter parties accounted for the remainder. Moderate conservative Democratic Rally (DISY), founded by Glafkos Clerides in 1976, won 35.8 percent of vote and twenty seats in 1991 parliamentary election. Democratic Party (DIKO), founded by Spyros Kyprianou in 1976, won 19.5 percent of vote and eleven parliamentary seats in 1991 election. Long a government party, DIKO was center right and close to Archbishop Makarios III. The social-democratic United Democratic Union of the Center (EDEK) founded in 1969 by Vassos Lyssarides, still its leader in 1992. EDEK won 10.9 percent of the vote and seven seats in 1991 elections. The Progressive Party of the Working People (AKEL) dates from 1941, but with historical ties to communist movement of 1920s. Although long doctrinaire and subservient to the former Soviet Union, AKEL moderate left wing in practice. In 1991, elections won 30.6 percent of vote and eighteen seats. Flexible on intercommunal problem, it often allied with DISY on this issue. EDEK and DIKO frequently advocated a more traditional approach to end the island's division.

[Three main Turkish Cypriot parties and a smaller right-wing party offered voters range of choices. For the 1990 Legislative Assembly election, unsuccessful electoral alliance against governing party, the conservative National Unity Party (UBP). The UBP won 55 percent of the vote and thirty-four seats in parliament. Founded in 1975 by Rauf Denktaş, this perennial governing party led in early 1990s by Prime Minister Derviş Eroğlu. Rightist New Dawn Party (YDP) formed in 1984 to represent Turkish settlers. Won two seats in 1990, which it subsequently occupied. Moderate Communal Liberation Party (TKP) often opposed UBP policies, urging greater contacts with Greek Cypriots. Founded in 1976 by Alpay Durduran, it was led in early 1990s by Mustafa Akinci. Some of the party boycotted the Legislative Assembly after the 1990 elections, refusing to take all of its five seats. Left-wing Republican Turkish Party (CTP) dated from 1970. Led by Özker Özgür, it won seven seats in 1990, but like TKP boycotted parliament. By-elections in 1991 to fill fourteen empty parliamentary seats resulted in UBP winning eleven of them. In 1992 ten UBP delegates left their party and founded the Democratic Party (DP).]

International Memberships: United Nations and its affiliated organizations; World Bank; International Monetary Fund; Commonwealth of Nations; Council of Europe; Conference on Security and Cooperation in Europe; associate membership in European Community.

[''Turkish Republic of Northern Cyprus'' an observer at the Organization of the Islamic Conference.]

National Security

Armed Forces: National Guard—13,000 active in 1989, 1,800 of whom officers and NCOs seconded from the Greek Army; 66,000 first-line and 30,000 second-line reserves as of 1990. Five active battalions: two mechanized; one armored; one artillery; one commando.

[The Turkish Cypriot Security Force consisted of an estimated 4,000 men; most officers seconded from the Turkish Army; 5,000 first-line and 10,000 second-line reserves as of 1989. The force organized into seven infantry battalions equipped with light weapons. The Turkish Cypriot Security Force, supported by an estimated 30,000 soldiers of the Turkish Army, organized into two infantry divisions and an armored brigade.]

Military Equipment: As of 1990, National Guard's weapons included 30 AMX B–2 tanks, 27 armored infantry fighting vehicles, over 100 armored personnel carriers, several hundred howitzers, mortars, recoilless rifles and other pieces of artillery, 20 SA–7 missiles, 6 Gazelle helicopters, and 3 coastal patrol boats.

[Turkish forces equipped with several hundred M–47 and M–48 tanks, 105 mm, 155mm, and 203mm guns and howitzers, and Bell Uh- 1D helicopters.]

Other Forces: United Nations Peace-keeping Force in Cyprus (UNICYP) consisted of about 2,000 men as of 1990, organized into four infantry battalions along national lines. As of 1990, British Army and Royal Air Force had about 4,000 troops stationed in two Sovereign Base Areas. Army organized into one infantry battalion and two infantry companies and one armed reconnaissance squadron; RAF unit consisted of one squadron with five Wessex helicopters. Army equipped with six Gazelle helicopters.

Military Budget: In 1990 about US$325 million.

[Planned Turkish Cypriot budget of US$3.9 million for 1990; most defense costs borne by Turkey.]

Police: Cyprus Police Force personnel amounted to 3,700 in 1989.

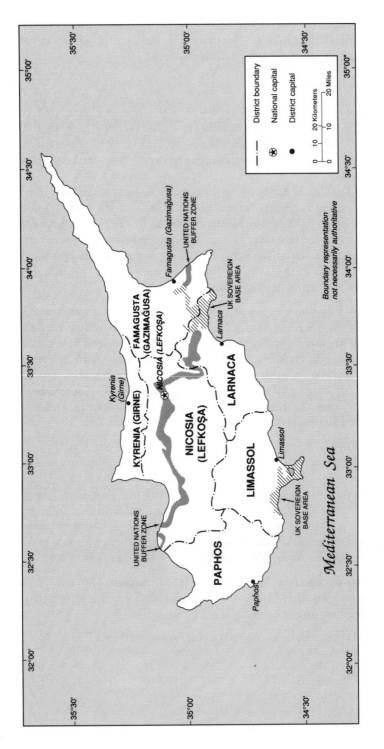

Figure 1. Administrative Divisions, 1991

Introduction

THE REPUBLIC OF CYPRUS came into being on August 16, 1960. The reluctant republic, as it has often been termed, was seen as a necessary compromise by Greek Cypriots and Turkish Cypriots, the two peoples who would live within it, and the three foreign powers who had been parties to its creation. Greek Cypriots preferred enosis, that is, the union of their island with the Greek motherland, rather than the creation of an independent state. Turkish Cypriots preferred that the island remain under British rule as it had been since 1878. If British governance were not possible, many Turkish Cypriots favored partition, or *taksim,* of the island and the union of the parts of the island in which they lived with Turkey—their ethnic motherland. Greece, for its part, preferred that enosis be achieved once again and that Cyprus, like a number of other islands, be united with the Hellenic motherland. Turkey's principal desire was that Cyprus not come under Greek control and be yet another island off the Turkish coast from which it could be attacked by its traditional enemy. Britain would have preferred a more measured cessation of its rule of the island, but the armed insurrection during the second half of the 1950s made the creation of an independent Cypriot republic seem a way out of a difficult situation. In addition, Britain's military needs could be met by arranging for bases on the island, rather than keeping the island of Cyprus itself as a base.

Negotiations between the Greek and Turkish foreign ministers in late 1958 and early 1959 resulted in three treaties that met to some degree the desires and needs of Greece, Turkey, and Britain. Representatives of the Greek Cypriot and Turkish Cypriot communities signed the treaties, but without enthusiasm. The three treaties—the Treaty of Guarantee, the Treaty of Alliance, and the Treaty of Establishment—went into effect on August 16, 1960.

The Treaty of Guarantee provides that Greece, Turkey, and Britain will ensure the independence and sovereignty of the Republic of Cyprus. It bans political or economic union of the republic with any foreign state and bans activities that would lead to such unions. Forty-eight of the basic articles of the constitution were incorporated into the Treaty of Guarantee, and the treaty's signatories were pledged to uphold the "state of affairs" established by the constitution. Article IV of the treaty states that if this "state of affairs" is endangered or altered, Greece, Turkey, and Britain are obliged to consult together and act to restore it. If joint consultations or actions are not possible, these states may act independently.

The Treaty of Alliance involves Cyprus, Greece, and Turkey. It establishes a tripartite headquarters on the island and permits the two latter states to deploy, respectively, 950 and 650 military personnel to Cyprus to protect the island and train its army. The Treaty of Establishment grants Britain sovereignty over a total of 256 square kilometers of territory on the island's southern coast for two military bases, Akrotiri and Dhekelia. Between the signing of these treaties in early 1959 and independence on August 16, 1960, a long and intricate constitution was worked out, with elaborate protections for the rights of the smaller Turkish Cypriot community.

Almost from the beginning, however, governing the island was difficult. Resentment within the Greek Cypriot community arose because Turkish Cypriots were given a larger share of government posts than the size of their population warranted. The disproportionate number of ministers and legislators assigned to Turkish Cypriots meant that their representatives could veto budgets or legislation and prevent essential government operations from being carried out. A Cypriot army, to be composed of both ethnic groups, was not formed because of disagreements about organizational matters. Nor was the crucial issue of municipal government settled to the satisfaction of Turkish Cypriots.

The complicated governmental system established by the constitution would have had difficulty functioning well even under normal conditions, but the withholding of support for the new republic on the part of many Cypriots made its smooth functioning even less likely. The acrimony, ill will, and suspicion that existed between the two ethnic communities made impossible the spirit of cooperation needed for the system to succeed. Not surprisingly, the early 1960s saw the resurgence of armed groups that had been active during the uprising against British rule. The Greek Cypriot National Organization of Cypriot Fighters (Ethniki Organosis Kyprion Agoniston—EOKA) rearmed, as did its Turkish Cypriot counterpart, the Turkish Resistance Organization (Türk Mukavemet Teşkilâtı—TMT). They were joined by growing contingents of Greek and Turkish soldiers from the mainland, whose numbers were much in excess of the limits set by the Treaty of Alliance. The frustrations of political impasse, coupled with the presence of armed bands, made for an explosive situation.

In late 1963, the republic's president, Archbishop Makarios III, proposed a series of constitutional changes that, if enacted, would have reduced the political rights and powers of the Turkish Cypriot community. These proposals worsened an already tense situation, and in December 1963 serious intercommunal violence broke out. In the next months, hundreds died. In March 1964, the first members of the United Nations Peace-keeping Force in Cyprus (UNFICYP) were deployed to Cyprus, but hostilities continued into August 1964. Only vigorous diplomacy from United States president Lyndon Johnson prevented a Turkish invasion in June 1964.

Several years of relative peace ensued, but the governing system established in 1960 no longer functioned. Turkish Cypriots had withdrawn from the republic's politics and were fashioning a governing system of their own. In addition, a good part of the Turkish Cypriot community lived in enclaves because many Turkish Cypriots had abandoned their homes out of fear of Greek Cypriot violence.

Intercommunal violence erupted in November 1967, when two dozen Turkish Cypriots were killed by Greek Cypriot forces under the command of Colonel George Grivas, the leader of the insurgency against the British in the 1950s. The threat of a Turkish invasion led the Greek government to remove Colonel Grivas and thousands of its troops from the island.

A coup d'état in Athens in 1967 established a military dictatorship that lasted until 1974. Elements of this regime pressed vigorously for enosis. Some members of the junta were even willing to cede parts of Cyprus to Turkey in exchange for a joining of the island with Greece. Greek pro-enosists, joined by like-minded rightist Greek Cypriot groups, put pressure on Archbishop Makarios. In 1970 there was an unsuccessful assassination attempt on the president. Makarios yielded to the junta on some points, once, for example, accepting the ''resignations'' of several members of his cabinet known to oppose the Athens government. He, however, would not compromise on the larger issue of the territorial integrity of the republic. Makarios, once a leading exponent of enosis, had come to place more value on the independence of Cyprus as a sovereign state than on union with Greece.

In July 1974, Greek Cypriot underground groups and the Greek Cypriot National Guard overthrew Archbishop Makarios and selected Nicos Sampson, a notorious EOKA terrorist, as his replacement. Makarios escaped with British help and appealed to world opinion at the United Nations (UN). Within a week of the rightist coup, Turkish forces invaded Cyprus. Turkish officials justified their country's actions by citing the terms of Article IV of the Treaty of Guarantee, noting the impossibility of joint action with Greece and the reluctance of Britain to use military force to restore the ''state of affairs'' established by the constitution of 1960. A brief truce permitted Turkish forces to consolidate their positions, and a quick second campaign in mid-August allowed them to occupy 37 percent of the republic.

The idea of enosis grew out of the successful Greek revolution of the 1820s. The dream of uniting all formerly Greek lands to the motherland spread during the nineteenth century. At first the movement was confined to the small educated segment of society, but as the general population became literate, the *megali idea* (grand idea in Greek), as it was often termed, found ever more adherents. The enosis movement had some notable successes. Crete was returned to Greece in the late nineteenth century, and after World War II a number of islands off the Turkish coast became Greek. The movement also suffered major reverses, most notably Kemal Atatürk's beating back the Greek Army when it invaded Turkey in the early 1920s.

By the mid-twentieth century, most Greek Cypriots desired that their island be united with Greece. The campaign for enosis was strengthened by the world-wide upsurge of anticolonialism after World War II. The enosis movement, which had become coupled with the goal of ending British rule of the island, erupted into armed rebellion in April 1955.

Cyprus's unification with Greece faced two significant obstacles: the island's proximity to Turkey and distance from Greece, and the presence of a substantial Turkish Cypriot minority who had lived on the island for hundreds of years. Either obstacle by itself could conceivably have been overcome, but together they posed in the end an insurmountable barrier to enosis.

The island's size and closeness to Turkey meant that the Turkish military would be opposed to its being occupied by Greek forces. In addition, the 800 kilometers that lay between Cyprus and the Greek mainland made it nearly impossible for Greek forces to seize and hold the island successfully.

The Turkish Cypriot community was the other significant barrier to enosis. Present on the island since it had been seized in 1571 from Venice, Turkish Cypriots were adamantly opposed to living as a minority under Greek rule. Few Turkish Cypriots had objected to British rule, and British policy had been to use them as a counterweight in colonial institutions in order to block Greek Cypriot efforts for enosis. The growing virulence of the enosist movement was noted with concern by the smaller community, and during the 1950s a Turkish Cypriot nationalism emerged that rivalled that of the enosists in intensity. Some Turkish Cypriots came to advocate *taksim,* that is, partition of the island, as a way to prevent their becoming a minority in a Greek state.

The gradually widening division of the two communities during the twentieth century was new to the island. For centuries the two groups had lived together in mixed villages or in separate villages close to villages of the other group. Intercommunal relations were harmonious if reserved; intermarriage was rare, but interethnic violence was even rarer. The two groups had even joined together at times to protest despotic rule from Constantinople.

During the twentieth century, however, the number of mixed villages declined, and the first instances of intercommunal violence occurred. Mounting pressure for enosis was the main cause of estrangement between the communities. Another cause was the increase in schooling and literacy. The two communities used textbooks from their respective motherlands, texts laden with chauvinistic comments emphasizing the rapacity, cruelty, and duplicity of the other community. Centuries of conflict between Greece and Turkey afforded an ample stock of atrocities to strengthen the aversion felt for the "traditional" enemy, be it Greek or Turkish. The commonly practiced British colonial policy of "divide and rule," of setting the two communities' interests against one another to maintain London's hold on Cyprus, also engendered intercommunal animosity. Some writers have charged that the British policy of emphasizing the role of the communities in governing encouraged the growth of ethnic as opposed to Cypriot nationalism. Some scholars have noted that the absence of Cypriot nationalism was perhaps the most fateful legacy of British rule and that it doomed the Republic of Cyprus from the outset. A sense of nationalism might well have muted ethnic differences and bound the island's inhabitants together.

As a result of these disparate factors, in the late 1950s intercommunal violence became common for the first time in Cypriot history. Violence of Cypriot against Cypriot flared even stronger in the 1960s and ended hopes that the Republic of Cyprus could work as planned in the elaborate and carefully crafted constitution of 1960.

At the end of his life, Archbishop Makarios stated in an interview with a Norwegian journalist that of all the mistakes he had made in his life, he most regretted the role he had played in the movement for enosis. Even before he became the first president of the Republic of Cyprus in 1960, Makarios was the dominant figure on Cyprus. His dominance extended from the early 1950s when he became head of the Greek Orthodox Church of Cyprus until his death in 1977. He had begun agitating for enosis as a young bishop. As archbishop he was the ethnarch or leader of the Greek Cypriot community, and in that role he continued working for union with Greece, even enduring exile for his role in the rebellion against British rule. He regarded the imposition of the Republic of Cyprus on the island by outside powers as a temporary setback on the way to enosis, and a setback that he could undo. In the late 1960s, however, Makarios stated publicly that he had come to regard enosis as still desirable but impossible to achieve, at least in the near future. Opposed in the 1969 presidential election by a die-hard enosist, Makarios won over 95 percent of the Greek Cypriot vote. The movement's extremists resorted to violence in the early 1970s, even mounting an assassination attempt against him. The movement to which Makarios had given so much had turned against him. In 1974 enosists and the Greek-led National Guard staged a coup d'état that caused Makarios to flee the country. The Turkish invasion a week later partitioned the country and resulted in one-third of the island's population being driven from their homes. The powerfully seductive ideal of enosis furthered by Makarios during most of his career had, in his words, "destroyed Cyprus" and made of him a tragic figure.

As of late 1992, Cyprus remained partitioned. The southern portion of the island was governed by the internationally recognized Republic of Cyprus and was home to the island's Greek Cypriot community. This community had made a remarkable recovery since 1974, despite the great material and psychological damage it had suffered from the Turkish invasion. Its economy had flourished and modernized and created a standard of living superior to that of some West European nations. This achievement was made possible by a versatile and skilled work force, a well-established entrepreneurial class, a sophisticated program of government planning, and a highly successful tourist industry that welcomed over a million tourists a year by the early 1990s. Foreign economic aid also contributed to the striking economic recovery, as did the collapse of Beirut as an international business center in the Middle East.

Prosperity led to social changes and permitted an expansion of the education system. Although Greek Cypriot society remained more traditional than most European societies, women worked more outside the home than their mothers did and young people displayed many of the characteristics of their West European counterparts. Education was widely available and esteemed. The Republic of Cyprus had one of highest rates of university graduates in the world. This was true despite the fact that, until the early 1990s, all Greek Cypriots wishing to study at the university level had to do so abroad because the Republic of Cyprus had no university.

Greek Cypriot politics matured after the invasion. During the first years of the republic's history, political parties more closely resembled groupings or factions around dominant individuals than organizations with political programs. After the events of 1974, new parties with a more clearly defined political ideology formed. Only the two left-wing parties pre-dated 1974: the Progressive Party of the Working People (Anorthotikon Komma Ergazomenou Laou—AKEL), a doctrinaire yet in practice a moderate and pragmatic communist party; and the United Democratic Union of Cyprus (Eniea Dimokratiki Enosis Kyprou—EDEK), usually referred to as the Socialist Party EDEK (Sosialistiko Komma EDEK), a left-wing party consisting mainly of urban white-collar employees and professionals. In 1976 two right-wing parties were formed: the Democratic Rally (Dimokratikos Synagermos—DISY), led by Glafkos Klerides; and the Democratic Party (Dimokratiko Komma—DIKO), headed by Spyros Kyprianou, who succeeded Archbishop Makarios as president. Kyprianou remained president until his defeat in 1988 by George Vassiliou, a businessman not tied to any party, who had the backing of AKEL and EDEK. In addition to these four main parties, several smaller groups were active as well.

Domestic politics mirrored those of most other prosperous democratic countries, with individual parties advocating policies in consonance with their political philosophy. The overriding issue in Cypriot politics, however, was the question of dealing with the de facto partition of the island. Here the parties' course was unusual. The right-wing DISY and the communist AKEL generally advocated a more flexible approach to negotiating with the Turkish Cypriots. These two parties favored making greater concessions than had former President Kyprianou, and they were frequently harsh in their criticism of what they regarded as his intransigence or insufficient sense of reality. DIKO and EDEK, for their part, were less willing to yield up long-held positions no matter how unacceptable they were to Turkish Cypriot negotiators. They often condemned what they saw as President Vassiliou's insufficient protection of the country's interests.

Greek Cypriot politics were stable. There were four main parties in the House of Representatives; the changing majorities in this body reflected the public's evolving opinion on main issues. Most analysts believed, for example, that the results of the May 1991 parliamentary elections indicated that overall the public supported President Vassiliou's willingness to break new ground in intercommunal negotiations. In the elections, DISY won twenty seats in the House of Representatives, one more than in the last parliamentary elections in 1985, and received 35.8 percent of the vote. AKEL increased its number of seats to eighteen, a gain of three, and got 30.6 percent of the vote. AKEL's win was all the more impressive because in May 1990 a faction of its membership, frustrated by a reform of AKEL that seemed too slow to them, had formed a new party, the Democratic Socialist Renewal Movement (Anorthotiko Dimokratiko Sosialistiko Kinima—ADISOK). The new party got 2.4 percent of vote, but won no seats. DIKO took a drubbing, losing eight of its nineteen seats and polling only 19.5 percent of the vote, compared with 27.6 percent in 1985. Although EDEK's share of the vote remained almost the same, falling slightly to 10.9 percent, it gained one parliamentary seat for a total of seven.

President Vassiliou's popularity would again be put the test by the presidential elections scheduled for February 1993 in which, as of late 1992, there were four candidates. Running once again as an independent, President Vassiliou had the support of AKEL. Glafkos Clerides, unsuccessful in several earlier attempts to win the republic's highest political office, had the support of DISY, the party he had founded and had led since the mid-1970s. DIKO and the Socialist Party EDEK formed an electoral front to back Paschalis Paschalides, a businessman active in Cypriot public affairs since the rebellion against British rule. The fourth candidate was an independent, Yiannakis Taliotis, a former deputy mayor of the western port of Paphos.

In the northern part of the island, 37 percent of Cyprus's territory was occupied by the "Turkish Republic of Northern Cyprus" ("TRNC"), unilaterally proclaimed in November 1983 by the Turkish Cypriots and recognized by no state other than Turkey. (Because this state is not recognized by the United States government, its name is within quotation marks.) Protected by an estimated 30,000 Turkish troops based on the island and bolstered by much Turkish aid, the Turkish Cypriot community had formed its own governing institutions, fashioned a functioning democracy with a free press, put in place an education system that extended from the pre-school to the university level, and laid the groundwork of an economy that, despite a Greek Cypriot economic blockade, had registered respectable growth rates and benefited from the visits of over 300,000 tourists a year.

As of late 1992, the Turkish Cypriot community was headed by the veteran politician Rauf Denktaş, a leading figure in Cypriot affairs since the mid-1950s. Denktaş was elected president of the "TRNC" in 1983 and again in 1990. Until mid-1992, he was supported by the National Unity Party (Ulusal Birlik Partisi—UBP), which had been the Turkish Cypriot governing party since its founding in 1975. After by-elections in 1991, the UBP controlled forty-four of the fifty seats in the National Assembly, the Turkish Cypriot legislative body.

Despite the UBP's virtual monopoly of parliamentary seats, there was a vigorous political opposition in the "TRNC." Two left-of-center parties, the Communal Liberation Party (Toplumcu Kurtuluş Partisi—TKP) and the Republican Turkish Party (Cumhuriyetçi Türk Partisi—CTP), along with the centrist New Dawn Party (Yeni Doğuş Partisi—YDP) and several smaller parties, forcefully condemned the policies, both foreign and domestic, pursued by the government and Denktaş. These parties generally recommended greater flexibility in negotiating with the Republic of Cyprus over issues relating to the island's partition. The TKP and CTP were also concerned about the role settlers from the Turkish mainland (estimated between 30,000 and 50,000) had in the "TRNC" and might have in a possibly negotiated new federal, bicommunal, and bizonal republic that could eventually replace the Cypriot state that had come into being in 1960.

The TKP, the CTP, and the YDP had formed an electoral alliance, the Democratic Struggle Party (Demokratik Mücadele Partisi—DMP), for the 1990 parliamentary elections. The party won sixteen seats. The TKP and CTP charged election irregularities and refused to occupy their fourteen seats. The 1991 by-election to fill these seats resulted in ten for the UBP, the remainder going to several smaller parties and independents. Many Turkish Cypriots were appalled at the results of this election, fearing that the election endangered the survival of democratic politics in their country. In the latter half of 1992, ten of the UPB's delegates withdrew from the party and formed a new group, the Democratic Party (Demokratik Parti—DP), headed by Hakkı Atun and having Serdar Denktaş, a son of Rauf Denktaş, as a member. Atun and his partners were generally in agreement with the UBP on the national issue, but charged the party's leadership with extensive financial and political corruption. At the end of 1992, the UBP still controlled thirty-four seats of the fifty-seat Legislative Assembly, but its political dominance and its leader, Derviş Eroğlu, were under vigorous attack from the DP, the TKP, the CTP, and some smaller parties.

This upheaval in Turkish Cypriot politics occurred against a backdrop of international controversy over the failure of intercommunal negotiations, sponsored by the UN in the summer and fall of 1992, to resolve the island's de facto partition. In the first half of 1992, there was more optimism than usual that these negotiations would yield a settlement of the island's division that was acceptable to both ethnic communities. Working from a "set of ideas" that incorporated many hard-won compromises from earlier negotiations, the new UN secretary general, Boutros Boutros-Ghali, thought that an agreement was finally within reach. Meetings in the summer and fall in New York between President Vassiliou and Turkish Cypriot leader Rauf Denktaş ended in early November, however, without success. Lack of agreement on the degree of sovereignty each component part of the new federal state was to possess, how much territory Turkish Cypriots would relinquish, and under what conditions Greek Cypriot refugees from areas remaining under Turkish Cypriot control were to return to their homes caused the failure. The secretary general issued a report that unequivocally blamed the Turkish Cypriot side for the failed negotiations. The Turkish Cypriots rejected his judgements as unfair. Talks were scheduled to resume in March 1993 after presidential elections in the Republic of Cyprus in February.

Intercommunal negotiations to arrange a new bicommunal, bizonal federal republic had been underway since 1975. In 1977 Makarios had agreed that the new Cypriot state would consist of the two communities, each with extensive local autonomy in discrete regions, but united via some degree of federation into a single state. In 1979 procedures that facilitated further dialogue were worked out by negotiators from the two communities. Aided by the good offices of the UN, negotiations continued at numerous venues through the 1980s and into the 1990s, but without significant accomplishments. In early 1985, an agreement was nearly achieved, but President Kyprianou backed off at the last moment. Although Kyprianou was censured in the House of Representatives for failure to reach an agreement, his party won the ensuing parliamentary elections. Voter discontent removed him from office in 1988. George Vassiliou, an independent, was elected president, probably because Greek Cypriots hoped he could bring a new openness and fresh initiatives to the negotiating process.

Over the years, Greek Cypriots had come to accept the concept of a bicommunal, bizonal, federal republic. This meant that some of Cyprus would remain under Turkish Cypriot control. Greek Cypriots would be allowed to return to properties they owned in this area before 1974, or be compensated for them, but attention would be paid to "certain practical difficulties." Also accepted was the principal Turkish Cypriot demand that the two communities be seen as political equals despite their differences in size. The Turkish Cypriot community was not to be seen as a minority, although it made up less than 20 percent of the island's population. It was to have exclusive management of its own communal affairs. Frequent demands that Turkish troops be withdrawn from the island before negotiations began had been abandoned because of hopes that intercommunal talks could have positive results.

As broad as these concessions were, Greek Cypriots remained adamant on a number of points. They demanded the eventual removal of Turkish troops from the island. Of even greater importance and more difficult to resolve was how to undo the losses suffered by Greek Cypriot refugees. An estimated 180,000 Greek Cypriots had fled or been driven from their homes and lost much property in what became the "TRNC," as compared with about 40,000 Turkish Cypriots who had moved out of areas under the control of the Republic of Cyprus. Greek Cypriot insistence on realizing the "three freedoms" of movement, settlement, and ownership throughout Cyprus for all Cypriots was intended to expunge the results of the Turkish invasion.

Greek Cypriot demands that the three freedoms eventually be realized throughout Cyprus challenged negotiators. The degree and quality of federation, or confederation, that Turkish Cypriots saw as a necessary underpinning for their political freedom also received much discussion.

Reconciling these varied aims would work only if both communities manifested patience, flexibility, and good faith. Given the great stakes involved and the power of pressure groups within communities (most notably refugee groups), these qualities were often lacking. Observers noted that both parties on occasion demonstrated a desire to win on all points rather than conceding some. A negotiating team having made some gains might suddenly renounce earlier concessions. Concessions granted often resulted in vitriolic attacks from within the negotiators' own community. Confidentiality of negotiations was rare; within hours full accounts of closed talks were available to the public.

As always in Cypriot history, the success of a new settlement would be affected by external forces. Turkey and Greece would almost certainly be involved in the final agreement and would sign treaties similar to the Treaties of Guarantee and Alliance. For both political and military reasons, neither Greek nor Turkish elites could ignore Cyprus because in recent decades events there had affected the larger states, sometimes in ways not to their liking. To reach his objectives, Archbishop Makarios, for example, frequently appealed to the Greek people over the heads of the Greek political leadership. Rauf Denktaş, for his part, had so much personal support among Turkey's political and military elites that only the strongest of Turkish governments could coerce him. In effect, he was to some degree independent of Turkey, the country that guaranteed his survival and that of the "TRNC." Conversely, Greek and

Turkish politicians often found the Cyprus issue a ready tool with which to attack their domestic opponents; hence there was a narrowing of the range of policy decisions relating to Cyprus available to the leaders of the two nations.

The end of the Cold War has lessened international concern with Cyprus. The disappearance of the Soviet Union meant, at least in the early 1990s, that Western Europe's security would no longer be threatened by a rupture of the North Atlantic Treaty Organization's southeastern flank in the event of a war between Greece and Turkey over Cyprus, as could have happened in 1964, 1967, and 1974. Cyprus's reduced geopolitical significance was reflected in the increasing reluctance of the UN to maintain forces on the island. In addition, instability elsewhere on the globe has taxed the resources of the organization and its member states. As part of a planned reduction of UNFICYP forces, the Danish contingent of several hundred personnel was scheduled to depart from Cyprus by mid-January 1993, leaving 1,500 UN soldiers to man the buffer zone that cuts across the island.

In the short run at least, the end of the Cold War would most likely benefit Turkey because its size and location made its goodwill and cooperation crucial to the Western powers, as was demonstrated in the Gulf Crisis of 1990-91. Given the continuing instability in the Middle East, in the Balkans, and in some of the former Soviet republics bordering these areas, Turkey's strategic importance would probably endure and make unlikely sustained and significant outside pressures to resolve the Cyprus question. Greece retained, however, its trump card: its ability to block Turkey's membership in the European Community if the Cyprus problem were not settled in a way it found satisfactory.

Despite the obstacles to a mutually acceptable settlement, hope remained that the creation of a new bicommunal, bizonal, federal state might someday be agreed on. In 1992 after the nearly twenty years of division, the younger members of each community had little or no first-hand knowledge of one another. Some observers believed this lack of familiarity would facilitate polite intercommunal relations along the formal lines established by a new settlement. Young Cypriots had an advantage their parents and grandparents had not had: they knew well how terrible the results would be of another failure to live together peacefully on their small island. Blessed with hindsight and aware of the immense gains a reasonable settlement would bring, perhaps young Cypriots would make their island whole again.

Eric Solsten   December 17, 1992

Chapter 1. Historical Setting

Artist's rendition of a sphinx, carved in ivory, from Salamis, eighth century B.C.

THE REPUBLIC OF CYPRUS was established in 1960, after the former colony gained independence from Britain. Since 1974, however, a de facto division of the island has existed, with the Greek Cypriot community controlling 63 percent of the territory, and the Turkish Cypriots, backed by Turkish Army units, 37 percent. The scene of anticolonial and intercommunal strife from the mid-1950s to the mid-1970s, Cyprus assumed an importance out of proportion to its size and population because of its strategic location and its impact on the national interests of other nations. The island's location in the eastern Mediterranean Sea has made it easily accessible from Europe, Asia, and Africa since the earliest days of ships. Its timber and mineral resources made it important as a source of trade goods in the ancient world, but attracted conquerors, pirates, and adventurers in addition to merchants and settlers. About the middle of the second millennium B.C., Cyprus was subjected to foreign domination for the first time, and from then until 1960, almost without interruption, outside powers controlled the island and its people.

Christianity was introduced early in the Christian Era, when Cyprus was under Roman rule, by the apostles Paul, Mark, and Barnabas. The martyrdom of Barnabas and the later discovery of his tomb are particularly important events in the history of the Church of Cyprus and were instrumental in the church's becoming autocephalous rather than remaining subordinate to the patriarchate of Antioch. After doctrinal controversies split Christianity between East and West, the church survived 400 years of attempts by Roman Catholic rulers to force recognition of the authority of the pope in Rome. After Cyprus's conquest by Ottoman Turks in the sixteenth century, the sees of the Orthodox bishops were reestablished, according to the Ottoman practice of governing through a *millet* (a community distinguished by religion) system. Provided a *millet* met the empire's demands, its leaders enjoyed a degree of autonomy. The head of the Greek Cypriot *millet,* the archbishop, was therefore both a religious and a secular leader, and it was entirely consistent with historical tradition that, in the anticolonial struggle of the mid-1950s, Archbishop Makarios III emerged as the leader of the Greek Cypriots and was subsequently elected president of the new republic.

After Greece had won its independence from the Ottoman Empire in 1821, the idea of enosis (union with Greece) took hold among

3

ethnic Greeks living in the Ionian and Aegean islands, Crete, Cyprus, and areas of Anatolia. Britain ceded the Ionian Islands to Greece in 1864, and after control of Cyprus passed from the Ottoman Empire to the British Empire in 1878, Greek Cypriots saw the ceding of the Ionian Islands as a precedent for enosis for themselves. Under British rule, agitation for enosis varied with time. After World War II, in the era of the breakup of colonial empires, the movement gained strength, and Greek Cypriots spurned British liberalization efforts. In the mid-1950s, when anticolonial guerrilla activities began, Turkish Cypriots—who until that time had only rarely expressed opposition to enosis—began to agitate for *taksim,* or partition, and Greece and Turkey began actively to support their respective ethnic groups on the island.

After four years of guerrilla revolt by Greek Cypriots against the British, a compromise settlement was reached in Zurich between the foreign ministers of Greece and Turkey and later in London among representatives of Greece, Turkey, Britain, and the Greek Cypriot and Turkish Cypriot communities. As a result of this settlement, Cyprus became an independent republic. Independence was marked on August 16, 1960. In separate communal elections, Makarios became president, and Fazıl Küçük, leader of the Turkish Cypriots, became vice president. In the early 1960s, political arguments over constitutional interpretation continually deadlocked the government. Greek Cypriots insisted on revision of the constitution and majority rule. Turkish Cypriots argued for strict constructionism, local autonomy, and the principle of minority veto. The result was stalemate. Intercommunal violence broke out in December 1963, and resulted in the segregation of the two ethnic communities and establishment of the United Nations Peacekeeping Force in Cyprus (UNFICYP). Even with United Nations (UN) troops as a buffer, however, intermittent conflict continued and brought Greece and Turkey to the brink of war in 1964 and 1967.

The irony of the divided Cyprus that has existed since 1974 is that the Greek government set the stage for Turkish intervention. The military junta that controlled Greece had come to view Archbishop Makarios as an obstacle to settlement of the Cyprus problem and establishment of better relations between Athens and Ankara. A successful coup was engineered in Cyprus in July 1974: Makarios was ousted, and a puppet president installed. Turkey, as one of the guarantor powers according to the agreements that led to Cypriot independence, sent troops into Cyprus to restore order. Britain, as another guarantor power, refused to participate. Meanwhile, in Greece the junta had collapsed, and a new government was being established. After a short cease-fire and a few days of hurried negotiations, the Turkish government reinforced its troops and ordered them to secure the northern part of the island.

Turkish forces seized 37 percent of the island and effected a de facto partition that was still in existence at the beginning of the 1990s. Turkish Cypriots declared the establishment of their own state in 1983, but as of 1990 only Turkey had recognized the "Turkish Republic of Northern Cyprus." Although more populous and considerably richer than the Turkish Cypriot state, and enjoying international recognition, the Republic of Cyprus had not been able to regain its lost territory. Increased military expenditures could not offset the considerable Turkish military presence on the island. Years of laborious negotiations at numerous venues had also achieved little toward ending the island's tragic division.

The Ancient Period

Human settlements existed on Cyprus as early as 5800 B.C., during the Neolithic Era or New Stone Age. The Neolithic Cypriots' origin is uncertain. Some evidence, including artifacts of Anatolian obsidian, suggests that the setters were related to the peoples of Asia Minor (present-day Turkey). The discovery of copper on the island around 3000 B.C. brought more frequent visits from traders. Trading ships were soon bringing settlers to exploit the mineral wealth.

During the long progression from stone to bronze, many Neolithic villages were abandoned, as people moved inland to settle on the great plain (the Mesaoria) and in the foothills of the mountains. Also during this era of transition, Cypriot pottery became distinctive in shape and design, and small figurines of fertility goddesses appeared for the first time. During the same period, Cypriots were influenced by traders from the great Minoan civilization that had developed on Crete, but, although trade was extensive, few settlers came to Cyprus. The Minoan traders developed a script for Cypriot commerce, but unfortunately extant examples still await decipherment. The cultural advances, thriving economy, and relative lack of defenses invited the attention of more powerful neighbors, and during the Late Bronze Age (about 1500 B.C.), the forces of the Egyptian pharaoh, Thutmose III, invaded the island.

After 1400 B.C., Mycenaean and Mycenaean-Achaean traders from the northeastern Peloponnesus began regular commercial visits to the island. Settlers from the same areas arrived in large numbers toward the end of the Trojan War (traditionally dated about 1184 B.C.). Even in modern times, a strip of the northern coast was known as the Achaean Coast in commemoration of those early

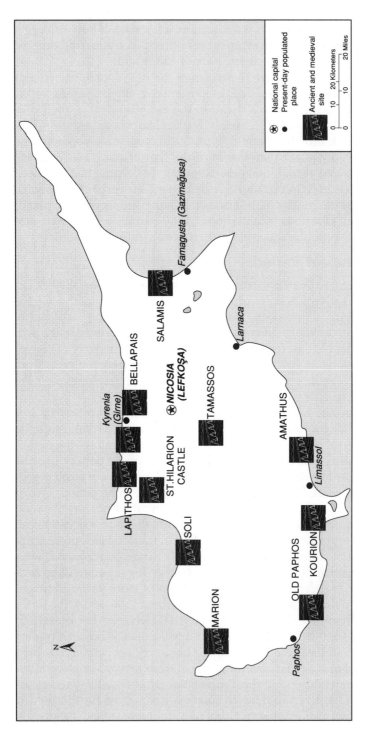

Figure 2. Ancient and Medieval Sites

settlers. The newcomers spread the use of their spoken language and introduced a script that greatly facilitated commerce. They also introduced the potter's wheel and began producing pottery that eventually was carried by traders to many mainland markets. By the end of the second millennium B.C., a distinctive culture had developed on Cyprus. The island's culture was tempered and enriched by its position as a crossroads for the commerce of three continents, but in essence it was distinctively Hellenic. It is to this 3,000 years of Hellenic tradition that the present-day Greek Cypriots refer when arguing either for enosis or for their own dominance in an independent state.

Later Greek poets and playwrights frequently mention the early influences of Cyprus. Aphrodite, Greek goddess of love and beauty, was said to have been born out of the sea foam on the island's west coast. The most important of many temples to Aphrodite was built at Paphos, where the love goddess was venerated for centuries, and even in modern times young women visited the ruins to make votive offerings and to pray for good marriages or fertility (see fig. 2). Aphrodite is mentioned by Homer in the *Iliad* and *Odyssey*, as is a Cypriot king, Kinyras, of Paphos.

The Late Bronze Age on Cyprus was characterized by a fusion of the indigenous culture and the cultures brought by settlers from the mainland areas. This fusion took place over a long period and was affected by shifting power relationships and major movements of peoples throughout the eastern Mediterranean area. Cyprus was affected particularly by the introduction of iron tools and weapons, signaling the end of the Bronze Age and the beginning of the Iron Age, near the end of the second millennium B.C. Iron did not displace bronze overnight, any more than one culture immediately displaced another (pockets of native Cypriot culture, for example, existed for several more centuries). The introduction of iron, however, heralded major economic changes, and the numbers of Greek settlers ensured the dominance of their culture.

An important eastern influence during the early part of the first millennium B.C. came from a Phoenician settlement. The principal Phoenician concentration was at Kition, the modern city of Larnaca, on the southeast coast. Three thousand years later some Turks and Turkish Cypriots would try to use such influences to prove that eastern cultures predated Greek influence on the island. On this basis, modern Cypriots were said to be descended from Phoenician Cypriot forebears. Greek Cypriots responded that, even though visits by Phoenician traders probably occurred as early as the third millennium B.C., colonists did not arrive until about

800 B.C. The Phoenicians settled in several areas and shared political control with the Greeks until the arrival of the Assyrians.

In 708 B.C. Cyprus encompassed seven independent kingdoms that were conquered by the Assyrian king, Sargon II. During the Assyrian dominance, about 100 years, Cypriot kings maintained considerable autonomy in domestic affairs and accumulated great wealth. The number of city-kingdoms increased to ten, one of which was Phoenician. The Cypriot kings were religious as well as secular leaders and generally commanded the city's defense forces. When Assyrian power and influence began to decline near the end of the seventh century B.C., Egypt filled the resulting vacuum in eastern Mediterranean affairs.

The Egyptian pharaohs had built a powerful fleet of warships that defeated the combined fleets of Phoenicia and Cyprus, setting the stage for Egypt's domination of the eastern Mediterranean. During the Egyptian ascendancy, the Cypriot kings were again allowed to continue in power after pledging themselves vassals of the pharaoh. The main impact of Egyptian domination was the reorientation of commerce, making Egypt the principal market for Cypriot minerals and timber.

When Egypt fell to the Persians in the late sixth century B.C., Cyprus was made part of a satrapy of King Darius. By the time of Persian domination, Salamis outshone the other city-kingdoms in wealth and splendor, and its kings were looked on as first among equals. Petty kings ruled at Amathus, Kition, Kyrenia, Lapithos, Kourion, Marion, Paphos, Soli, and Tamassos, but leadership in the fifth- and fourth-century struggles against the Persians stemmed from Salamis. The king of Salamis, Onesilos, is remembered as the hero who died leading the revolt against the Persians in 498 B.C.

The Cypriot kings continued to enjoy considerable autonomy while paying tribute to Persia, and were even allowed to strike their own coinage. They remained culturally oriented toward Greece, and when the Ionians revolted against the Persians, those of the Cypriot kings who were Greek also rebelled. The revolt was suppressed quickly, apparently without retaliation.

In 411 B.C. another Greek Cypriot, Evagoras, established himself as king of Salamis and worked for a united Cyprus that would be closely tied to the Greek states. By force and by guile, the new king brought other Cypriot kingdoms into line and led forces against Persia. He also allied the Cypriots with Athens, and the Athenians honored him with a statue in the agora. As the Salamisian king gained prominence and power in the eastern Mediterranean (even attacking Persian positions in Anatolia), the Persians tried to rid themselves of this threat and eventually defeated the Cypriots.

Through diplomacy Evagoras managed to retain the throne of Salamis, but the carefully nurtured union of the Cypriot kingdoms was dissolved. Although Cyprus remained divided at the end of his thirty-seven-year reign, Evagoras is revered as a Greek Cypriot of uncommon accomplishment. He brought artists and learned men to his court and fostered Greek studies. He was instrumental in having the ancient Cypriot syllabary replaced by the Greek alphabet. He issued coins of Greek design and in general furthered the integration of Greek and Cypriot culture.

Cypriot freedom from the Persians finally came in 333 B.C. when Alexander the Great decisively defeated Persia at the Battle of Issus. A short time later, the Cypriot kings were granted autonomy in return for helping Alexander at the siege of Tyre. The death of Alexander in 323 B.C. signaled the end of that short period of self-government. Alexander's heirs fought over Cyprus, a rich prize, for several years, but in 294 B.C. it was taken by Ptolemy, one of Alexander's generals, who had established himself as satrap (and eventual king) of Egypt. Under the rule of the Ptolemies, which lasted for two and one-half centuries, the city-kingdoms of Cyprus were abolished and a central administration established. The Ptolemaic period, marked by internal strife and intrigue, was ended by Roman annexation in 58 B.C..

At first Rome governed the island as part of the province of Cilicia, and for a time Cicero, the famous orator, was governor. Later, when administration was vested in the Roman Senate, the island was governed by a proconsul and divided into four districts: Amathus, Lapithos, Paphos, and Salamis. The government seat was at Paphos, and the center of commerce at Salamis.

Although the object of Roman occupation was to exploit the island's resources for the ultimate gain of the Roman treasury, the new rulers also brought a measure of prosperity, as their enforced peace allowed the mines, industries, and commercial establishments to increase their activities. The Romans soon began building new roads, harbors, and public buildings. Although Paphos supplanted Salamis as the capital, the latter retained its glory, remaining a center of culture and education as well as of commerce. An earthquake leveled much of Salamis in 15 B.C., but the Emperor Augustus bestowed his favor on the city and had it rebuilt in the grand Roman fashion of the time.

Salamis was shattered by earthquakes again in the fourth century. Again reconstructed, although on a smaller scale, the city never achieved its former magnificence. When its harbor silted up in medieval times, it was abandoned to the drifting coastal sand that eventually buried it. Twentieth-century archaeologists have

9

uncovered much of ancient Salamis, revealing glories from every epoch, from the Bronze Age to its final abandonment.

The single most important event during Roman rule was the introduction of Christianity during the reign of the Emperor Claudius. According to tradition, the apostle Paul landed at Salamis in A.D. 45, accompanied by Barnabas, also a convert to Christianity and an apostle. Barnabas's arrival was a homecoming; he was a native of Salamis, of Hellenized Jewish parentage. The two missionaries traveled across Cyprus preaching the new religion and making converts. At Paphos they converted the Roman proconsul, Sergius Paulus, who became the first Roman of noble birth to accept Christianity, thus making Cyprus the first area of the empire to be governed by a Christian.

In 285 the Emperor Diocletian undertook the reorganization of the Roman Empire, dividing its jurisdiction between its Latin-speaking and Greek-speaking halves. Diocletian's successor, Constantine, accepted conversion and became the first Christian Roman emperor. In 324 he established his imperial residence at Byzantium, on the shore of the Bosporus. Byzantium was renamed Constantinople and eventually became the capital of the Byzantine (Eastern) Empire.

The Medieval Period

From Constantine's establishment of the Byzantine Empire until the crusaders arrived more than 800 years later, the history of Cyprus is part of the history of that empire. Under Byzantine rule, the Greek orientation that had been prominent since antiquity developed the strong Hellenistic-Christian character that continues to be a hallmark of the Greek Cypriot community.

Byzantine Rule

By the time Constantine accepted Christianity for himself, the new religion was probably already predominant on Cyprus, owing mainly to the early missionary work of Paul, Barnabas, and Mark. Earthquakes in the early fourth century created havoc on the island, and drought seriously damaged the economy. However, the most significant event of the century was the struggle of the Church of Cyprus to maintain its independence from the patriarchs of Antioch. Three bishops represented Cyprus at the first Ecumenical Council of Nicaea in 325. At the second council (Sardica, 343), there were twelve Cypriot bishops, indicating a great increase in the number of communicants in the intervening years.

A major struggle concerning the status of the Church of Cyprus occurred at the third council, at Ephesus, in 431. The powerful

Kourion Theater, west of Limassol on Episkopi Bay, dates from the second century B.C. and was later enlarged by the Romans.
Courtesy Embassy of Cyprus, Washington

patriarch of Antioch argued forcefully that the small Cypriot church belonged in his jurisdiction, but the Cypriot bishops held their ground, and the council decided in their favor. Antioch still did not relinquish its claim, however, and it was not until after the discovery of the tomb of Saint Barnabas containing a copy of the Gospel of St. Matthew allegedly placed there by the apostle Mark that Emperor Zeno intervened and settled the issue. The Church of Cyprus was confirmed as being autocephalous, that is, ecclesiastically autonomous, enjoying the privilege of electing and consecrating its own bishops and archbishops and ranking equally with the churches of Antioch, Jerusalem, Alexandria, and Constantinople.

Except for the religious disputes, a period of calm prevailed on Cyprus during the early Byzantine centuries. The social structure was rigid and codified in law. Under a law issued by Constantine, tenant farmers were made serfs and forbidden to leave the land on which they were born. A later law allowed runaways to be returned in chains and punished. Administration was highly centralized, with government officials responsible directly to the emperor. The wealthy landlord and merchant classes retained their age-old privileges. The connection between church and state grew closer. The pervasive organization and authority of the church,

11

however, sometimes benefited the common man by interceding in cases of abuse of power by public officials or wealthy persons. During the fifth and sixth centuries, the level of prosperity permitted the construction of major cathedrals in several of the island's cities and towns. Salamis, renamed Constantia, again became the capital and witnessed another era of greatness. Archaeologists have uncovered an enormous fourth-century basilica at the site.

The peace that many generations of Cypriots enjoyed during the middle centuries of the first millennium A.D. was shattered by Arab attacks during the reign of Byzantine emperor Constans II (641–68). Sometime between 647 and 649, Muawiyah, the amir of Syria (later caliph of the Muslim empire), led a 1,700-ship invasion fleet against Cyprus. Constantia was sacked, and most of its population massacred. Muawiyah's destructive raid was only the first of a long series of attacks over the next 300 years. Many were merely quick piratical raids, but others were large-scale attacks in which many Cypriots were slaughtered and great wealth carried off or destroyed. No Byzantine churches survived the Muslim attacks. In 965, General Nicephorus Phocas (later emperor), leading the Byzantine imperial forces, drove the Arabs out of Crete and Cilicia and scored a series of victories on land and sea that led to the liberation of Cyprus after more than three centuries of constant turmoil.

The pitiable condition of the Cypriots during the three centuries of the Arab wars can only be imagined. Thousands upon thousands were killed, and other thousands were carried off into slavery. Death and destruction, rape and rampage were the heritage of unnumbered generations. Many cities and towns were destroyed, never to be rebuilt.

In the twelfth century, Isaac Comnenos, a Byzantine governor, set himself up in the capital as the emperor of Cyprus, and the authorities in Constantinople were either too weak or too busy to do anything about the usurper. When an imperial fleet was eventually sent against Cyprus, Comnenos was prepared and, in league with Sicilian pirates, defeated the fleet and retained control of the island. Comnenos, a tyrant and murderer, was unlamented when swept from power by the king of England, Richard I the Lion-Heart.

After wintering in Sicily, Richard set sail en route to the Holy Land as a leader of the Third Crusade. But in April 1191 his fleet was scattered by storms off Cyprus. Two ships were wrecked off the southern coast, and a third, carrying Richard's fiancée Berengaria of Navarre, sought shelter in Lemesos (Limassol). The wrecked ships were plundered and the survivors robbed by the forces of Comnenos, and the party of the bride-to-be was prevented from obtaining provisions and fresh water. When Richard arrived and learned of these affronts, he took time out from crusading, first to marry Berengaria in the chapel of the fortress at Lemesos and then to capture Cyprus and depose Comnenos. The capture of Cyprus, seemingly a footnote to history, actually proved beneficial to the crusaders whose foothold in the Holy Land had almost been eliminated by the Muslim commander Saladin. Cyprus became a strategically important logistic base and was used as such for the next 100 years.

When Richard defeated Comnenos, he extracted a huge bounty from the Cypriots. He then appointed officials to administer Cyprus, left a small garrison to enforce his rule, and sailed on to the Holy Land. A short time later, the Cypriots revolted against their new overlords. Although the revolt was quickly put down, Richard decided that the island was too much of a burden, so he sold it to the Knights Templars, a Frankish military order whose grand master was a member of Richard's coterie. Their oppressive, tyrannical rule made that of the avaricious Comnenos seem mild in comparison. The people again rebelled and suffered a massacre, but their persistence led the Templars, convinced that they would have no peace on Cyprus, to depart. Control of the island was turned over to Guy de Lusignan, the controversial ruler of the Latin (see Glossary) kingdom of Jerusalem, who evidently agreed to pay Richard the amount still owed him by the Templars. More than 800 years of Byzantine rule ended as the Frankish Lusignan dynasty established a Western feudal system on Cyprus.

The Lusignan and Venetian Eras

Guy de Lusignan lived only two years after assuming control in 1192, but the dynasty that he founded ruled Cyprus as an independent kingdom for more than three centuries. In religious matters, Lusignan was tolerant of the Cypriot adherence to Orthodoxy, but his brother Amaury, who succeeded him, showed no such liberality. The stage was hence set for a protracted struggle, which dominated the first half of the Lusignan period. At issue was the paramountcy of the Roman Catholic Church over the Orthodox church. Latin sees were established at Famagusta, Limassol, Nicosia, and Paphos; land was appropriated for churches; and authority to collect tithes was granted to the Latins. The harshness with which the Latin clergy attempted to gain control of the Church of Cyprus exacerbated the uneasy relationship between Franks and Cypriots. In 1260 Pope Alexander IV issued the *Bulla Cypria,* declaring the Latin church to be the official church of Cyprus, forcing the

Cypriot clergy to take oaths of obedience, and claiming the right to all tithes. The papal ordinance had no more effect than the constant persecution or the frequent visits of high-ranking papal legates sent to convert the islanders. The Cypriots remained loyal to their Orthodox heritage, and by the middle of the fourteenth century the Latin clergy had become less determined in its efforts to Latinize the population. The dominance of the Latin church officially continued for another 200 years, but Cypriots followed the lead of their own clergy and refused to accept the imposition of their Western rulers' form of Christianity.

In the thirteenth century, the kings of Cyprus, particularly Hugh III (reigned 1267-84), tried to assist the Latin Christians of the Syrian mainland in their final efforts to retain their holdings. The Mamluks of Egypt, however, proved to be the decisive defeating factor, capturing Christian fortresses one after another as they moved along the eastern Mediterranean littoral toward Acre. With the fall of Acre in 1291, the remaining Christian positions were given up, and the Frankish lords and merchants retreated to Cyprus, which became a staging area for spasmodic and unprofitable attacks on Syria.

For a century after the fall of Acre, Cyprus attained and held a position of influence and importance far beyond that which such a small kingdom would normally enjoy. As the only remaining eastern base of operations against the Muslims, the island prospered, and its kings gained importance among the ruling families of Europe. Under the rigid feudal system that prevailed, however, the new-found prosperity fell to the Franks; the native Cypriots, who were mostly serfs, benefited little or not at all. This was a period of great architectural achievement, as the Frankish lords directed the construction of beautiful castles and palaces, and the Latin clergy ordered the building of magnificent cathedrals and monasteries. The prosperity of the island attracted adventurers, merchants, and entrepreneurs. Two Italian trading conglomerates from the republics of Genoa and Venice gained particular importance in the kingdom's economy. Through intrigue, force, and financial power, the two Italian republics gained ever-increasing privileges, and at one point in the fourteenth century Famagusta was ceded to Genoa, which exercised suzerainty over the thriving port for ninety-one years.

The Lusignans' ability to control Cypriot cultural, economic, and political life declined rapidly in the first half of the fifteenth century. The situation was particularly desperate after the capture of King Janus I by the Mamluks in 1426. The captors demanded an enormous ransom, putting Cyprus again in the position of paying

*St. Chryssostomos Monastery near the Castle of Buffavento in the
Kyrenia Range was built in the eleventh century.
Kolossi Castle and its domed sugar storehouse, west of Limassol,
were built by Crusaders in the thirteenth century.
Courtesy Embassy of Cyprus, Washington*

15

tribute to Egypt. Janus was succeeded by his son John II, whose reign was marked by dissension and intrigue.

The most important event in the reign of John II was his marriage to Helena Palaeologos, a Greek who was a granddaughter of a Byzantine emperor and a follower of the Orthodox faith. Queen Helena, stronger in character than her husband, took over the running of the kingdom and brought Greek culture out of the oblivion in which it had languished for three centuries. Her actions in favor of the Orthodox faith and Greek culture naturally disturbed the Franks, who came to consider her a dangerous enemy, but she had become too powerful to attack. Greek Cypriots have always revered Queen Helena as a great heroine because of her boldness. John II and Helena died within a few months of each other in 1458 and were succeeded by their seventeen-year-old daughter Charlotte, but the succession was contested by John's illegitimate son. After six years of treachery and conniving (even with the Mamluks), James ousted his half sister and ascended the throne as James II. He is generally known as James the Bastard and was renowned for his political amorality.

After years of enduring rapacious forays by neighboring states, the weakened Kingdom of Cyprus was forced to turn to its ally Venice to save itself from being dismembered. In 1468, by virtue of a marriage between James II and Caterina Cornaro, daughter of a Venetian noble family, the royal house of Cyprus was formally linked with Venice. James died in 1473, and the island came under Venetian control. Caterina reigned as a figurehead until 1489, when Venice formally annexed Cyprus and ended the 300-year Lusignan epoch.

For ordinary Cypriots, the change from Lusignan to Venetian rule was hardly noticeable. The Venetians were as oppressive as their predecessors and aimed to profit as much as possible from their new acquisition. One difference was that the wealth that had been kept on the island by the Frankish rulers was taken to Venice—Cyprus was only one outpost of the far-flung Venetian commercial empire.

During the long Lusignan period and the eighty-two years of Venetian control, foreign rulers unquestionably changed the Cypriot way of life, but it was the Cypriot peasant with his Greek religion and Greek culture who withstood all adversity. Throughout the period, almost three centuries, there were two distinct societies, one foreign and one native. The first society consisted primarily of Frankish nobles with their retinues and Italian merchants with their families and followers. The second society, the majority of the population, consisted of Greek Cypriot serfs and laborers. Each of these societies had its own culture, language, and religion. Although a decided effort was made to supplant native customs and beliefs, the effort failed.

Ottoman Rule

Throughout the period of Venetian rule, Ottoman Turks raided and attacked at will. In 1489, the first year of Venetian control, Turks attacked the Karpas Peninsula, pillaging and taking captives to be sold into slavery. In 1539 the Turkish fleet attacked and destroyed Limassol. Fearing the ever-expanding Ottoman Empire, the Venetians had fortified Famagusta, Nicosia, and Kyrenia, but most other cities were easy prey.

In the summer of 1570, the Turks struck again, but this time with a full-scale invasion rather than a raid. About 60,000 troops, including cavalry and artillery, under the command of Lala Mustafa Pasha landed unopposed near Limassol on July 2, 1570, and laid siege to Nicosia. In an orgy of victory on the day that the city fell— September 9, 1570—20,000 Nicosians were put to death, and every church, public building, and palace was looted. Word of the massacre spread, and a few days later Mustafa took Kyrenia without having to fire a shot. Famagusta, however, resisted and put up a heroic defense that lasted from September 1570 until August 1571.

The fall of Famagusta marked the beginning of the Ottoman period in Cyprus. Two months later, the naval forces of the Holy League, composed mainly of Venetian, Spanish, and papal ships under the command of Don John of Austria, defeated the Turkish fleet at Lepanto in one of the decisive battles of world history. The victory over the Turks, however, came too late to help Cyprus, and the island remained under Ottoman rule for the next three centuries.

The former foreign elite was destroyed—its members killed, carried away as captives, or exiled. The Orthodox Christians, i.e., the Greek Cypriots who survived, had new foreign overlords. Some early decisions of these new rulers were welcome innovations. The feudal system was abolished, and the freed serfs were allowed to acquire land and work their own farms. Although the small landholdings of the peasants were heavily taxed, the ending of serfdom changed the lives of the island's ordinary people. Another action of far-reaching importance was the granting of land to Turkish soldiers and peasants who became the nucleus of the island's Turkish community.

Although their homeland had been dominated by foreigners for many centuries, it was only after the imposition of Ottoman rule that Orthodox Christians began to develop a really strong sense of cohesiveness. This change was prompted by the Ottoman practice of ruling the empire through *millets,* or religious communities. Rather than suppressing the empire's many religious communities, the Turks allowed them a degree of automony as long as they complied with the demands of the sultan. The vast size and the ethnic variety of the empire made such a policy imperative. The system of governing through *millets* reestablished the authority of the Church of Cyprus and made its head the Greek Cypriot leader, or ethnarch. It became the responsibility of the ethnarch to administer the territories where his flock lived and to collect taxes. The religious convictions and functions of the ethnarch were of no concern to the empire as long as its needs were met.

In 1575 the Turks granted permission for the return of the archbishop and the three bishops of the Church of Cyprus to their respective sees. They also abolished the feudal system, for they saw it as an extraneous power structure, unnecessary and dangerous. The autocephalous Church of Cyprus could function in its place for the political and fiscal administration of the island's Christian inhabitants. Its structured hierarchy put even remote villages within easy reach of the central authority. Both parties benefited. Greek Cypriots gained a measure of autonomy, and the empire received revenues without the bother of administration.

Ottoman rule of Cyprus was at times indifferent, at times oppressive, depending on the temperaments of the sultans and local officials. The island fell into economic decline both because of the empire's commercial ineptitude and because the Atlantic Ocean had displaced the Mediterranean Sea as the most important avenue of commerce. Natural disasters such as earthquakes, infestations of locusts, and famines also caused economic hardship and contributed to the general condition of decay and decline.

Reaction to Turkish misrule caused uprisings, but Greek Cypriots were not strong enough to prevail. Occasional Turkish Cypriot uprisings, sometimes with their Christian neighbors, against confiscatory taxes also failed. During the Greek War of Independence in 1821, the Ottoman authorities feared that Greek Cypriots would rebel again. Archbishop Kyprianos, a powerful leader who worked to improve the education of Greek Cypriot children, was accused of plotting against the government. Kyprianos, his bishops, and hundreds of priests and important laymen were arrested and summarily hanged or decapitated on July 9, 1821. After a few years, the archbishops were able to regain authority in religious matters, but as secular leaders they were unable to regain any substantial power until after World War II.

The military power of the Ottomans declined after the sixteenth century, and hereditary rulers often were inept. Authority gradually shifted to the office of the grand vizier, the sultan's chief minister. During the seventeenth century, the grand viziers acquired an official residence in the compound that housed government ministries in Constantinople. The compound was known to the Turks as Babiali (High Gate or Sublime Porte). By the nineteenth century, the grand viziers were so powerful that the term Porte became a synonym for the Ottoman government. Efforts by the Porte to reform the administration of the empire were continual during the nineteenth century; similar efforts by local authorities on Cyprus failed, as did those of the Porte. Various Cypriot movements arose in the 1820s and the 1830s and worked to gain greater self-government, but because the imperial treasury took most of the island's wealth and because local officials were often corrupt, reform efforts failed. Cypriots had little recourse through the courts because Christian testimony was rarely accepted.

The Ottoman Turks became the enemy in the eyes of the Greek Cypriots, and this enmity served as a focal point for uniting the major ethnic group on the island under the banner of Greek identity. Centuries of neglect by the Turks, the unrelenting poverty of most of the people, and the ever-present tax collectors fueled Greek nationalism. The Church of Cyprus stood out as the most significant Greek institution and the leading exponent of Greek nationalism.

During the period of Ottoman domination, Cyprus had been a backwater of the empire, but in the nineteenth century it again drew the attention of West European powers. By the 1850s, the decaying Ottoman Empire was known as ''the sick man of Europe,'' and various nations sought to profit at its expense. Cyprus itself could not fight for its own freedom, but the centuries of Frankish and Turkish domination had not destroyed the ties of language, culture, and religion that bound the Greek Cypriots to other Greeks. By the middle of the nineteenth century, enosis, the idea of uniting all Greek lands with the newly independent Greek mainland, was firmly rooted among educated Greek Cypriots. By the time the British took over Cyprus in 1878, Greek Cypriot nationalism had already crystalized.

British Rule

The sultan ceded the administration of Cyprus to Britain in exchange for guarantees that Britain would use the island as a base to protect the Ottoman Empire against possible Russian aggression.

The British had been offered Cyprus three times (in 1833, 1841, and 1845) before accepting it in 1878.

In the mid-1870s, Britain and other European powers were faced with preventing Russian expansion into areas controlled by a weakening Ottoman Empire. Russia was trying to fill the power vacuum by expanding the tsar's empire west and south toward the warm-water port of Constantinople and the Dardanelles. British administration of Cyprus was intended to forestall such an expansion. In June 1878, clandestine negotiations between Britain and the Porte culminated in the Cyprus Convention, by which "His Imperial Majesty the Sultan further consents to assign the island of Cyprus to be occupied and administered by England."

There was some opposition to the agreement in Britain, but not enough to prevent it, and colonial administration was established on the island. Greek Cypriot nationalism made its presence known to the new rulers, when, in a welcoming speech at Larnaca for the first British high commissioner, the bishop of Kition expressed the hope that the British would expedite the unification of Cyprus and Greece as they had previously done with the Ionian Islands. Thus, the British were confronted at the very beginning of their administration with the reality that enosis was vital to many Greek Cypriots.

The terms of the convention provided that the excess of the island's revenue over the expenditures for government should be paid as an "annual fixed payment" by Britain to the sultan. This proviso enabled the Porte to assert that it had not ceded or surrendered Cyprus to the British, but had merely temporarily turned over administration. Because of these terms, the action was sometimes described as a British leasing of the island. The "Cyprus Tribute" became a major source of discontent underlying later Cypriot unrest.

Negotiations eventually determined the sum of the annual fixed payment at exactly 92,799 pounds sterling, eleven shillings, and three pence. The governor of the island, Ronald Storrs, later wrote that the calculation of this sum was made with "all that scrupulous exactitude characteristic of faked accounts." The Cypriots found themselves not only paying the tribute, but also covering the expenses incurred by the British colonial administration, creating a steady drain on an already poor economy.

From the start, the matter of the Cyprus Tribute was severely exacerbated by the fact that the money was never paid to Turkey. Instead it was deposited in the Bank of England to pay off Turkish Crimean War loans (guaranteed by both Britain and France) on which Turkey had defaulted. This arrangement greatly disturbed the Turks as well as the Cypriots. The small sum left over went into a contingency fund, which further irritated the Porte. Public opinion on Cyprus held that the Cypriots were being forced to pay a debt with which they were in no way connected. Agitation against the tribute was incessant, and the annual payment became a symbol of British oppression.

There was also British opposition to the tribute. Undersecretary of State for the Colonies Winston Churchill visited Cyprus in 1907 and, in a report on his visit, declared, "We have no right, except by force majeure, to take a penny of the Cyprus Tribute to relieve us from our own obligations, however unfortunately contracted." Parliament soon voted a permanent annual grant-in-aid of 50,000 pounds sterling to Cyprus and reduced the tribute accordingly.

British Annexation

Britain annulled the Cyprus Convention and annexed the island when Turkey joined forces with Germany and its allies in 1914. In 1915 Britain offered the island to Greece as an inducement to enter the war on its side, but King Constantine preferred a policy of benign neutrality and declined the offer. Turkey recognized the British annexation through the 1923 Treaty of Lausanne. The treaty brought advantages to the new Turkish state that compensated it for its loss of the island. In 1925 Cyprus became a crown colony, and the top British administrator, the high commissioner, became governor. This change in status meant little to Greek Cypriots, and some of them continued to agitate for enosis.

The constitution of 1882, which was unchanged by the annexation of 1914, provided for a Legislative Council of twelve elected members and six appointees of the high commissioner. Three of the elected members were to be Muslims (Turkish Cypriots) and the remaining nine non-Muslims. This distribution was devised on the basis of a British interpretation of the census taken in 1881. These arrangements favored the Muslims. In practice, the three Muslim members usually voted with the six appointees, bringing about a nine to nine stalemate that could be broken by the vote of the high commissioner. Because Turkish Cypriots were generally supported by the high commissioners, the desires of the Greek Cypriot majority were thwarted. When Cyprus became a crown colony after 1925, constitutional modifications enlarged the Legislative Council to twenty-four, but the same balance and resulting stalemate prevailed.

There also remained much discontent with the Cyprus Tribute. In 1927 Britain had raised the annual grant-in-aid to cover the entire amount, but on the condition that Cyprus pay the crown an annual sum of 10,000 pounds sterling toward "imperial defense."

Cypriots, however, were not placated. They pressed two further claims for sums they considered were owed to them: the unexpended surplus of the debt charge that had been held back and invested in government securities since 1878 and all of the debt charge payments since 1914, which, after annexation, the Cypriots considered illegal.

The British government rejected those pleas and made a proposal to raise Cypriot taxes to meet deficits brought on by economic conditions on the island and throughout the world at the beginning of the 1930s. These proposals aroused dismay and discontent on Cyprus and resulted in mass protests and mob violence in October 1931. A riot resulted in the death of six civilians, injuries and wounds to scores of others, and the burning of the British Government House in Nicosia. Before it was quelled, incidents had occurred in a third of the island's 598 villages. In ensuing court cases, some 2,000 persons were convicted of crimes in connection with the violence.

Britain reacted by imposing harsh restrictions. Military reinforcements were dispatched to the island, the constitution suspended, press censorship instituted, and political parties proscribed. Two bishops and eight other prominent citizens directly implicated in the riot were exiled. In effect, the governor became a dictator, empowered to rule by decree. Municipal elections were suspended, and until 1943 all municipal officials were appointed by the government. The governor was to be assisted by an Executive Council, and two years later an Advisory Council was established; both councils consisted only of appointees and were restricted to advising on domestic matters only.

The harsh measures adopted by the British on Cyprus seemed particularly incongruous in view of the relaxation of strictures in Egypt and India at the same time. But the harsh measures continued; the teaching of Greek and Turkish history was curtailed, and the flying of Greek or Turkish flags or the public display of portraits of Greek or Turkish heroes was forbidden. The rules applied to both ethnic groups, although Turkish Cypriots had not contributed to the disorders of 1931.

Perhaps most objectionable to the Greek Cypriots were British actions that Cypriots perceived as being against the church. After the bishops of Kition and Kyrenia had been exiled, only two of the church's four major offices were occupied, i.e., the archbishopric in Nicosia and the bishopric of Paphos. When Archbishop Cyril III died in 1933 leaving Bishop Leontios of Paphos as locum tenens, church officials wanted the exiled bishops returned for the election of a new archbishop. The colonial administration refused, stating that the votes could be sent from abroad; the church authorities objected, and the resulting stalemate kept the office vacant from 1933 until 1947. Meanwhile, in 1937, in an effort to counteract the leading role played by the clergy in the nationalist movement, the British enacted laws governing the internal affairs of the church. Probably most onerous was the provision subjecting the election of an archbishop to the governor's approval. The laws were repealed in 1946. In June 1947, Leontios was elected archbishop, ending the fourteen-year British embarrassment at being blamed for the vacant archbishopric.

Under the strict rules enforced on the island, Cypriots were not allowed to form nationalist groups; therefore, during the late 1930s, the center of enosis activism shifted to London. In 1937 the Committee for Cyprus Autonomy was formed with the avowed purpose of lobbying Parliament for some degree of home rule. But most members of Parliament and of the Colonial Office, as well as many colonial officials on the island, misread the situation just as they had sixty years earlier, when they assumed administration from the Ottoman Turks and were greeted with expressions of the Greek Cypriot desire for enosis. The British were still not able to understand the importance of that desire to the majority community.

Although there was growing opposition to British rule, colonial administration had brought some benefits to the island. Money had gone into modernization projects. The economy, stagnant under the Ottomans, had improved, and trade increased. Financial reforms eventually broke the hold money lenders had over many small farmers. An honest and efficient civil service was put in place. New schools were built for the education of Cypriot children. Whereas only one hospital had existed during the Ottoman era, several were built by the British. Locusts were eradicated, and after World War II malaria was eliminated. A new system of roads brought formerly isolated villages into easy reach of the island's main cities and towns. A reforestation program to cover the colony's denuded hills and mountains was begun. Still, there was much poverty, industry was almost nonexistent, most manufactures were imported from Britain, and Cypriots did not govern themselves.

World War II and Postwar Nationalism

Whatever their misgivings about British rule, Cypriots were staunch supporters of the Allied cause in World War II. This was particularly true after the invasion of Greece in 1940. Conscription was not imposed on the colony, but 6,000 Cypriot volunteers fought under British command during the Greek campaign. Before the war ended, more than 30,000 had served in the British forces.

As far as the island itself was concerned, it escaped the war except for limited air raids. As it had twenty-five years earlier, the island became important as a supply and training base and as a naval station. This time, however, its use as an air base made it particularly significant to the overall Allied cause. Patriotism and a common enemy did not entirely erase enosis in the minds of Greek Cypriots, and propagandists remained active during the entire war, particularly in London, where they hoped to gain friends and influence lawmakers. Hopes were sometimes raised by the British government during the period when Britain and Greece were practically alone in the field against the Axis. British foreign secretary Anthony Eden, for example, hinted that the Cyprus problem would be resolved when the war had been won. Churchill, then prime minister, also made some vague allusions to the postwar settlement of the problem. The wartime governor of the island stated without equivocation that enosis was not being considered, but it is probable that the Greek Cypriots heard only those voices that they wanted to hear.

During the war, Britain made no move to restore the constitution that it had revoked in 1931, to provide a new one, or to guarantee any civil liberties. After October 1941, however, political meetings were condoned, and permission was granted by the governor for the formation of political parties. Without delay Cypriot communists founded the Progressive Party of the Working People (Anorthotikon Komma Ergazomenou Laou—AKEL) as the successor to an earlier communist party that had been established in the 1920s and proscribed during the 1930s. Because of Western wartime alliances with the Soviet Union, the communist label in 1941 was not the anathema that it later became; nevertheless, some Orthodox clerics and middle-class merchants were alarmed at the appearance of the new party. At the time, a loose federation of nationalists backed by the church and working for enosis and the Panagrarian Union of Cyprus (Panagrotiki Enosis Kyprou—PEK), the nationalist peasant association, opposed AKEL.

In the municipal elections of 1943, the first since the British crackdown of 1931, AKEL gained control of the important cities of Famagusta and Limassol. After its success at the polls, AKEL supported strikes, protested the absence of a popularly elected legislature, and continually stressed Cypriot grievances incurred under the rigid regime of the post-1931 period. Both communists and conservative groups advocated enosis, but for AKEL such advocacy was an expediency aimed at broadening its appeal. On other matters, communists and conservatives often clashed, sometimes violently. In January 1946, eighteen members of the communist-oriented Pan-Cyprian Federation of Labor (Pankypria Ergatiki Omospondia—PEO) were convicted of sedition by a colonial court and sentenced to varying prison terms. Later that year, a coalition of AKEL and PEO was victorious in the municipal elections, adding Nicosia to the list of cities having communist mayors.

In late 1946, the British government announced plans to liberalize the colonial administration of Cyprus and to invite Cypriots to form a Consultative Assembly for the purpose of discussing a new constitution. Demonstrating their good will and conciliatory attitude, the British also allowed the return of the 1931 exiles, repealed the 1937 religious laws, and pardoned the leftists who had been convicted of sedition in 1946. Instead of rejoicing, as expected by the British, the Greek Cypriot hierarchy reacted angrily because there had been no mention of enosis.

Response to the governor's invitations to the Consultative Assembly was mixed. The Church of Cyprus had expressed its disapproval, and twenty-two Greek Cypriots declined to appear, stating that enosis was their sole political aim. In October 1947, the fiery bishop of Kyrenia was elected archbishop to replace Leontios, who had died suddenly of natural causes.

As Makarios II, the new archbishop continued to oppose British policy in general and any policy in particular that did not actively promote enosis. Nevertheless, the assembly opened in November with eighteen members present. Of these, seven were Turkish Cypriots, two were Greek Cypriots without party affiliations, one was a Maronite from the small minority of non-Orthodox Christians on the island, and eight were AKEL-oriented Greek Cypriots—usually referred to as the "left wing." The eight left-wing members proposed discussion of full self-government, but the presiding officer, Chief Justice Edward Jackson, ruled that full self-government was outside the competence of the assembly. This ruling caused the left wing to join the other members in opposition to the British. The deadlocked assembly adjourned until May 1948, when the governor attempted to break the deadlock by advancing new constitutional proposals.

The new proposals included provisions for a Legislative Council with eighteen elected Greek Cypriot members and four elected Turkish Cypriot members in addition to the colonial secretary, the attorney general, the treasurer, and the senior commissioner as appointed members. Elections were to be based on universal adult male suffrage, with Greek Cypriots elected from a general list and

Turkish Cypriots from a separate communal register. Women's suffrage was an option to be extended if the assembly so decided. The presiding officer was to be a governor's appointee, who could not be a member of the council and would have no vote. Powers were reserved to the governor to pass or reject any bill regardless of the decision of the council, although in the event of a veto he was obliged to report his reasons to the British government. The governor's consent was also required before any bill having to do with defense, finance, external affairs, minorities, or amendments to the constitution could be introduced in the Legislative Council.

In the political climate of the immediate post-World War II era, the proposals of the British did not come close to fulfilling the expectations and aspirations of the Greek Cypriots. The idea of "enosis and only enosis" became even more attractive to the general population. Having observed this upsurge in popularity, AKEL felt obliged to shift from backing full self-government to supporting enosis, although the right-wing government in Greece was bitterly hostile to communism.

Meanwhile, the Church of Cyprus solidified its control over the Greek Cypriot community, intensified its activities for enosis and, after the rise of AKEL, opposed communism. Prominent among its leaders was Bishop Makarios, spiritual and secular leader of the Greek Cypriots. Born Michael Christodoulou Mouskos in 1913 to peasant parents in the village of Pano Panayia, about thirty kilometers northeast of Paphos in the foothills of the Troodos Mountains, the future archbishop and president entered Kykko Monastery as a novice at age thirteen. His pursuit of education over the next several years took him from the monastery to the Pancyprian Gymnasium in Nicosia, where he finished secondary school. From there he moved to Athens University as a deacon to study theology. After earning his degree in theology, he remained at the university during the World War II occupation, studying law. He was ordained as a priest in 1946, adopting the name Makarios. A few months after ordination, he received a scholarship from the World Council of Churches that took him to Boston University for advanced studies at the Theological College. Before he had completed his studies at Boston, he was elected in absentia bishop of Kition. He returned to Cyprus in the summer of 1948 to take up his new office.

Makarios was consecrated as bishop on June 13, 1948, in the Cathedral of Larnaca. He also became secretary of the Ethnarchy Council, a position that made him chief political adviser to the archbishop and swept him into the mainstream of the enosis struggle. His major accomplishment as bishop was planning the plebiscite that brought forth a 96 percent favorable vote for enosis in January 1950. In June Archbishop Makarios II died, and in October the bishop of Kition was elected to succeed him. He took office as Makarios III and, at age thirty-seven, was the youngest archbishop in the history of the Church of Cyprus. At his inauguration, he pledged not to rest until union with "Mother Greece" had been achieved.

The plebiscite results and a petition for enosis were taken to the Greek Chamber of Deputies, where Prime Minister Sophocles Venizelos urged the deputies to accept the petition and incorporate the plea for enosis into national policy. The plebiscite data were also presented to the United Nations (UN) Secretariat in New York, with a request that the principle of self-determination be applied to Cyprus. Makarios himself appeared before the UN in February 1951 to denounce British policy, but Britain held that the Cyprus problem was an internal issue not subject to UN consideration.

In Athens, enosis was a common topic of coffeehouse conversation, and Colonel George Grivas, a Cypriot native, was becoming known for his strong views on the subject. Grivas, born in 1898 in the village of Trikomo about fifty kilometers northeast of Nicosia, was the son of a grain merchant. After elementary education in the village school, he was sent to the Pancyprian Gymnasium. Reportedly a good student, Grivas went to Athens at age seventeen to enter the Greek Military Academy. As a young officer in the Greek army, he saw action in Anatolia during the Greco-Turkish War of 1920–22, in which he was wounded and cited for bravery. Grivas's unit almost reached Ankara during the Anatolian campaign, and he was sorely disappointed as the Greek campaign turned into disaster. However, he learned much about war, particularly guerrilla war. When Italy invaded Greece in 1940, he was a lieutenant colonel serving as chief of staff of an infantry division.

During the Nazi occupation of Greece, Grivas led a right-wing extremist organization known by the Greek letter X (Chi), which some authors describe as a band of terrorists and others call a resistance group. In his memoirs, Grivas said that it was later British propaganda that blackened the good name of X. At any rate, Grivas earned a reputation as a courageous military leader, even though his group was eventually banned. Later, after an unsuccessful try in Greek politics, he turned his attention to his original home, Cyprus, and to enosis. For the rest of his life, Grivas was devoted to that cause.

In anticipation of an armed struggle to achieve enosis, Grivas toured Cyprus in July 1951 to study the people and terrain (his first visit in twenty years). He discussed his ideas with Makarios

27

but was disappointed by the archbishop's reservations about the effectiveness of a guerrilla uprising. From the beginning, and throughout their relationship, Grivas resented having to share leadership with the archbishop. Makarios, concerned about Grivas's extremism from their very first meeting, preferred to continue diplomatic efforts, particularly efforts to get the UN involved. Entry of both Greece and Turkey into the North Atlantic Treaty Organization (NATO) made settlement of the Cyprus issue more important to the Western powers, but no new ideas were forthcoming. One year after the reconnaissance trip by Grivas, a secret meeting was arranged in Athens to bring together like-minded people in a Cyprus liberation committee. Makarios chaired the meeting. Grivas, who saw himself as the sole leader of the movement, once again was disappointed by the more moderate views of the archbishop. The feelings of uneasiness that arose between the soldier and the cleric never dissipated. In the end, the two became bitter enemies.

In July 1954, Henry L. Hopkinson, minister of state for the colonies, speaking in the British House of Commons, announced the withdrawal of the 1948 constitutional proposals for Cyprus in favor of an alternative plan. He went on to state, "There are certain territories in the Commonwealth which, owing to their peculiar circumstances, can never expect to be fully independent." Hopkinson's "never" and the absence of any mention of enosis doomed the alternative from the beginning.

In August 1954, Greece's UN representative formally requested that self-determination for the people of Cyprus be included on the agenda of the General Assembly's next session. That request was seconded by a petition to the secretary general from Archbishop Makarios. The British position continued to be that the subject was an internal issue. Turkey rejected the idea of the union of Cyprus and Greece; its UN representative maintained that "the people of Cyprus were no more Greek than the territory itself." The Turkish Cypriot community had consistently opposed the Greek Cypriot enosis movement, but had generally abstained from direct action because under British rule the Turkish minority status and identity were protected. The expressed attitude of the Cyprus Turkish Minority Association was that, in the event of British withdrawal, control of Cyprus should simply revert to Turkey. (This position ignored the fact that Turkey gave up all rights and claims in the 1923 Treaty of Lausanne.) Turkish Cypriot identification with Turkey had grown stronger, and after 1954 the Turkish government had become increasingly involved as the Cyprus problem became an international issue. On the island, an underground political organization known as Volkan (volcano) was

Turkish quarter of Nicosia
Courtesy Office of the "Turkish Republic of Northern Cyprus," Washington

formed. Volkan eventually established in 1957 the Turkish Resistance Organization (Türk Mukavemet Teşkilâtı—TMT), a guerrilla group that fought for Turkish Cypriot interests. In Greece, enosis was a dominant issue in politics, and pro-enosis demonstrations became commonplace in Athens. Cyprus was also bombarded with radio broadcasts from Greece pressing for enosis.

In the late summer and fall of 1954, the Cyprus problem intensified. On Cyprus the colonial government threatened advocates of enosis with up to five years' imprisonment and warned that antisedition laws would be strictly enforced. The archbishop defied the law, but no action was taken against him.

Anti-British sentiments were exacerbated when Britain concluded an agreement with Egypt for the evacuation of forces from the Suez Canal zone and began moving the headquarters of the British Middle East Land and Air Forces to Cyprus. Meanwhile, Grivas had returned to the island surreptitiously and made contact with Makarios. In December the UN General Assembly, after consideration of the Cyprus item placed on the agenda by Greece, adopted a New Zealand proposal that, using diplomatic jargon, announced the decision "not to consider the problem further for the time being, because it does not appear appropriate to adopt a resolution on the question of Cyprus." Reaction to the setback at the UN was immediate and violent. Greek Cypriot leaders called a general strike, and schoolchildren left their classrooms to demonstrate in the streets. These events were followed by the worst rioting since 1931. Makarios, who was at the UN in New York during the trouble, returned to Nicosia on January 10, 1955. At a meeting with Makarios, Grivas stated that their group needed a name and suggested that it be called the National Organization of Cypriot Fighters (Ethniki Organosis Kyprion Agoniston—EOKA). Makarios agreed, and, within a few months, EOKA was widely known.

The Emergency

On April 1, 1955, EOKA opened a campaign of violence against British rule in a well-coordinated series of attacks on police, military, and other government installations in Nicosia, Famagusta, Larnaca, and Limassol. In Nicosia the radio station was blown up. Grivas circulated his first proclamation as leader of EOKA under his code name Dighenis (a hero of Cypriot mythology), and the four-year revolutionary struggle was launched. According to captured EOKA documents, Cypriot communists were not to be accepted for membership and were enjoined to stand clear of the struggle if they were sincerely interested in enosis. The Turkish Cypriots were described as compatriots in the effort against an alien ruler; they too were simply asked to stand clear, to refrain from opposition, and to avoid any alliance with the British.

During a difficult summer of attacks and counterattacks, the Tripartite Conference of 1955 was convened in London in August at British invitation; representatives of the Greek and Turkish governments met with British authorities to discuss Cyprus—a radical departure from traditional British policy. Heretofore the British had considered colonial domestic matters internal affairs not to be discussed with foreigners. Greece accepted the invitation with some hesitation because no Cypriots had been invited, but reluctantly decided to attend. The Turks also accepted. The meeting broke up in September, having accomplished nothing. The Greeks were dissatisfied because Cypriot self-determination (a code word for enosis) was not offered; the Turks because it was not forbidden.

A bombing incident at the Turkish consulate in Salonika, Greece, a day before the meeting ended led to serious rioting in Istanbul and İzmir. It was later learned that the bombing had been carried out by a Turk, and that the riots had been prearranged by the government of Turkey to bring pressure on the Greeks and to show the world that Turks were keenly interested in Cyprus. The Turkish riots got so out of hand and destroyed so much Greek property in Turkey that Premier Adnan Menderes called out the army and declared martial law. Greece reacted by withdrawing its representatives from the NATO headquarters in Turkey, and relations between the two NATO partners became quite strained.

Shortly after the abortive tripartite meeting, Field Marshal John Harding, chief of the British imperial general staff, was named governor of Cyprus and arrived on the island to assume his post in October 1955. Harding immediately began talks with Makarios, describing a multimillion-pound development plan that would be adopted contingent on acceptance of limited self-government and postponement of self-determination. Harding wanted to leave no doubt that he was there to restore law and order, and Grivas wanted the new governor to realize that a get-tough policy was not going to have any great effect on EOKA. In November Harding declared a state of emergency, banning public assemblies, introducing the death penalty for carrying a weapon, and making strikes illegal. British troops were put on a wartime footing, and about 300 British policemen were brought to the island to replace EOKA sympathizers purged from the local force.

Further talks between Harding and Makarios in January 1956 began favorably but degenerated into a stalemate and broke up in March, with each side accusing the other of bad faith and intransigence. A few days later, Makarios was seized, charged with complicity in violence, and, along with the bishop of Kyrenia and two other priests, exiled to the Seychelles. This step removed the archbishop's influence on EOKA, leaving less moderate forces in control. The level of violence on Cyprus increased, a general strike was called, and Grivas had political leadership thrust on him by the archbishop's absence.

In July the British government appointed Lord Radcliffe, a jurist, to the post of commissioner for constitutional reform. Radcliffe's proposals, submitted in December, contained provisions for a balanced legislature, as in former schemes. But the proposals also included an option of self-determination at some indefinite time in the future and safeguards for the Turkish Cypriot minority. Turkey accepted the plan, Greece rejected it outright, and Makarios refused to consider it while in exile.

Makarios was allowed to leave the Seychelles in April, but could not return to Cyprus. In Athens he received a tremendous welcome. During the rest of the year, Grivas kept the situation boiling through various raids and attacks. Makarios also went once again to New York to argue his case before the UN. Harding retired to be replaced by Hugh Foot.

In early 1958, intercommunal strife became severe for the first time, and tension mounted between the governments of Greece and Turkey. Grivas tried to enforce an island-wide boycott of British goods and increased the level of sabotage attacks. In June 1958, British prime minister Harold Macmillan proposed a seven-year partnership scheme of separate communal legislative bodies and separate municipalities, which became known as the Macmillan Plan. Greece and Greek Cypriots rejected it, calling it tantamount to partition.

The Macmillan Plan, although not accepted, led to discussions of the Cyprus problem between representatives of Greece and Turkey, beginning in December 1958. Participants for the first time discussed the concept of an independent Cyprus, i.e., neither enosis nor partition. This new approach was stimulated by the understanding that Makarios was willing to discuss independence in exchange for abandonment of the Macmillan Plan. Subsequent talks between the foreign ministers of Greece and Turkey, in Zurich in February 1959, yielded a compromise agreement supporting independence. Thus were laid the foundations of the Republic of Cyprus. The scene then shifted to London, where the Greek and Turkish representatives were joined by representatives of the Greek Cypriots, the Turkish Cypriots, and the British. In London Makarios raised certain objections to the agreements, but, failing to get Greek backing, he accepted the position papers. The Zurich-London agreements, which were ratified by the official participants of the London Conference and became the basis for the Cyprus constitution of 1960, were the Treaty of Establishment, the Treaty of Guarantee, and the Treaty of Alliance.

The Republic of Cyprus

The general tone of the agreements was one of compromise. Greek Cypriots, especially members of organizations such as EOKA, expressed disappointment because enosis had not been attained. Turkish Cypriots, however, welcomed the agreements and set aside their earlier defensive demand for partition. According to the Treaty of Establishment, Britain retained sovereignty over about 256 square kilometers, which became the Dhekelia Sovereign Base Area, to the northwest of Larnaca, and the Akrotiri Sovereign Base Area, to the west of Limassol. Britain also retained certain access and communications routes.

According to constitutional arrangements, Cyprus was to become an independent republic with a Greek Cypriot president and a Turkish Cypriot vice president; a council of ministers with a ratio of seven Greeks to three Turks and a House of Representatives of fifty members, also with a seven-to-three ratio, were to be separately elected by communal balloting on a universal suffrage basis. The judicial system would be headed by a Supreme Constitutional Court, composed of one Greek Cypriot and one Turkish Cypriot and presided over by a contracted judge from a neutral country. In addition, separate Greek Cypriot and Turkish Cypriot Communal Chambers were provided to exercise control in matters of religion, culture, and education. The entire structure of government was strongly bicommunal in composition and function, and thus perpetuated the distinctiveness and separation of the two communities.

The aspirations of the Greek Cypriots, for which they had fought during the emergency, were not realized. Cyprus would not be united with Greece, as most of the population had hoped, but neither would it be partitioned, which many had feared. The unsatisfactory but acceptable alternative was independence. The Turkish Cypriot community, which had fared very well at the bargaining table, accepted the agreements willingly. The provisions of the constitution and the new republic's territorial integrity were ensured by Britain, Greece, and Turkey under the Treaty of Guarantee. The Treaty of Alliance gave Greece and Turkey the rights to station military forces on the island (950 and 650 men, respectively). These forces were to be separate from Cypriot national forces, numbering 2,000 men in a six-to-four ratio of Greek Cypriots to Turkish Cypriots (see Armed Forces, ch. 5).

Makarios, accepting independence as the pragmatic course, returned to Cyprus on March 1, 1959. Grivas, still an ardent supporter of enosis, agreed to return to Greece after having obtained amnesty for his followers. The state of emergency was declared over on December 4, 1959. Nine days later, Makarios was elected president, despite opposition from right-wing elements who claimed that he had betrayed enosis and from AKEL members who objected to the British bases and the stationing of Greek and Turkish troops on the island. On the same day, Fazıl Küçük, leader of the Turkish Cypriot community, was elected vice president without opposition.

The first general election for the House of Representatives took place on July 31, 1960. Of the thirty-five seats allotted to Greek Cypriots, thirty were won by supporters of Makarios and five by AKEL candidates. The fifteen Turkish Cypriot seats were all won by Küçük supporters. The constitution became effective August 16, 1960, on the day Cyprus formally shed its colonial status and became a republic. One month later, the new republic became a member of the UN, and in the spring of 1961 it was admitted to membership in the Commonwealth. In December 1961, Cyprus became a member of the International Monetary Fund (IMF—see Glossary) and the World Bank (see Glossary).

Independence did not ensure peace. Serious problems concerning the working and interpretation of the constitutional system appeared immediately. These problems reflected the sharp bicommunal division in the constitution and the historical and continuing distrust between the two communities. Turkish Cypriots, after eight decades of passivity under the British, had become a political entity. In the words of political scientist Nancy Crawshaw, "Turkish Cypriot nationalism, barely perceptible under British rule, came to equal that of the Greeks in fanaticism." One major point of contention concerned the composition of units under the six-to-four ratio decreed for the Cypriot army. Makarios wanted complete integration; Küçük favored segregated companies. On October 20, 1961, Küçük used his constitutional veto power as vice president to halt the development of an integrated force. Makarios then stated that the country could not afford an army anyway; planning and development of the national army ceased. Other problems developed in the application of the seven-to-three ratio of employment in government agencies.

Underground organizations of both communities revived during 1961 and 1962. EOKA and the TMT began training again, smuggling weapons in from Greece and Turkey, and working closely with national military contingents from Greece and Turkey that were stationed on the island in accordance with the Treaty of Alliance. Friction increased in 1962 regarding the status of municipalities. Each side accused the other of constitutional infractions, and the Supreme Constitutional Court was asked to rule on municipalities and taxes. The court's decisions were unsatisfactory to both sides, and an impasse was reached. Government under the terms of the 1960 constitution had come to appear impossible to many Cypriots.

Some Greek Cypriots believed the constitutional impasse could be ended through bold action. Accordingly, a plan of action—the Akritas Plan—was drawn up sometime in 1963 by the Greek Cypriot minister of interior, a close associate of Archbishop Makarios. The plan's course of action began with persuading the international community that concessions made to the Turkish Cypriots were too extensive and that the constitution had to be reformed if the island were to have a functioning government. World opinion had to be convinced that the smaller community had nothing to fear from constitutional amendments that gave Greek Cypriots political dominance. Another of the plan's goals was the revocation of the Treaty of Guarantee and the Treaty of Alliance. If these aims were realized, enosis would become possible. If Turkish Cypriots refused to accept these changes and attempted to block them by force, the plan foresaw their violent subjugation "in a day or two" before foreign powers could intervene.

On November 30, 1963, Makarios advanced a thirteen-point proposal designed, in his view, to eliminate impediments to the functioning of the government. The thirteen points involved constitutional revisions, including the abandonment of the veto power by both the president and the vice president, an idea that certainly would have been rejected by the Turkish Cypriots, who thought of the veto as a form of life insurance for the minority community. Küçük asked for time to consider the proposal and promised to respond to it by the end of December. Turkey rejected it on December 16, declaring the proposal an attempt to undermine the constitution.

Intercommunal Violence

The atmosphere on the island was tense. On December 21, 1963, serious violence erupted in Nicosia when a Greek Cypriot police patrol, ostensibly checking identification documents, stopped a Turkish Cypriot couple on the edge of the Turkish quarter. A hostile crowd gathered, shots were fired, and two Turkish Cypriots were killed. As the news spread, members of the underground organizations began firing and taking hostages. North of Nicosia, Turkish forces occupied a strong position at St. Hilarion Castle, dominating the road to Kyrenia on the northern coast. The road became a principal combat area as both sides fought to control it. Much intercommunal fighting occurred in Nicosia along the line separating the Greek and Turkish quarters of the city (known later as the Green Line). Turkish Cypriots were not concentrated in one area, but lived throughout the island, making their position precarious. Vice President Küçük and Turkish Cypriot ministers and members of the House of Representatives ceased participating in the government.

In January 1964, after an inconclusive conference in London among representatives of Britain, Greece, Turkey, and the two Cypriot communities, UN Secretary General U Thant, at the request of the Cyprus government, sent a special representative to the island. After receiving a firsthand report in February, the Security Council authorized a peace-keeping force under the direction of the secretary general. Advance units reached Cyprus in March, and by May the United Nations Peace-keeping Force in Cyprus (UNFICYP) totaled about 6,500 troops. Originally authorized for a three-month period, the force, at decreased strength, was still in position in the early 1990s.

Severe intercommunal fighting occurred in March and April 1964. When the worst of the fighting was over, Turkish Cypriots—sometimes of their own volition and at other times forced by the TMT—began moving from isolated rural areas and mixed villages into enclaves. Before long, a substantial portion of the island's Turkish Cypriot population was crowded into the Turkish quarter of Nicosia in tents and hastily constructed shacks. Slum conditions resulted from the serious overcrowding. All necessities as well as utilities had to be brought in through the Greek Cypriot lines. Many Turkish Cypriots who had not moved into Nicosia gave up their land and houses for the security of other enclaves.

In June 1964, the House of Representatives, functioning with only its Greek Cypriot members, passed a bill establishing the National Guard, in which all Cypriot males between the ages of eighteen and fifty-nine were liable to compulsory service. The right of Cypriots to bear arms was then limited to this National Guard and to the police. Invited by Makarios, General Grivas returned to Cyprus in June to assume command of the National Guard; the purpose of the new law was to curb the proliferation of Greek Cypriot irregular bands and bring them under control in an organization commanded by the prestigious Grivas. Turks and Turkish Cypriots meanwhile charged that large numbers of Greek regular troops were being clandestinely infiltrated into the island to lend professionalism to the National Guard. Turkey began military preparations for an invasion of the island. A brutally frank warning from United States president Lyndon B. Johnson to Prime Minister İsmet İnönü caused the Turks to call off the invasion. In August, however, Turkish jets attacked Greek Cypriot forces besieging Turkish Cypriot villages on the northwestern coast near Kokkina.

In July veteran United States diplomat Dean Acheson met with Greek and Turkish representatives in Geneva. From this meeting emerged what became known as the Acheson Plan, according to which Greek Cypriots would have enosis and Greece was to award the Aegean island of Kastelorrizon to Turkey and compensate Turkish Cypriots wishing to emigrate. Secure Turkish enclaves and a Turkish sovereign military base area were to be provided on Cyprus. Makarios rejected the plan because it called for what he saw as a modified form of partition.

Throughout 1964 and later, President Makarios and the Greek Cypriot leadership adopted the view that the establishment of UNFICYP by the UN Security Council had set aside the rights of intervention granted to the guarantor powers—Britain, Greece, and Turkey—by the Treaty of Guarantee. The Turkish leadership, on the other hand, contended that the Security Council action had reinforced the provisions of the treaty. These diametrically opposed views illustrated the basic Greek Cypriot and Turkish Cypriot positions; the former holding that the constitution and the other provisions of the treaties were flexible and subject to change under changing conditions, and the latter, that they were fixed agreements, not subject to change.

Grivas and the National Guard reacted to Turkish pressure by initiating patrols into the Turkish Cypriot enclaves. Patrols surrounded two villages, Ayios Theodhoros and Kophinou, about twenty-five kilometers southwest of Larnaca, and began sending in heavily armed patrols. Fighting broke out, and by the time the Guard withdrew, twenty-six Turkish Cypriots had been killed. Turkey issued an ultimatum and threatened to intervene in force to protect Turkish Cypriots. To back up their demands, the Turks massed troops on the Thracian border separating Greece and Turkey and began assembling an amphibious invasion force. The ultimatum's conditions included the expulsion of Grivas from Cyprus, removal of Greek troops from Cyprus, payment of indemnity for the casualties at Ayios Theodhoros and Kophinou, cessation of pressure on the Turkish Cypriot community, and the disbanding of the National Guard.

Grivas resigned as commander of the Greek Cypriot forces on November 20, 1967, and left the island, but the Turks did not reduce their readiness posture, and the dangerous situation of two NATO nations on the threshold of war with each other continued. President Johnson dispatched Cyrus R. Vance as his special envoy to Turkey, Greece, and Cyprus. Vance arrived in Ankara in late November and began ten days of negotiations that defused the situation. Greece agreed to withdraw its forces on Cyprus except for the contingent allowed by the 1960 treaties, provided that Turkey did the same and also dismounted its invasion force. Turkey agreed, and the crisis passed. During December 1967 and early January 1968, about 10,000 Greek troops were withdrawn. Makarios did not disband the National Guard, however, something he came to regret when it rebelled against him in 1974.

Political Developments after the Crisis of 1967

Seizing the opportune moment after the crisis had ended, Turkish Cypriot leaders, in late December 1967, announced the establishment of a "transitional administration" to govern their community's affairs "until such time as the provisions of the Constitution of 1960 have been fully implemented." The body's president was Fazıl Küçük, vice president of the republic; the body's vice president was Rauf Denktaş, president of the Turkish Cypriot Communal Chamber. Nineteen governing articles, called the Basic Principles, were announced, and the provisional administration organized itself along lines that were similar to a cabinet. The provisional administration also formed a legislative assembly composed of the Turkish Cypriot members-in-absentia of the republic's House of Representatives and the members of the Turkish Cypriot Communal Chamber. The provisional administration did not state that the Communal Chamber was being abolished. Nor did it seek recognition as a government. Such actions would have been contrary to the provisions of the constitution and the Zurich-London agreements, and the Turkish Cypriots as well as the Turks scrupulously avoided any such abrogation. The Greek Cypriots immediately concluded that the formation of governing bodies was in preparation for partition. U Thant was also critical of the new organizations.

President Makarios, seeking a fresh mandate from his constituency, announced in January 1968 that elections would be held during February. Küçük, determined to adhere to the constitution, then announced that elections for vice president would also be held. Elections, which the Greek Cypriot government considered invalid, were subsequently held in the Turkish Cypriot community; Küçük was returned to office unopposed. Two weeks later, Makarios received 220,911 votes (about 96 percent), and his opponent, Takis Evdokas, running on a straight enosis platform, received 8,577 votes. Even though there were 16,215 abstentions, Makarios's overwhelming victory was seen as a massive endorsement of his personal leadership and of an independent Cyprus. At his investiture, the president stated that the Cyprus problem could not be solved by force, but had to be worked out within the framework of the UN. He also said that he and his followers wanted to live peacefully in a unitary state where all citizens enjoyed equal rights. Some Cypriots opposed Makarios's conciliatory stance, and there would be an unsuccessful attempt to assassinate him in 1970.

In mid-1968 intercommunal talks under UN auspices began in Beirut. Glafkos Clerides, president of the House of Representatives, and Rauf Denktaş were involved in the first stages of these talks, which lasted until 1974. Although many points of agreement were arrived at, no lasting agreements were reached. Turkish Cypriot proposals emphasized the importance of the local government of each ethnic community at the expense of the central government,

Archbishop Makarios III, first president of the Republic of Cyprus
Courtesy Embassy of Cyprus, Washington

whereas the Greek Cypriot negotiating teams stressed the dominance of the central authorities over local administration.

In the parliamentary elections that took place on July 5, 1970, fifteen seats went to the Unified Democratic Party (Eniaion), nine to AKEL, seven to the Progressive Coalition, two to a socialist coalition, and two to the Independents. The enosis opposition did not capture any seats. Eniaion, led by Clerides and based on an urban constituency, was a moderate party of the right that generally supported Makarios. The Progressive Coalition had an ideological base almost the same as Eniaion's, but was based in the rural areas. The socialist group was led by Vassos Lyssarides, personal physician to Makarios; its two seats in the House of Representatives did not reflect its significant influence in Cypriot affairs and the personal power of its leader. The Independents were a left-wing noncommunist group similar to EDEK but lacking its dynamic leadership. The fifteen seats reserved for Turkish Cypriots went to followers of Denktaş.

In the early 1970s, Cyprus was in fact a partitioned country. Makarios was the president of the republic, but his authority did not extend into the Turkish enclaves. The House of Representatives sat as the legislature, but only the thirty-five Greek Cypriot seats were functioning as part of a central government. De facto, the partition sought for years by Turks and Turkish Cypriots existed, but intercommunal strife had not ended.

In the summer of 1971, tension built up between the two communities, and incidents became more numerous. Sometime in the late summer or early fall, Grivas (who had attacked Makarios as a traitor in an Athens newspaper) returned secretly to the island and began to rebuild his guerrilla organization, which became known as the National Organization of Cypriot Fighters (Ethniki Organosis Kyprion Agoniston B—EOKA B). Three new newspapers advocating enosis were also established at the same time. All of these activities were funded by the military junta that controlled Greece. The junta probably would have agreed to some form of partition similar to the Acheson Plan to settle the Cyprus question, but at the time the overthrow of Makarios was the primary objective, and the junta backed Grivas toward that end. From hiding, Grivas directed terrorist attacks and propaganda assaults that shook the Makarios government, but the president remained a powerful, popular leader.

In January 1972, a new crisis rekindled intercommunal tensions when an Athens newspaper reported that the Makarios government had received a shipment of Czechoslovakian arms. The guns were intended for Makarios's own elite guard; the Greek government, hoping to overthrow Makarios through Grivas, EOKA B, and the National Guard, objected to the import of the arms. The authorities in Ankara were more than willing to join Athens in such a protest, and both governments demanded that the Czechoslovakian munitions be turned over to UNFICYP. Makarios was eventually forced to comply.

Relations between Nicosia and Athens were at such a low ebb that the colonels of the Greek junta, recognizing that they had Makarios in a perilous position, issued an ultimatum for him to reform his government and rid it of ministers who had been critical of the junta. The colonels, however, had not reckoned with the phenomenal popularity of the archbishop, and once again mass demonstrations proved that Makarios had the people behind him. In the end, however, Makarios bowed to Greek pressure and reshuffled the cabinet.

Working against Makarios was the fact that most officers of the Cypriot National Guard were Greek regulars who supported the junta and its desire to remove him from office and achieve some degree of enosis. Grivas was also a threat to the archbishop. He remained powerful and to some extent was independent of the junta that had permitted his return to Cyprus. Whereas the Greek colonels were at times prepared to make a deal with Turkey about Cyprus, Grivas was ferociously opposed to any arrangement that did not lead to complete enosis.

In the spring of 1972, Makarios faced an attack from another quarter. The three bishops of the Church of Cyprus demanded that he resign as president because his temporal duties violated canon law. Moving astutely, Markarios foiled the three bishops and had them defrocked in the summer of 1973. Before choosing their replacements, he increased the number of bishoprics to five, thereby reducing the power of individual bishops.

Grivas and his one-track pursuit of enosis through terrorism had become an embarrassment to the Greek Cypriot government, as well as to the Greek government that had sponsored his return to the island. His fame and popularity in both countries, however, prevented his removal. That problem was solved on January 27, 1974, when the general died of a heart attack. Makarios granted his followers an amnesty, hoping that EOKA B would disappear after the death of its leader. Terrorism continued, however, and the 100,000 mourners who attended Grivas's funeral indicated the enduring popularity of his political aims.

The Greek Coup and the Turkish Invasion

A coup d'état in Athens in November 1973 had made Brigadier

General Dimitrios Ioannides leader of the junta. Rigidly anticommunist, Ioannides had served on Cyprus in the 1960s with the National Guard. His experiences convinced him that Makarios should be removed from office because of domestic leftist support and his visits to communist capitals. During the spring of 1974, Cypriot intelligence found evidence that EOKA B was planning a coup and was being supplied, controlled, and funded by the military government in Athens. EOKA B was banned, but its operations continued underground. Early in July, Makarios wrote to the president of Greece demanding that the remaining 650 Greek officers assigned to the National Guard be withdrawn. He also accused the junta of plotting against his life and against the government of Cyprus. Makarios sent his letter (which was released to the public) to the Greek president on July 2, 1974; the reply came thirteen days later, not in the form of a letter but in an order from Athens to the Cypriot National Guard to overthrow its commander in chief and take control of the island.

Makarios narrowly escaped death in the attack by the Greek-led National Guard. He fled the presidential palace and went to Paphos. A British helicopter took him to the Sovereign Base Area at Akrotiri, from where he went to London. Several days later, Makarios addressed a meeting of the UN Security Council, where he was accepted as the legal president of the Republic of Cyprus.

In the meantime, the notorious EOKA terrorist Nicos Sampson was declared provisional president of the new government. It was obvious to Ankara that Athens was behind the coup, and major elements of the Turkish armed forces went on alert. Turkey had made similar moves in 1964 and 1967, but had not invaded. At the same time, Turkish prime minister Bülent Ecevit flew to London to elicit British aid in a joint effort in Cyprus, as called for in the 1959 Treaty of Guarantee, but the British were either unwilling or unprepared and declined to take action as a guarantor power. The United States took no action to bolster the Makarios government, but Joseph J. Sisco, Under Secretary of State for Political Affairs, went to London and the eastern Mediterranean to stave off the impending Turkish invasion and the war between Greece and Turkey that might follow. The Turks demanded removal of Nicos Sampson and the Greek officers from the National Guard and a binding guarantee of Cypriot independence. Sampson, of course, was expendable to the Athens regime, but Sisco could get an agreement only to reassign the 650 Greek officers.

As Sisco negotiated in Athens, Turkish invasion ships were already at sea. A last-minute reversal might have been possible had the Greeks made concessions, but they did not. The intervention began early on July 20, 1974. Three days later, the Greek junta collapsed in Athens, Sampson resigned in Nicosia, and the threat of war between NATO allies was over. The Turkish army, however, remained on Cyprus.

Constantinos Karamanlis, in self-imposed exile in France since 1963, was called back to head the Greek government once more. Clerides was sworn in as acting president of the Republic of Cyprus, and the foreign ministers of the guarantor powers met in Geneva on July 25 to discuss the military situation on the island. Prime Minister Ecevit publicly welcomed the change of government in Greece and seemed genuinely interested in eliminating the tensions that had brought the two countries so close to war. Nevertheless, during the truce that was arranged, Turkish forces continued to take territory, to improve their positions, and to build up their supplies of war matériel.

A second conference in Geneva began on August 10, with Clerides and Denktaş as the Cypriot representatives. Denktaş proposed a bizonal federation, with Turkish Cypriots controlling 34 percent of the island. When this proposal was rejected, the Turkish foreign minister proposed a Turkish Cypriot zone in the northern part of the island and five Turkish Cypriot enclaves elsewhere, all of which would amount once again to 34 percent of the island's area. Clerides asked for a recess of thirty-six to forty-eight hours to consult with the government in Nicosia and with Makarios in London. His request was refused, and early on August 14 the second phase of the Turkish intervention began. Two days later, after having seized 37 percent of the island above what the Turks called the "Atilla Line," the line that ran from Morphou Bay in the northwest to Famagusta (Gazimağusa) in the east, the Turks ordered a cease-fire.

Developments since 1974

The de facto partition of Cyprus resulting from the Turkish invasion, or intervention, as the Turks preferred to call their military action, caused much suffering in addition to leaving thousands dead, many of whom were unaccounted for even years later. An estimated one-third of the population of each ethnic community had to flee their homes. The island's economy was devastated.

Efforts were undertaken immediately to remedy the effects of the catastrophe. Intensive government economic planning and intervention on both sides of the island soon improved living standards and allowed the construction of housing for refugees. Both communities benefited greatly from the expansion of the tourist industry, which brought millions of foreign visitors to the island during the 1980s. The economic success of the Republic of Cyprus was significant enough to seem almost miraculous. Within just a few years, the refugees had housing and were integrated into the bustling economy, and Greek Cypriots enjoyed a West European standard of living. Turkish Cypriots did not do as well, but, working against an international embargo imposed by the Republic of Cyprus and benefiting from extensive Turkish aid, they managed to ensure a decent standard of living for all members of their community—a standard of living, in fact, that was higher than that of Turkey. Both communities established government agencies to provide public assistance to those who needed it and built modern education systems extending to the university level.

Both communities soon developed political systems on the European model, with parties representing mainstream political opinion from right to the left. Greek Cypriots had two older parties dating from before 1970, the Progressive Party of the Working People (Anorthotikon Komma Ergazomenou Laou—AKEL) and the United Democratic Union of Cyprus (Eniea Dimokratiki Enosis Kyprou—EDEK), generally called the Socialist Party EDEK (Socialistiko Komma EDEK), and some formed after the events of 1974. The two most important of these newer parties were the Democratic Party (Dimokratiko Komma—DIKO) and the Democratic Rally (Dimokratikos Synagermos—DISY). Both of these parties were on the right, with DIKO headed by Spyros Kyprianou, who replaced Makarios as president after the latter's death in 1977, and DISY led by veteran politician Glafkos Clerides. Parliamentary elections held in 1976, 1981, and 1985 resulted in stable patterns in the House of Representatives that permitted coalition-building and a serious opposition to the government in power (see table 3, Appendix). Kyprianou was reelected president in 1983, but lost in 1988 to George Vassiliou, a successful businessman and a political outsider who had the support of AKEL and EDEK. Vassiliou won election by promising to bring a new spirit to politics and break the deadlocked negotiations to end the island's division.

The Turkish Cypriots' progress to parliamentary democracy was not as easy. First they had to build a new state. In 1975 the "Turkish Federated State of Cyprus" was proclaimed. In 1983, by means of a unilateral declaration of independence, Turkish Cypriots created the "Turkish Republic of Northern Cyprus" ("TRNC"), but by the early 1990s, only Turkey had recognized it as a nation. Rauf Denktaş, who had been the political leader of the Turkish Cypriot community since the 1970s, was elected president of the "TRNC." A number of political parties were active in the area occupied by the "TRNC." They included both left- and right-wing parties, which both supported and opposed the settlement of mainland Turks on the island and the politics of partition. The largest party, the National Unity Party (Ulusal Birlik Partisi—UBP), was founded and controlled by Denktaş (see table 4, Appendix). The UBP supported a resolutely separatist stance. The second party of the "TRNC," the Communal Liberation Party (Toplumcu Kurtuluş Partisi—TKP) advocated closer relations with the Greek Cypriot community. The left-wing Republican Turkish Party (Cumhuriyetçi Türk Partisi—CTP) was even more forthright in its opposition to the government's policy of restricted relations with the Republic of Cyprus.

Negotiations began in the mid-1970s to end the de facto partition and to bring the two communities together again. Two major compromises on the part of the Republic of Cyprus occurred in the second half of the 1970s. First, in 1977, four guidelines for future intercommunal talks were accepted by both communities; their thrust was that Cyprus would become a bicommunal federal republic, a departure from the terms of the constitution of 1960. Second, the ten-point agreement of 1979, achieved at a meeting between Kyprianou and Denktaş, worked out policies to ease further intercommunal talks.

A possible settlement was missed in 1985 when Kyprianou refused to sign a recently worked-out accord, fearing it conceded too much to the other side. The stalemate continued up to the election of Vassiliou in 1988. Agreement on some major points had slowly evolved, but the practical steps to realize an actual settlement were still not attainable. Differences in the two communities' view of the desirable mixture of federation or confederation and the powers of a central government seemed unbridgeable.

* * *

The four-volume work by the British historian George Hill, *The History of Cyprus,* although completed in 1952, is still considered the most definitive history of the island. Stavros Panteli's *A New History of Cyprus* covers events up to the mid-1980s. H.D. Purcell's *Cyprus,* available in many libraries, is a balanced but dated survey of Cypriot history. *Footprints in Cyprus,* edited by Sir David Hunt, is also a good introduction to the island's past.

Cyprus: Nationalism and International Politics by Michael Attalides is a thoughtful analysis of the background and development of Cypriot nationalism. *The Cyprus Revolt* by Nancy Crawshaw is a detailed study of the struggle against British rule. Also valuable is *The Rise and Fall of the Cyprus Republic* by Kyriacos C. Markides, which covers the period of independence and events after the Turkish invasion of 1974. *Makarios: A Biography* by Stanley Mayes is a sympathetic yet objective portrait of the republic's first president. Pierre Oberling's *The Road to Bellapais* presents a Turkish Cypriot perspective on the island's recent history. John Reddaway, a former British colonial official in Cyprus, examines many of the controversies surrounding recent history in *Burdened with Cyprus*. Parker T. Hart's *Two NATO Allies at the Threshold of War* offers a first-hand American account of diplomatic efforts to defuse the crisis of 1967. A highly controversial account of the international background of the events of 1974 is Christopher Hitchens's *Cyprus*. (For further information and complete citations, see Bibliography.)

Chapter 2. The Society and Its Environment

Mosque of Lala Mustafa Pasha (once the Cathedral of Saint Nicholas), built by the Lusignans, Famagusta (Gazimağusa)

CYPRUS WAS BITTERLY DIVIDED at the beginning of the 1990s. The island's 9,200 square kilometers encompassed two separate societies: one Greek Cypriot and the other Turkish Cypriot. Until 1974 the two peoples had lived side by side throughout the island. Although they had kept their separate languages and religions, they had become in many respects similar, most of the two peoples being small farmers or peasants. Relations were generally harmonious, if reserved, during the four centuries they shared the island.

The rise of Greek Cypriot nationalism, most clearly demonstrated in the ever-increasing strength of the dream of enosis—the unification of Cyprus with the Greek motherland—engendered a Turkish reaction, the doctrine of *taksim,* or partition. The Greek and Turkish Cypriot communities became estranged within a single generation. The Greek-backed coup of 1974 resulted in a Turkish invasion and the de facto partition of the island. Afterward, the two communities lived virtually without contact. Greek and Turkish Cypriot societies appeared relatively successful at the beginning of the 1990s, but their centuries-long intercourse was ended.

Republic of Cyprus

The Turkish invasion of 1974 was a calamity, but Greek Cypriot society was able to overcome its effects. The economy of the Republic of Cyprus quickly recovered, and went on to flourish into the early 1990s. Greek Cypriot society also withstood the loss of homeland and broken social relations. Greek Cypriots built shelters and found work for the 180,000 displaced people who had fled their homes and villages. During the 1980s, a more prosperous and modern society emerged. Education was made more accessible, and government help to those needing it was improved. Like other societies, Greek Cypriot society became more urbanized, yet mostly avoided the ill effects of a too rapid transition to city life. Ties to the countryside remained strong, even as Greek Cypriots became better connected with the world beyond the island.

As the Republic of Cyprus modernized, social relations changed, but not as quickly as in Western Europe. The Church of Cyprus, rather conservative in its doctrine, remained the dominant religion, although it played a smaller role than formerly in the lives of most Greek Cypriots. Marriage and family remained stronger than in the United States, and relations between the sexes were not as relaxed. However, Greek Cypriot women were better educated than their mothers and were more likely to work outside the home. Although they were well represented in some professions, Greek Cypriot women suffered some sex discrimination in employment, and the republic's feminist movement was not yet influential.

These developments occurred against the backdrop of the tragedy of partition. The barrier between Greek and Turkish Cypriots was virtually impenetrable. The older generation of the two peoples had experienced the terrors of intercommunal conflict, but they had had some contact with one another. A new generation of Greek Cypriots did not know members of the other community. Some had never seen a Turkish Cypriot.

Geography

The physical setting for life on the island is dominated by the mountain masses and the central plain they encompass, the Mesaoria (see fig. 3). The Troodos Mountains cover most of the southern and western portions of the island and account for roughly half its area. The narrow Kyrenia Range, extending along the northern coastline, occupies substantially less area, and elevations are lower. The two mountain systems run generally parallel to the Taurus Mountains on the Turkish mainland, whose silhouette is visible from northern Cyprus. Coastal lowlands, varying in width, surround the island.

Terrain

The rugged Troodos Mountains, whose principal range stretches from Pomos Point in the northwest almost to Larnaca Bay on the east, are the single most conspicuous feature of the landscape. Intensive uplifting and folding in the formative period left the area highly fragmented, so that subordinate ranges and spurs veer off at many angles, their slopes incised by steep-sided valleys. In the southwest, the mountains descend in a series of stepped foothills to the coastal plain.

Whereas the Troodos Mountains are a massif formed of molten igneous rock, the Kyrenia Range is a narrow limestone ridge that rises suddenly from the plains. Its easternmost extension becomes a series of foothills on the Karpas Peninsula. That peninsula points toward Asia Minor, to which Cyprus belongs geologically.

Even the highest peaks of the Kyrenia Range are hardly more than half the height of the great dome of the Troodos massif, Mount Olympus (1,952 meters), but their seemingly inaccessible, jagged slopes make them considerably more spectacular. British writer Lawrence Durrell, in *Bitter Lemons*, wrote of the Troodos as ''an

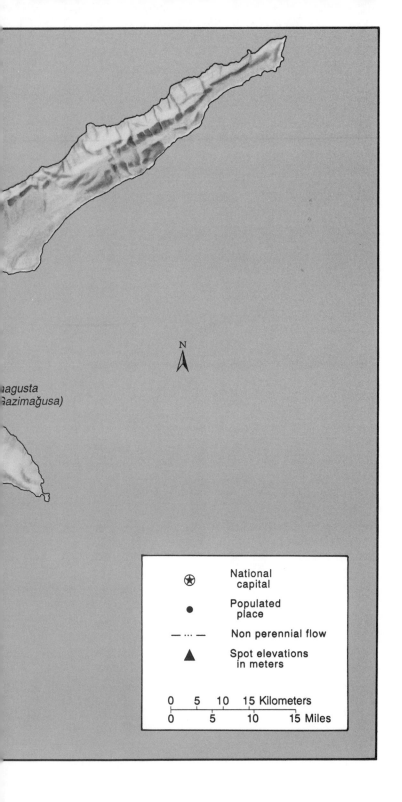

amagusta
(Gazimağusa)

⊛		National capital
●		Populated place
— … —		Non perennial flow
▲		Spot elevations in meters

0   5   10   15 Kilometers
0   5   10   15 Miles

Figure 3. Topography and Drainage

unlovely jumble of crags and heavyweight rocks'' and of the Kyrenia Range as belonging to "the world of Gothic Europe, its lofty crags studded with crusader castles.''

Rich copper deposits were discovered in antiquity on the slopes of the Troodos. Geologists speculate that these deposits may have originally formed under the Mediterranean Sea, as a consequence of the upwelling of hot, mineral-laded water through a zone where plates that formed the ocean floor were pulling apart.

Drainage

Deforestation over the centuries has damaged the island's drainage system and made access to a year-round supply of water difficult. A network of winter rivers rises in the Troodos Mountains and flows out from them in all directions. The Yialias River and the Pedhieos River flow eastward across the Mesaoria into Famagusta Bay; the Serakhis River flows northwest through the Morphou plain. All of the island's rivers, however, are dry in the summer. An extensive system of dams and waterways has been constructed to bring water to farming areas.

The Mesaoria is the agricultural heartland of the island, but its productiveness for wheat and barley depends very much on winter rainfall; other crops are grown under irrigation. Little evidence remains that this broad, central plain, open to the sea at either end, was once covered with rich forests whose timber was coveted by ancient conquerors for their sailing vessels. The now-divided capital of the island, Nicosia, lies in the middle of this central plain.

Climate

The Mediterranean climate, warm and rather dry, with rainfall mainly between November and March, favors agriculture. In general, the island experiences mild wet winters and dry hot summers. Variations in temperature and rainfall are governed by altitude and, to a lesser extent, distance from the coast.

The higher mountain areas are cooler and moister than the rest of the island. They receive the heaviest annual rainfall, which may be as much as 1,000 millimeters. Sharp frost also occurs in the higher districts, which are usually blanketed with snow during the first months of the year. Plains along the northern coast and in the Karpas Peninsula area average 400 to 450 millimeters of annual rainfall. The least rainfall occurs in the Mesaoria, with 300 to 400 millimeters a year. Variability in annual rainfall is characteristic for the island, however, and droughts are frequent and sometimes severe. Earthquakes, usually not destructive, occur from time to time.

Summer temperatures are high in the lowlands, even near the sea, and reach particularly uncomfortable readings in the Mesaoria. Because of the scorching heat of the lowlands, some of the villages in the Troodos have developed as resort areas, with summer as well as winter seasons. The mean annual temperature for the island as a whole is about 20°C. The amount of sunshine the island enjoys enhances the tourist industry. On the Mesaoria in the eastern lowlands, for example, there is bright sunshine 75 percent of the time. During the four summer months, there is an average of eleven and one-half hours of sunshine each day, and in the cloudiest winter months there is an average of five and one-half hours per day.

Ethnicity

Cyprus has been home to many peoples in its history. At the beginning of the 1990s, five ethnic communities lived on the island: Greek Cypriots, Turkish Cypriots, Maronites, Armenians, and Latins. The events of 1974 resulted in a de facto partition of the island, and by the early 1990s virtually all Turkish Cypriots lived in the "Turkish Republic of Northern Cyprus" ("TRNC"). Nearly all members of the other groups lived in the Republic of Cyprus; only about 600 Greek Cypriots lived outside the government-controlled area.

Greek Cypriots

Greek Cypriots formed the island's largest ethnic community, nearly 80 percent of the island's population. They were the descendants of Achaean Greeks who settled on the island during the second half of the second millennium B.C. The island gradually became part of the Hellenic world as the settlers prospered over the next centuries (see The Ancient Period, ch. 1). Alexander the Great freed the island from the Persians and annexed it to his own empire in 333 B.C. Roman rule dating from 58 B.C. did not erase Greek ways and language, and after the division of the Roman Empire in A.D. 285 Cypriots enjoyed peace and national freedom for 300 years under the jurisdiction of the Eastern Empire of Byzantium (see Byzantium Rule, ch. 1). The most important event of the early Byzantine period was that the Greek Orthodox Church of Cyprus became independent in 431. Beginning in the middle of the seventh century, Cyprus endured three centuries of Arab attacks and invasions. In 965, it became a province of Byzantium, and remained in that status for the next 200 years.

The Byzantine era profoundly molded Cypriot culture. The Greek Orthodox Christian legacy bestowed on Greek Cypriots in this period would live on during the succeeding centuries of oppressive foreign domination. English, Lusignan, and Venetian feudal lords ruled Cyprus with no lasting impact on its culture (see The Lusignan and Venetian Eras, ch. 1). Because Cyprus was never the final goal of any external ambition, but simply fell under the domination of whichever power was dominant in the eastern Mediterranean, destroying its civilization was never a military objective or necessity.

Nor did the long period of Ottoman rule (1570–1878) change Greek Cypriot culture (see Ottoman Rule, ch. 1). The Ottomans tended to administer their multicultural empire with the help of their subject *millets,* or religious communities. The tolerance of the *millet* system permitted the Greek Cypriot community to survive, administered for Constantinople by the Archbishop of the Church of Cyprus, who became the community's head, or ethnarch.

However tolerant Ottoman rule may have been with regard to religion, it was otherwise generally harsh and rapacious, tempered mainly by inefficiency. Turkish settlers suffered alongside their Greek Cypriot neighbors, and the two groups endured together centuries of oppressive governance from Constantinople.

In the light of intercommunal conflict since the mid-1950s, it is surprising that Cypriot Muslims and Christians generally lived harmoniously. Some Christian villages converted to Islam. In many places, Turks settled next to Greeks. The island evolved into a demographic mosaic of Greek and Turkish villages, interspersed with many mixed communities (see fig. 4). The extent of this symbiosis could be seen in the two groups' participation in commercial and religious fairs, pilgrimages to each other's shrines, and the occurrence, albeit rare, of intermarriage despite Islamic and Greek laws to the contrary. There was also the extreme case of the *linobambakoi* (linen-cottons), villagers who practiced the rites of both religions and had a Christian as well as a Muslim name. In the minds of some, such religious syncretism indicates that religion was not a source of conflict in traditional Cypriot society.

The rise of Greek nationalism in the 1820s and 1830s affected Greek Cypriots, but for the rest of the century these sentiments were limited to the educated. The concept of enosis—unification with the Greek motherland, by then an independent country, having freed itself from Ottoman rule—became important to literate Greek Cypriots. A movement for the realization of enosis gradually formed, in which the Church of Cyprus had a dominant role.

During British rule (1878–1960), the desire for enosis intensified. The British brought an efficient and honest colonial administration, but maintained the *millet* system. Government and education were administered along ethnic lines, accentuating differences. For

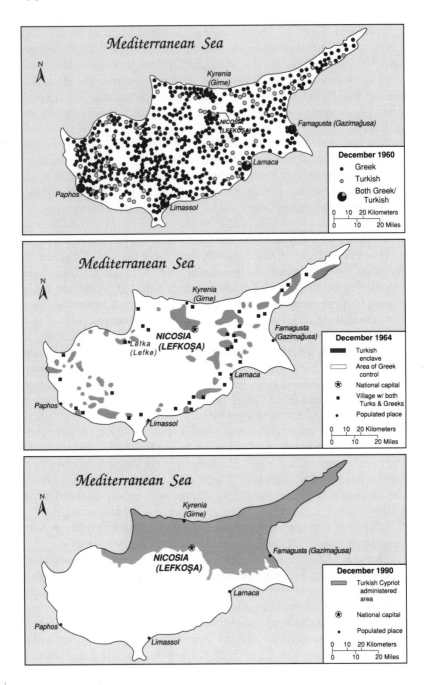

Figure 4. Ethnic Distribution of the Population, 1960, 1964, and 1990

example, the education system was organized with two Boards of Education, one Greek and one Turkish, controlled by Athens and Constantinople, respectively. The resulting education emphasized linguistic, religious, cultural, and ethnic differences and ignored traditional ties between the two Cypriot communities. The two groups were encouraged to view themselves as extensions of their respective motherlands, and the development of two distinct nationalities with antagonistic loyalties was ensured.

By the 1950s, the growing attraction of enosis for ever larger segments of Greek Cypriot society caused a Turkish Cypriot reaction, a desire for *taksim*—partition of the island. The smaller ethnic community had well-founded reasons for fearing rule from the Greek mainland. In the mid-1950s, Greek Cypriot agitation for enosis went beyond manifestos and demonstrations, and Turkish Cypriots responded in kind (see The Emergency, ch. 1). Within twenty years, the island was tragically divided.

By the early 1990s, Greek Cypriot society enjoyed a high standard of living, and, to a degree unknown in its past, was educated and open to influences from the outside world. Economic modernization created a more flexible and open society and caused Greek Cypriots to share the concerns and hopes of other secularized West European societies. The Archbishop of the Church of Cyprus was the ethnarch, or leader, of the Greek Cypriot community in name only because religion had lost much of its earlier power. Finally, the dream of enosis was irrevocably shattered by the events of 1974, and Greek Cypriots sought to deal with the consequences of the Turkish invasion.

Other Ethnic Groups

Cyprus had three other ethnic groups at the beginning of the 1990s: Maronites, Armenians, and Latins. Together they numbered only about 6,000, less than 1 percent of the island's population, but they maintained social institutions of their own and were represented in organs of government. The Maronites and Armenians had come during the Byzantine period, and the Latins slightly later. The Maronites, Arabic-speaking peasants from around Syria and Lebanon, were already an important ethnic group at the time of the Turkish conquest in 1571. By the mid-twentieth century, they lived mainly in four villages in northwestern Cyprus. Armenian Cypriots were primarily urban and mercantile, most of whom had arrived after the collapse of the Armenian nationalist movement in the Caucasus at the end of World War I. Latins were concentrated among merchant families of the port towns on the southern coast and were descendants of the Lusignan and Venetian upper classes.

The Ottomans had suppressed Roman Catholicism, and Latins were largely Greek Orthodox, but retained their French or Italian names. Some Latins reverted to the group's original religion.

Population

In 1960, the last year for which there was an official census for the entire population of Cyprus, the island was home to 573,566 people. Official estimates held that there were 441,568 Greek Cypriots, 3,627 Armenians, 2,706 Maronites (in the future these two groups were to be counted as part of the Greek Cypriot community, according to the terms of the constitution of 1960), 103,822 Turkish Cypriots, and 24,408 others (mostly foreigners) (see table 5, Appendix). According to government statistics, 81.14 percent of Cypriots in 1960 were Greek Cypriot (including Armenians and Maronites) and 18.86 percent were Turkish Cypriot. Republic of Cyprus statistics estimated the 1988 population of the whole island at 687,500, and that of the government-controlled area at 562,700 (see table 6, Appendix). It was estimated that the island's population consisted of 550,400 (80.1 percent) Greek Cypriots (including 6,300 Armenians and Maronites), 128,200 (18.6 percent) Turkish Cypriots, and 8,900 (1.3 percent) who belonged to other groups (mainly British). Cypriot population estimates were often controversial because they could have significant bearing on political settlements. Thus, population figures from the "Turkish Republic of Northern Cyprus" differed markedly from those of the Republic of Cyprus (see table 7, Appendix).

Birth Rates

At the end of the 1980s, the Republic of Cyprus had a fertility rate (births per woman) of 2.4, the highest in Western Europe. But this spurt in births was a new development, and it was uncertain how long it would continue. In the troubled 1970s, the reverse had been the case. Substantial migration and a decline in the fertility rate resulted in a negative growth rate of −0.9 percent in the years 1973–76 (see fig. 5). In the period 1976–82, while the economy was being restructured, population growth gradually reached an average rate of 0.8 percent, and in 1984 peaked at 1.4 percent. In the second half of the 1980s, the growth rate remained above 1 percent.

The long-term decline in the fertility rate was first noted after World War II, when the crude birth rate dropped from 32 per thousand in 1946 to an average of 25 per thousand during the 1950s. The main contributing factor in this remarkable fall in fertility was the rapid postwar economic development. This downward trend continued in the following decades, and a rate of 18 per thousand was recorded in the first part of the 1970s. After a further decline to 16 per thousand in the years after the 1974 invasion, the Greek Cypriot birth rate increased to a rate of 20 to 21 per thousand during the period 1980–86, and then continued its decline, reaching 19.2 per thousand in 1985–88.

This change in the reproductive behavior of the Greek Cypriot population was generally attributed to improvement of the standard of living, expansion of education to all sections of the population, and the consequent wider participation by women in the work force. In addition, there was the traditional Cypriot concern to provide a better future for offspring, which, in a modern social context, entailed increased expenditure for education and a striving to amass a larger material inheritance. As a result, the average family size has declined, from 3.97 persons in 1946 to 3.51 in 1982.

A final cause of declining birth rates is the disappearance in Cyprus of the rural-urban dichotomy, in which higher birth rates are registered in the countryside. The postwar period saw an increasing movement of people to the towns, on either a daily or a permanent basis. This fact, together with the compactness of the island, has resulted in "the near fusion of urban and rural life," in the words of L.W. St. John-Jones, a student of Cypriot demography. The rapid and effective dissemination of typical urban attitudes contributed to a rural fertility rate not much higher than the urban one. Contraceptives were easily available at modest cost all over the island; abortions, widely carried out in private clinics, were seen not as matters of moral or religious controversy, but simply as another means of family planning, albeit a drastic one.

Emigration

Emigration of Cypriots abroad has often been on a large enough scale to affect population growth. As a demographic phenomenon, it has been viewed as an extension of rural to urban movement. At times when a future in the towns was unpromising for those intent on escaping rural poverty, there was the additional safety valve of emigration. Cypriots frequently availed themselves of this opportunity instead of living in crowded slums in their country's towns, and their relatively small numbers meant that recipient countries could easily absorb them. Although there was emigration as early as the 1930s, there is no available data before 1955.

The periods of greatest emigration were 1955–59, the 1960s, and 1974–79, times of political instability and socioeconomic insecurity when future prospects appeared bleak and unpromising. Between 1955 and 1959, the period of anticolonial struggle, 29,000 Cypriots,

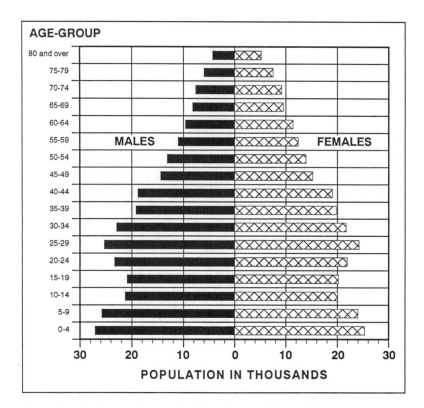

Source: Based on information from Republic of Cyprus, Ministry of Finance, Department of Statistics and Research, *Demographic Report, 1988,* Nicosia, 1989, 83.

Figure 5. Republic of Cyprus: Population by Age and Sex, 1988

5 percent of the population, left the island. In the 1960s, there were periods of economic recession and intercommunal strife, and net emigration has been estimated at about 50,000, or 8.5 percent of the island's 1970 population. Most of these emigrants were young males from rural areas and usually unemployed. Some 5 percent were factory workers, and only 5 percent were university graduates. Britain headed the list of destinations, taking more than 75 percent of the emigrants in 1953–73; another 8 to 10 percent went to Australia, and about 5 percent to North America.

During the early 1970s, economic development, social progress, and relative political stability contributed to a slackening of emigration. At the same time, there was immigration, so that the net immigration was 3,200 in 1970–73. This trend ended with the 1974 invasion. During the 1974–79 period, 51,500 persons left as emigrants, and another 15,000 became temporary workers abroad.

The new wave of emigrants had Australia as the most common destination (35 percent), followed by North America, Greece, and Britain. Many professionals and technical workers emigrated, and for the first time more women than men left. By the early 1980s, the government had rebuilt the economy, and the 30 percent unemployment rate of 1974 was replaced by a labor shortage. As a result, only about 2,000 Cypriots emigrated during the years 1980–86, while 2,850 returned to the island.

Although emigration slowed to a trickle during the 1980s, so many Cypriots had left the island in preceding decades that in the late 1980s an estimated 300,000 Cypriots (a number equivalent to 60 percent of the population of the Republic of Cyprus) resided in seven foreign countries.

Internal Migration

Major demographic changes could also be seen in the distribution of the population between urban and rural areas in the past fifty years. From 1881 to 1911, there was almost no internal migration, and the rural population constituted 81 percent of the total. The first change was noted in the 1931 census, when 22 percent of the population was classified as town dwellers. In the following decades, especially in the period 1946–60, the urban proportion grew increasingly rapidly; the urban population increased by 78 percent in that period, whereas that of rural areas grew by only 10 percent. Some 36 percent of the island's population was concentrated in towns in 1960. The urban share increased to 42 percent by 1973. In this same period, the rural population actually declined by 0.7 percent.

Following the displacement of one-third of the population in 1974, the urban population in the government-controlled area rose to 52 percent in 1976 and 63.5 percent in 1983. Urbanization did not abate in the following years, for in 1986 fully 64 percent of the population living in government-controlled areas of Cyprus was urban-based. According to the republic's 1988 Demographic Report for those areas controlled by the government, 363,000 persons lived in urban areas and 199,300 in rural areas. Such a phenomenal change in the island's demographic composition could not fail to have significant repercussions in all areas of life.

The Nicosia district, historically the largest of the island's six districts, continued to expand at a faster rate than the other districts. In 1881 its population constituted 30 percent of the total; in 1973, it constituted 37 percent, and in 1986, it was up to 42 percent. In the late 1980s, the district's population was estimated at 234,000, despite the fact that a large part of it is in the occupied north; Limassol, the second largest district, had 91,500; Paphos, 49,500; and Famagusta, most of which is under Turkish occupation, 29,100.

Urbanization and Occupational Change

Cyprus experienced a rapid and intense economic transformation after World War II. The traditional economy of subsistence agriculture and animal husbandry was replaced by a commercial economy, centered in expanding urban areas. These economic changes resulted from extensive construction of housing and other facilities for British military personnel during World War II; exports of minerals (60 percent of all exports), which became the island's most valuable export in the 1950s; and the fourteenfold increase in British military spending through the postwar period. (Cyprus became Britain's most important base in the eastern Mediterranean after the loss of bases in the Arab countries.) Independence brought such an acceleration of economic development, the so-called "economic explosion," that by the end of the 1960s the objectives of the government's economic planning were not only fulfilled, but overtaken.

In this context of economic growth, agriculture modernized: farm machinery became common, irrigation increased, and the scientific use of pesticides and fertilizers became widespread. Farming, however, became less important in the economy as a whole. Although agricultural income tripled during the 1950s, and then doubled in the 1960s, earnings from industry, construction, trade, tourism, and telecommunications grew even more; and agriculture's share of the gross domestic product (GDP—see Glossary) declined. This decline brought with it changes in employment for many. The increasing fragmentation of farms through inheritance and a shortage of water caused Cypriots to leave farming for full-time or part-time jobs in other economic sectors. The proximity of employment opportunities in urban areas only made the transition easier.

The flight from agriculture, which became noticeable in the decade and a half after World War II, continued after independence and reached a peak in 1974, when the best and most productive agricultural land fell under Turkish occupation. In 1960 some 40.3 percent of the economically active population were agricultural workers; in 1973, the figure was down to 33.6 percent employed in this sector. In 1988 government figures estimated only 13.9 percent of the work force earned a living from farming full time. Although changes in accounting principles explain some of the lower figures,

Kakopetria, a village in the Troodos Mountains
Courtesy Republic of Cyprus, Press and Information Office, Nicosia

the decline of agricultural employment since the late 1940s was striking.

Urbanization in Cyprus did not result in the annihilation of traditional values and practices, but in their preservation. Urbanization took place under conditions that generally spared the island the problems often connected with migration of large numbers of unemployed farm workers to urban centers. For one thing, urbanization occurred in a period of prosperity and increasing economic activity, and employment was available. In addition, farm workers generally left their villages only when they had found work in urban areas. Another happy circumstance was that the island's small size and its good road system linked most villages to the towns, so that many rural workers could commute daily to their new jobs. The capital and largest city was especially well connected to the countryside. Finally, rural migrants unable to afford housing in Nicosia and other towns were able to settle in nearby villages, a circumstance that reduced the likelihood of slums.

Many migrants regarded access to secondary education as a principal reason for moving to the city. Traditional Cypriot agricultural society valued land above all else and considered education a wasteful luxury; a modern and diversified economy, however, made education a necessity. Migrants came to value education as the principal means of improving their material and social positions. Expansion of education contributed immensely to the dissemination of urban values and organizations to rural Cyprus.

Postwar population redistribution in Cyprus was so extensive that most urban dwellers were born in rural areas. These migrants maintained close ties with the countryside, and many owned plots of land in their places of origin. The satisfaction of owning land went beyond increasing property values, a fact that is easy to understand in Cypriots, who were an agricultural people until just a generation ago.

Class Structure

Cypriot class structure traditionally has been free of vast disparities of wealth and status. During Ottoman rule, Venetian estates were broken up and given to Turkish settlers, who soon were indistinguishable from their Greek Cypriot neighbors, until one heard them speak. A small Ottoman bureaucracy governed the island, aided by the Greek Orthodox clergy, who, under the *millet* system, were the leaders of their people. Some Greek Cypriots engaged in commerce, but the island's population consisted mostly of small farmers. This pattern continued until the early decades of this century, when, under British rule, the economy became more diversified and living standards slowly began to rise.

During this period, a small Greek commercial class formed, often drawing its money from working for the British. In addition to profiting from government service and increased commerce, some Cypriots acquired wealth as moneylenders. Taking advantage of frequent droughts and plagues, moneylenders could become dominant figures and landowners in the countryside. Their fortunes were relatively small, however, for Cyprus was a poor country, with most people living at subsistence levels. The founding of the cooperative movement in the early years of the twentieth century and British reforms in later decades broke the power of these small financiers and permitted farmers to repay their debts at reasonable rates. The cities had no wealthy class, but only more prosperous groups that earned their living in government service, the professions, and business.

From the 1950s to the invasion of 1974, the Cypriot economy bloomed, and many prospered. The average living standard increased markedly in both the countryside and the city. Workers commuted to urban areas for employment, yet lived in their home villages; thus, no slums were created. Some businessmen in the cities earned substantial amounts of money through hotels, real estate, and commerce. Although some of these businessmen became quite wealthy, their money was new. Fortunes in Cyprus rarely went back beyond a generation.

The substantial economic growth of the Republic of Cyprus since the mid-1970s furthered these trends. All government-controlled areas benefited from the prosperous economy, and new modern houses were seen in every village. Land become very valuable, and fortunes could be earned from land earlier regarded as worthless. Many became rich from the explosive growth of the tourist industry. Fortunes were also earned from manufacturing, trade and shipping, and financial services, and at the beginning of the 1990s the republic had a highly visible class of the newly wealthy.

The republic's prosperity was widely shared, however. The average standard of living matched those of some other West European countries. At the beginning of the 1990s, even working-class Cypriots regarded vacations abroad as necessities. A welfare system along West European lines supported Cypriots in need.

Education was a common means of rising in social status, and most Cypriots respected higher education and white-collar professions. The expanding economy allowed many Cypriots to do more sophisticated work than had their parents. To move in one generation from farmer to urban professional became, if not the rule, at least not extraordinary. Given the small size of the republic, and the still strong tradition of the extended family, virtually all Cypriots could number among their relatives farmers, teachers, government employees, small businessmen, and other professional workers.

Family and Marriage

The structure of the family was affected by the postwar changes. The family was traditionally the most important institution in Cypriot society. Especially in village life, people thought of themselves primarily as members of families, and rarely, according to sociologist Peter Loizos, spoke of "themselves as individuals in the existential sense." Others have noted that Greek Cypriots traditionally identified themselves first as members of families, then according to their places of origin, and lastly as citizens of a nation.

The typical traditional Greek Cypriot households consisted of a father, a mother, and their unmarried children. At marriage, the parents gave their children a portion of land, if available, along with money and household items. Traditionally, the bridegroom provided the house and the bride's family the furniture and linens. These gifts were the dowry, the allocation of an equal portion of the parents' property to the children, male or female, at the time of marriage, rather than after the death of the parents. Until the

1950s, this transfer of property at marriage was agreed to orally by the parties involved; more recently the so-called dowry contract has been introduced. A formal agreement specifying the amount of property to be given to the couple, the dowry contract is signed by all parties and enforced by religious authorities. At the engagement, for example, a priest will ask if such a contract has been considered.

After World War II, it became the bride's obligation to provide the house. Ownership of a house, given the scarcity of land (especially after the invasion of 1974) and the considerable expense of building, became a great advantage for a single woman seeking to marry. For this reason, a great part of the wages of a working woman went to the construction of a house, for a "good marriage" was as important at the beginning of the 1990s as it was in the past.

Traditionally, all marriages were arranged, generally through the mediation of a matchmaker. The latter, although unrelated to either family, knew the families well enough to be confident that their children were well suited. Opportunities for the young themselves to meet were rare and restricted. They met at church, in the presence of their parents; at the village fountain; and during "Sunday afternoon walks," where girls and boys strolled separately. Couples were matched with a few qualities in mind, and in larger settlements were often relative strangers. Love was not seen as a good reason for marriage, for romantic love was not highly esteemed in traditional Cypriot society. Divorce and separation were virtually unknown. Through the system of marriage and dowry, kinship and economic ties were so rigidly defined that neither partner could opt out of a marriage without devastating social consequences.

Urbanization and modernization have altered Greek Cypriot attitudes toward marriage. The expansion of the school system has meant that boys and girls meet from an early age and are exposed to modern ideas about social and sexual relations. The great increase in the number of women in the work force also has liberated them from strict parental control.

Even at the beginning of the 1990s, however, economic considerations remained a decisive factor in matters of sexual morality and marriage settlements. In farming communities, for example, where daughters were financially dependent on parents, the latter could still regulate premarital behavior. Among the lower middle class of wage earners, where there was little property to divide among the children, parents still retained considerable authority over their daughters, for a "good name" was thought to increase the chances of a marriage bringing upward social mobility. Among affluent urban classes, where girls associated with boys of similar economic background, parents relaxed their vigilance considerably, and more typically modern Western attitudes toward sexual morality emerged.

In traditional Cypriot society, full manhood was attained through marriage and becoming the main support for a family. Similarly, it was only through marriage that a woman could realize what was seen as her main purpose in life, becoming a mother and homemaker. Remaining single reduced a woman to the marginal role of looking after aged parents and being on the periphery of her married siblings' lives.

The great importance of a separate "dwelling unit" for the nuclear family has always been recognized as a prerequisite for the couple's economic independence. Accordingly, the head of the family has been seen as morally justified in pursuing the interest of his dependents in all circumstances. This principle of *symferon,* that is, self-interest, overrides every other consideration. Acting in accordance with the principle of *symferon,* Greek Cypriot parents do all in their power to equip their children for the future. In present-day Cyprus, this involves providing the best possible education for sons and securing a house as well as an acceptable education for daughters.

In traditional Cypriot villages, houses were built close to one another, encouraging the close contact and cooperation that were necessary for survival in a context of general poverty. The closely knit community of families provided a sense of belonging and security, but also greatly restricted individuals within accepted norms and boundaries in all aspects of life. Urbanization had a liberating effect. As people became wage earners, the self-sufficiency of the nuclear family grew at the expense of community interdependence.

Despite changes in its structure, however, the family remained strong in Greek Cypriot society. In the period 1985–89, the country's marriage rate was 9.5 per thousand, the highest in Europe. The period saw a rising trend in the marriage age for men and women, about one year older for both than in earlier years. In 1988 the mean age at marriage was 28.7 for grooms, and 25.2 for brides. Grooms and brides in rural areas still tended to marry younger than their urban counterparts. On the other hand, the divorce rate had almost doubled from 42 per thousand in 1980 to 68 per thousand in 1988. The number of extramarital births remained very low by European standards; in 1988 only seventy-two children were born out of wedlock, a mere 0.7 percent of the total number of births.

Status of Women

Postwar changes greatly affected Greek Cypriot women's place in society. Especially influential were changes that gave women expanded access to education and increased participation in the work force. At the beginning of the century, the proportion of girls to boys enrolled in primary education was one to three. By 1943 some 80 percent of girls attended primary school. When, in 1960, elementary education was made compulsory, the two sexes were equally enrolled. By the 1980s, girls made up 45 percent of those receiving secondary education. Only after the mid-1960s did women commonly leave Cyprus to receive higher education. In the 1980s, women made up about 32 percent of those studying abroad.

Cyprus had long had a high degree of female participation in the work force. In the period 1960–85, women's share of the work force rose only slightly, from 40.8 percent to 42.2 percent. However, where women worked changed greatly. Women's share of the urban work force rose from 22 percent to 41 percent, and their share of the rural work force fell from 51 percent to 44.4 percent. The decline in rural areas stemmed from the overall shift away from agricultural work, where women's contribution had always been vital, to employment in urban occupations.

Cypriot women enjoyed the same rights to social welfare as men in such matters as social security payments, unemployment compensation, vacation time, and other common social provisions. In addition, after 1985 women benefited from special protective legislation that provided them with marriage grants and with maternity grants that paid them 75 percent of their insurable earnings. Still, a large number of women, the self-employed and unpaid family workers on farms, were not covered by the Social Insurance Scheme (see Health and Welfare, this ch.). These women constituted 28 percent of the economically active female population.

In 1985 the Republic of Cyprus ratified the United Nations Convention on the Elimination of all Forms of Discrimination against Women. Despite ratification of this agreement, as of late 1990 there was no legislation in the Republic of Cyprus that guaranteed the right to equal pay for work of equal value, nor the right of women to the same employment opportunities.

The occupational segregation of the sexes was still persistent in Cyprus at the beginning of the 1990s. Even though the participation of women in clerical jobs had more than doubled since the late 1970s, only one woman in fifteen was in an administrative or managerial position in 1985. Women's share of professional jobs increased to 39 percent by the mid-1980s, compared with 36 percent

Breadbaking in a Cypriot village
Courtesy Republic of Cyprus, Press and Information Office, Nicosia
Traditional Cypriot wedding
Courtesy Embassy of Cyprus, Washington

ten years earlier, but these jobs were concentrated in medicine and teaching, where women had traditionally found employment. In fields where men were dominant, women's share of professional positions amounted to only 11 percent, up from 8 percent in 1976. In the fields where women were dominant, men took just under half the professional positions.

Although most Cypriot women worked outside the home, they were expected to fulfill the traditional domestic roles of housewife and mother. They could expect little help from their spouses, for most Cypriot men were not ready to accept any domestic duties, and most women did not expect them to behave otherwise. Nonetheless, even women with full-time jobs were judged by the traditional standards of whether they kept a clean house and provided daily hot meals.

Moreover, even at the beginning of the 1990s, Cypriot women were still burdened with the expectation of safeguarding the honor of the family. According to tradition, a woman's duty was to protect herself against all criticism of sexual immodesty. A study carried out in a farming community in the mid-1970s found that women were still expected to avoid any social contact with men that could be construed to have a sexual content. An expressed desire for male society was seen to reflect poorly on a woman's honor, and virginity was seen by many villagers, both men and women, to be a precondition for marriage. The honor of a family, that is, the sense of dignity of its male members, depended on the sexual modesty and virtue of its women. These traditional attitudes have waned somewhat in recent decades, especially in urban areas, but were still prevalent in the early 1990s. Another indication of the conservative nature of Greek Cypriot society at the beginning of the 1990s was that the feminist movement in Cyprus was often the object of ridicule from both sexes. Nevertheless, women's increasing economic independence was a force for liberation in all sections of the population.

Religion

The most important church in Cyprus, the Church of Cyprus, is an autocephalous church in the Orthodox tradition using the Greek liturgy. It recognizes the seniority and prestige of the ecumenical patriarch in Constantinople, but retains complete administrative autonomy under its own archbishop. The Great Schism, as the split between Catholic and Orthodox became known, had major consequences for the Church of Cyprus. Under Lusignan and Venetian rule, the Church of Cyprus was pressured to recognize the authority of the Roman pope. The imposed Roman hierarchy attempted to remold the Church of Cyprus in the image of the Western church. Under the Muslim Ottomans, Cypriots were no longer considered schismatics, but merely unbelievers and followers of an inferior religion. As such they were allowed considerable autonomy, and the archbishop was the officially recognized secular as well as religious leader of his community. Under the British, there was an attempt to secularize all public institutions, but this move was bitterly opposed by church authorities, who used the conflict with the state to gain leadership of the Greek nationalist movement against colonial rule. At independence Archbishop Makarios III, a young, Western-educated former monk, was elected president of the republic, holding this position until his death in 1977. His successor, Archbishop Chrysostomos, was still head of the Church of Cyprus at the beginning of the 1990s. He was a conservative leader, both in religious and political matters, well-suited for a church that had never undergone reforms such as those instituted by the Second Vatican Council for the Roman Catholic Church.

The church had long been composed of four episcopal sees: the archbishopric of Nicosia, and the metropolitanates of Paphos, Kition, and Kyrenia. New metropolitanates were created by Makarios in 1973 for Limassol and Morphou, with a suffragan, or assistant, bishop in Salamis under the archbishop. A bishop had to be a graduate of the Orthodox theological seminary in Greece and be at least thirty years of age. Because Orthodox bishops were sworn to a vow of celibacy and parish clergy were usually married, bishops were recruits from monasteries rather than parish churches. Bishops were not appointed by the archbishop, but, like him, were elected through a system granting representation to laymen, other bishops, abbots, and regular clergy.

Individual churches, monasteries, dioceses, and charitable educational institutions organized by the Church of Cyprus were independent legal entities enjoying such rights and obligations as holding property. In exchange for the acquisition of many church lands, the government assumed responsibility for church salaries. Parish clergy, traditionally married men chosen by their fellow villagers, were sent for brief training before ordination. In the twentieth century, modernizers, most notably Archbishop Makarios, were instrumental in strengthening the quality and training of priests at the Cypriot seminary in Nicosia.

The monasteries of Cyprus had always been very important to the Church of Cyprus. By the twentieth century, many had long lain in ruins, but their properties were among the most important holdings of the church, the island's largest landowner. Although the number of monks decreased in the postwar era, at the beginning of the 1990s there were at least ten active monasteries in the government-controlled areas.

In the Orthodox church, ritual was to a great extent the center of the church's activity, for Orthodox doctrine emphasizes the mystery of God's grace rather than salvation through works and knowledge. Seven sacraments are recognized: baptism in infancy, confirmation with consecrated oil, penance, the Eucharist, matrimony, ordination, and unction in times of sickness or when near death.

Formal services are lengthy and colorful, with singing, incense, and elaborate vestments, according to the occasion, worn by the presiding priest. Statues are forbidden, but the veneration of icons, located on the church's walls and often covered with offerings of the faithful, is highly developed. Easter is the focus of the church year, closing the Lenten fasting with an Easter Eve vigil and procession.

Religious observance varied. In traditional rural villages, women attended services more frequently than men, and elderly family members were usually responsible for fulfilling religious duties on behalf of the whole family. Church attendance was less frequent in urban areas and among educated Cypriots. For much of the population, religion centered on rituals at home, veneration of icons, and observance of certain feast days of the Orthodox calendar.

Education

One of the most important institutional changes introduced during the period of British rule was the allocation of a small subsidy for the establishment of primary schools. A great increase in the number of primary schools throughout the island was made possible by the Education Law of 1895, which permitted local authorities to raise taxes to finance schools. In 1897 there were only 76 schools, run by voluntary and church donations; twenty years later, there were 179. Colonial officials also subsidized teacher training and agricultural courses, but did not interfere with local and church authorities in the area of secondary education.

As a result of a campaign against illiteracy launched by British authorities, the percentage of illiterate adult Cypriots fell from 33 percent in 1946 to 18 percent in 1960. After independence the illiteracy rate dropped still further, to 9.5 percent in 1976, the last year for which there are statistics. In that year, 15 percent of women were illiterate, as were 3.2 percent of men. This improvement reflected the growing school enrollment. In 1960 as much as 25 percent of the population had never attended school, but by 1986–87 this figure had dropped to 6 percent. Another indication of the expansion of education was that in 1946 only 5 percent of adult women had attended secondary schools; forty years later, 30 percent had.

During the colonial period, the main educational goal was the inculcation of national ideals and the strengthening of ethnic identity. After independence, goals became more practical. A well-educated population was seen as the best way of guaranteeing a thriving economy, a rise in overall living standards, and a vigorous cultural life. The great importance attached to education could be seen in the significant rise in government spending on it during the period since independence. In 1960 education accounted for 3.4 percent of the gross national product (GNP—see Glossary). By 1987 education accounted for 5.6 percent of GNP and 11.6 percent of the government's budget.

At the beginning of the 1990s, qualified teachers and administrative personnel for all levels and types of schools were in good supply. All teachers were accredited by a special committee of the Ministry of Education. All public schools had uniform curricula; the preparation of school textbooks was the responsibility of committees of teachers and administrators, working in close cooperation with educational authorities in Greece. Some instructional material for both primary and secondary education was donated by the Greek government. Cypriot schools were also well provided with modern teaching equipment.

A principal challenge at the beginning of the 1990s was providing education more responsive to the needs of the economy. The first vocational-technical schools were established after independence in an attempt to provide the rapidly expanding economy with technicians and skilled workers. However, Cypriots retained a tendency to choose academic rather than technical courses, for reasons of social prestige. Cyprus therefore faced a chronic shortage of skilled workers and a high rate of unemployment for university graduates. By the second half of the 1980s, this trend had ended. In the 1986–87 academic year, only 5.3 percent of students opted for the classical academic course of studies, compared with 46.2 percent in the 1965–66 academic year. About half of all students chose to concentrate on economic and commercial courses; about one-fifth chose scientific courses; and one-fifth, vocational-technical courses.

The Greek Cypriot education system consisted of preprimary and primary schools, secondary general and secondary technical/vocational schools, and special schools for the blind, deaf, and other teachable handicapped persons. In addition, there were institutions for teacher training, specialized instruction, and informal education. As of 1990, there was no university in the Republic of Cyprus, and until one opened in the early 1990s, further studies had to be pursued abroad. There were a small number of private schools.

The constitution of 1960 assigned responsibility for education to the Greek Cypriot and Turkish Cypriot communal chambers. After withdrawal of the Turkish Cypriots from all state institutions, the government proceeded with the establishment of the Ministry of Education in 1965. Under this ministry, the education system evolved its present structure: one to two and one-half years of preprimary schooling for children aged three to five and one-half years; six years of primary school for children aged five and one-half to eleven and one-half years; six years of secondary schooling, followed by two to three years of higher education for those who did not go to study abroad.

The development of preprimary education was a relatively recent phenomenon in Cyprus. In 1973 only 11 percent of children under five years of age attended public or private nurseries or kindergartens. Following the 1974 invasion, the state became much more involved with preprimary education through its establishment of nurseries and kindergartens for the thousands of refugees from northern areas. The 1980s saw a further expansion of public education of this kind (see table 8, Appendix).

Primary education was always free in Cyprus and aimed at the all-around education of young children. After 1962 primary education was compulsory, and primary schools were found in all communities, even remote villages. In the 1986–87 academic year, there were 357 public primary schools, and 16 private ones (most of the latter for the children of foreign residents).

Secondary education, which was also free, but not compulsory, was open without examination to all children who had completed primary schooling. It was divided into two stages, each consisting of three grades. During the first stage, the gymnasium, all students were taught the same general subjects, with a special emphasis on the humanities. The second stage consisted of either the lyceum, which offered five main fields of specialization (classical studies, science, economics, business, and languages), or a vocational-technical course. Schools of the second category aimed at providing industry with technicians and craftsmen. Vocational schools trained many students for work in the country's important tourist industry; technical schools emphasized mathematics, science, and training in various technologies.

After independence the number of students at the secondary level increased rapidly, rising from 26,000 in the 1960–61 academic year to 42,000 ten years later. By the second half of the 1980s, 98 percent of those who completed primary school attended secondary schools, compared with about 75 percent twenty years earlier.

Although Cyprus had no university of its own (the long-planned University of Cyprus was expected to begin enrolling students for some courses in 1991), many Cypriots were at foreign universities. The percentage of students studying at the university level, 29 percent, was among the highest in the world. During the 1970s and 1980s, an average of more than over 10,000 Cypriots studied abroad annually. During the 1970s, more than half of these students were in Greece, and about one-fifth were in Britain. In the 1980s, the United States became an important destination for students going abroad, generally surpassing Britain. The number of women studying abroad increased markedly during the 1970s and 1980s, going from 24 percent in 1970 to 40 percent in 1987.

Cyprus did, however, provide some opportunities for third-level training, and in the late 1980s attracted some of those who earlier would have studied abroad. In 1987 there were seven public and ten private institutions of higher learning, which enrolled about one-fourth of the island's secondary-school graduates. The public institutions were the Pedagogical Academy of the Ministry of Education, which trained kindergarten and primary-school teachers; the Higher Technical Institute of the Ministry of Labor and Social Insurance, which trained mechanical, electrical, and civil engineers; the College of Forestry under the Ministry of Agriculture and Natural Resources; the School of Nursing, the School of Midwifery, and the Psychiatric School of Nursing under the Ministry of Health; and the Hotel and Catering Institute under the Ministry of Labor and Social Insurance. Private institutions offered courses in business administration, secretarial studies, mechanical and civil engineering, banking and accounting, hotel and catering, and communications.

Health and Welfare

A Cambridge professor, visiting Cyprus in 1801, wrote that "there is hardly upon earth a more wretched spot" than Cyprus, with its "pestiferous air" and contagion. A few years after the British came into possession of the country, it was officially reported that the island was generally healthy; this assessment could be attributed to the disappearance of the plague around the middle of the nineteenth century. According to testimony of the chief medical officer in the mid-1880s, however, the island's situation was far from healthy. Because the towns and villages were often surrounded by marshes, drainage was often impossible and water

75

supplies were often contaminated. The draining of marshes, destruction of the anopheles mosquito, securing of sanitary water, and introduction of elementary health measures freed Cyprus entirely of the plague, typhus, and other virulent diseases by the end of the century. Malaria remained a serious concern, whose effects were widely evident. The eradication of this disease after World War II contributed greatly to the well-being of the island, so much so that some observers have regarded it as the most important event in the modern history of Cyprus.

Health Care

Mortality rates and the health of Greek Cypriots improved steadily in the postwar era. The eradication of malaria was an important cause for this improvement, as were material prosperity and the diffusion of up-to-date health information. Since independence in 1960, the Ministry of Health has been responsible for improving public health and providing public medical services, as well as overseeing the extensive private health-care sector.

Government medical services were available to all at the beginning of the 1990s. The poor were entitled to free services; middle-income families paid for care at reduced rates. These two groups accounted for well over half the population; upper-income persons paid for the full costs of medical services. In addition, employers and trade unions subsidized a number of health plans. Civil servants and members of police and military units received free medical care. Cypriots needing care not available in the republic were sent abroad at government expense.

At the beginning of the 1990s, the Republic of Cyprus had six general hospitals, all in the main towns. In addition, there were twenty-one rural health centers and a psychiatric hospital in Nicosia. In 1987 there were 1,870 hospital beds, compared with 1,592 in 1960. The private health sector was extensive, and more than three-quarters of all doctors and dentists had their own practices or practiced part time in private clinics. Taking both public and private care into account, in 1989 Cyprus had 1 hospital bed per 166 inhabitants, 1 doctor per 482 inhabitants, and 1 dentist for every 1,356 inhabitants.

The improvement in the island's health care during the postwar period was reflected by increased life expectancy. In the 1983–87 period, Cypriot women could expect to live 77.8 years and men 73.9 years, compared with 69 and 64 years, respectively, for the period 1948–50. The improvement in the infant mortality rate was even more striking, with 11 deaths per 1,000 births in the mid-1980s, compared with 63 per 1,000 at mid-century.

Refugee housing project in Strovolos, a suburb of Nicosia
Courtesy Republic of Cyprus, Press and Information Office, Nicosia

The main reasons for improved health conditions on the island were the Cypriots' constant pursuit of better living standards, their consuming concern with their family's welfare, the close urban-rural ties, and the rapid diffusion of and receptiveness to innovative ideas in health care.

Social Insurance

The five-year development plans adopted by the Republic of Cyprus increasingly stressed that a developing economy was the best means to improve the welfare and living standards of all sectors of the population. The plan covering the 1989–93 period had as its major objectives improving living standards, attaining higher levels of social welfare, and instituting a more equitable distribution of national income and economic burdens.

Beginning with independence, the state, trade unions, and the employers' associations had cooperated in establishing an extensive network of social security that included social insurance, death benefits, medical treatment and hospitalization, education, and housing. The crowning success of this effort was the national Social Insurance Scheme. As introduced by colonial authorities in 1957, it was limited with regard to both the number of persons covered and the benefits it could provide. In 1964 the plan was improved and expanded to cover every person gainfully employed on the island, including even the self-employed. The welfare program included maternity leave and assistance for sickness and work-related injuries. Legislation providing for annual paid vacations was introduced in 1967. By 1987 Cypriots working five days a week were entitled to fifteen days of annual leave a year; those working six days a week had the right to eighteen days. Supporting this entitlement was a central vacation fund to which all participating employers were required to contribute 6 percent of insurable earnings.

A system of unemployment compensation was introduced in 1968. Its main objectives were protecting employees against arbitrary dismissal, regulating how much advance notice was required before dismissal, and setting the amount of unemployment compensation.

The Social Insurance Scheme was fundamentally improved in 1973. For the first time, the plan included a disability pension, and coverage of the self-employed was extended. The social insurance program now included a whole range of benefits. Some benefits were short-range, such as unemployment, sickness, or injury benefits, marriage and maternity benefits, and disablement and funeral grants. Long-term benefits included pensions for the elderly, widows and invalids, and payments to orphans and survivors.

In June 1974, social insurance payments were increased 25 percent to reach West European standards and meet relevant International Labor Organisation criteria. The economic crisis stemming from the Turkish invasion, with its 30 percent unemployment, compelled the government to reduce all pensions by 20 percent and suspend the payment of unemployment benefits, as well as marriage, birth, and funeral grants. By 1977 benefits were restored to their preinvasion levels, partly through the establishment of a separate fund for unemployment benefits.

The Social Insurance Law of 1980 set contributions and benefits according to the incomes of the insured. The new program maintained the previous flat-rate principle for basic benefits, but introduced supplementary benefits with contributions directly related to the incomes of insured persons. In addition to compulsory coverage of all gainfully employed persons, the new program allowed those formerly employed to continue their social insurance on a voluntary basis. In the second half of the 1980s, participants had amounts equal to 15.5 percent of their insurable earnings paid into the central fund. For employees, the contributions came from three sources: 6 percent from employees themselves, 6 percent from employers, and 3.5 percent from the government. For the self-employed, the government paid 3.5 percent, and the insured the rest.

Apart from the state Social Insurance Scheme, an increasing number of insurance or pension funds were being registered with the Income Tax Department of the Ministry of Finance. In 1987 there were 1,065 such funds, with a total of C£25.1 million (for value of the Cyprus pound—see Glossary) in benefit payments. The number of insured contributors to all funds, public and private, amounted to 214,522 in 1987, compared with 183,000 in 1973. In this period, the government's annual contribution increased from C£21.7 million to C£223.7 million. In 1986 the government's payments of social insurance benefits constituted 4.5 percent of GNP, compared with 1.6 percent in 1970.

Social Welfare

Social welfare policy was introduced for the first time in Cyprus in 1946, when legislation was enacted to regulate the supervision of juvenile offenders, the aftercare of reform-school boys, and the protection of deprived children. After independence social welfare became the responsibility of the Department of Social Welfare Services under the Ministry of Labor and Social Insurance. The government committed itself to an active role in social policy when it stated in 1967 that "it recognizes that health, education and other social considerations affect and are interdependent with a vast complex of variables which determine both the social and economic welfare of the island."

By the 1970s, social welfare had evolved into a body of activities designed to enable individuals, family groups, and communities to cope with social problems. In the late 1980s, the state provided five main categories of services: delinquency and social defense; child and family welfare; community work and youth services; social services to other departments; and public assistance.

Delinquency and social defense services were concerned with juvenile and adult offenders. They included pretrial reports on juveniles, supervision of persons placed on probation, follow-up care for those leaving detention centers (obligatory for juveniles, voluntary for adults), and supervision of juveniles involved in antisocial behavior when requested by parents or school authorities.

The primary recipients of child and family welfare were children removed from families where conditions could no longer be remedied. Also served were children needing protection, but remaining with their families, and children threatened by such problems as chronic illness, marriage breakdown, and homelessness.

In these cases, the department could supervise fostering arrangements and adoptions. Service of this kind also involved inspecting and licensing homes for children, day nurseries, and childcare personnel. In 1986 there were 207 day-care centers, 164 of them privately run; state and local governments operated the rest. Children placed in the state's care lived in the department's four children's homes; delinquent youths (aged thirteen to eighteen) lived in four youth hostels. There was also a home for retarded children, one section of which was reserved for retarded adults.

Community work and youth services involved the department in providing expert advice, and occasionally financial assistance, to voluntary community and youth organizations. Especially after 1974, the department provided much support for youth centers, where recreational facilities were available for working young people. In the late 1980s, there were ninety-eight of these youth centers, eighty-three of which were run by local governments.

Social services to other departments included long-term care for persons released from psychiatric institutions and, on occasion, for former medical patients; prison welfare measures; and assistance for students having difficulty adjusting to school.

Public assistance was first instituted in 1952 to reduce poverty by offering economic assistance to very poor families, the aged, and the disabled. This service was greatly expanded in 1973, when every Cypriot citizen was made eligible for financial assistance "for the maintenance of a minimum standard of living, and the satisfaction of his basic needs," and promised social services for solving "his personal problems and the improvement of his living conditions." The ultimate objective of these services was to make their recipients socially and economically self-sufficient. By the time of the Turkish invasion in 1974, public assistance expenditures were minimal, given full employment and comparatively high living standards. The years immediately after the invasion saw a swelling of public assistance services. By 1987, when the economy was fully restored, there were only 5,087 recipients of public assistance, half of whom were aged or disabled.

Refugees and Social Reconstruction

During and immediately after the 1974 invasion, the Department of Social Welfare Services undertook the housing, clothing, and feeding of the 180,000 refugees. The social needs stemming from the invasion were so great, however, that a new agency, the Special Service for the Care and Rehabilitation of Displaced Persons, was established in September 1974. Initially this agency concentrated on emergency relief by distributing food and clothing and providing medical assistance to the refugee camps. After a few months, it became clear that the thousands of displaced people would not return to their homes in the foreseeable future. As a result, the agency gradually expanded its scope, to aid the reintegration of the displaced into the new society forming in the government-controlled area, once their immediate physical survival had been ensured.

Housing for the wave of refugees was initially provided by the construction of twenty-three camps housing 20,000 displaced persons in tents. Thousands, however, remained outside the camps in shacks, makeshift barracks, public buildings, and half-finished houses. By the end of 1975, the service had replaced its tents with wooden barracks, built by the occupants themselves with materials or money provided by the service.

Another initiative that contributed to solving the refugee problem was the Incentive Scheme for the Reactivation of Refugees. Instituted in 1976, this program provided financial incentives to help refugees get back on their feet. Funds were available to all refugees, but special emphasis was placed on certain occupational groups that could soon become economically self-reliant, such as farmers in remote areas. By fostering economic recovery, the program successfully combated a culture of despair in the refugee community and spared the government a considerable drain on its public assistance funds. Despite the magnitude of the refugee problem, the government concluded that by 1977 its measures had succeeded in rehabilitating all groups affected by the invasion.

The Special Service for the Care and Rehabilitation of Displaced Persons also undertook the construction of low-cost housing projects. In the 1975–86 period, 12,500 low-income families found housing in such projects, which also provided social services in the form of day-care centers, schools, and community and commercial centers. Other government programs that enabled thousands of refugees to live in acceptable housing involved "self-housing" on either private or state-owned land. In the period 1975-86, nearly 10,500 houses were built on private properties, and 11,000 on state-owned sites, at a cost to the government of C£280 million. By 1987 more than 43,000 families, about 80 percent of displaced persons, had been housed.

Once the refugee housing problem had been resolved, the government extended its housing program to include low- and middle-income groups, who also faced serious housing problems because of a tremendous increase in the cost of land and construction. Through a combination of controls on the value of land and housing loans, the government succeeded in significantly improving housing conditions.

Also introduced were a number of programs such as child care and youth recreation centers, hostels for the aged, assistance for invalids, and community welfare centers, all of which were incorporated in the existing services of the Department of Social Welfare Services. In this way, the objectives of social policy were redefined as the ''systematization, institutionalization, and legalization of public assistance, and the reconstruction of personal, family and social life in the island.''

"The Turkish Republic of Northern Cyprus"

Turkish Cypriot society, in the decades after World War II, experienced a series of trials almost cataclysmic in scope and intensity. Earlier, the Turkish Cypriot minority had lived quietly and securely under British rule. During the war, many Cypriots left the island for the first time to fight in His Majesty's forces. The burgeoning of Greek Cypriot nationalism in the 1950s at first only aroused misgivings in Turkish Cypriots, but within a few years it drew them into what they saw as a struggle for their survival as an independent community. In the 1960s, Turkish Cypriots often feared for their physical survival, and fled into fortified enclaves around the island. The Turkish intervention of 1974 led to the de facto partition of Cyprus, with Turkish Cypriots controlling 37 percent of its territory.

The partition disrupted many lives, and more than half of the Turkish Cypriots had to abandon their homes and find new places of residence. Once in possession of their own territory, they set about constructing a new state and creating a functioning economy. Old habits and ways of life had to be discarded, for now all aspects of society became the responsibility of the Turkish Cypriots themselves. Education expanded, a new professional class emerged, a growing economy created new kinds of occupations, women left their homes to work, life in formerly isolated villages was altered by the pull of the urban areas, and the Turkish Cypriot community entered a phase of its existence unimaginable a generation earlier.

Population

Except for a few Maronites in the Kormakiti (Koruçam) area, at the western end of the Kyrenia range, and several hundred Greek Cypriots in the Karpas Peninsula, the people living in the "Turkish Republic of Northern Cyprus" ("TRNC") were Turkish Cypriots, descendants of Turks who settled in Cyprus following the Ottoman conquest in 1571. As a result of the Ottoman conquest, the ethnic and cultural composition of Cyprus changed drastically. Although the island had been ruled by Venetians, its population was mostly Greek. Turkish rule brought an influx of settlers speaking a different language and entertaining other cultural traditions and beliefs. In accordance with the decree of Sultan Selim II, some 5,720 households left Turkey from the Karaman, İçel, Yozgat, Alanya, Antalya, and Aydın regions of Anatolia and migrated to Cyprus. The Turkish migrants were largely farmers, but some earned their livelihoods as shoemakers, tailors, weavers, cooks, masons, tanners, jewelers, miners, and workers in other trades. In addition, some 12,000 soldiers, 4,000 cavalrymen, and 20,000 former soldiers and their families stayed in Cyprus.

The Ottoman Empire allowed its non-Muslim ethnic communities (or *millets,* from the Arabic word for religion, *millah*) a degree of autonomy if they paid their taxes and were obedient subjects. The *millet* system permitted Greek Cypriots to remain in their villages and maintain their traditional institutions. The Turkish immigrants often lived by themselves in new settlements, but many lived in the same villages as Greek Cypriots. For the next four centuries, the two communities lived side by side throughout the island. Despite this physical proximity, each ethnic community had its own culture and there was little intermingling. Both communities, for example, considered interethnic marriage taboo, although it did sometimes occur. Also, in spite of relations that were often cordial, there was little possibility of serious intimacy between the two communities. In fact, according to the American psychologist, Vamik Volkan, the two groups seemed to have a psychological need to remain separate from each other.

Until the island came under British administration in 1878, there were only rough estimates of Cyprus's population and its ethnic breakdown. In more recent times, population figures became highly controversial after it was agreed that the government established in 1960 was to be staffed at a 70-to-30 ratio of Greek and Turkish Cypriots, although the latter made up only 18 to 20 percent of the island's population. For this reason, the population figures were a vital issue in the island's government, likely to affect any far-reaching political settlements in the 1990s.

About 40,000 to 60,000 Turks lived on Cyprus in the late sixteenth century, according to Ottoman migration figures. In the eighteenth century, the British consul in Syria, DeVezin, believed that the Turkish population on the island outnumbered the Greek population by a ratio of two to one. According to his estimates, the Greek Cypriots numbered between 20,000 to 30,000 and the Turkish population around 60,000. Not all historians accept his estimate, however. If there was a Turkish majority, it did not last. By the time of the first British census of the island in 1881, Greek Cypriots numbered 140,000 and Turkish Cypriots 42,638. One reason suggested for the small number of Turkish Cypriots was that many of them sold their property and migrated to mainland Turkey when the island was placed under British administration according to the Cyprus Convention of 1878.

There was a significant Turkish Cypriot exodus from the island between 1950 and 1974 when thousands left the island, mainly for Britain and Australia. The migration had two phases. The first lasted from 1950 to 1960, when Turkish Cypriots benefited from liberal British immigration policies as the island gained its independence and many Turkish Cypriots settled in London. Emigration would have been higher in this period had there not been pressure from the Turkish Cypriot leadership to remain in Cyprus and participate in building the new republic.

The second and more intense phase of Turkish Cypriot emigration began after intercommunal strife increased in late 1963. Living conditions for Turkish Cypriots worsened as about 25,000 of them, faced with Greek Cypriot violence, gathered in several enclaves around the island. In addition, all Turkish Cypriots working for the government of the Republic of Cyprus lost their civil service positions. Aid from Turkey allowed those in the enclaves to survive, but life at a subsistence level and the constant threat of violence caused numerous Turkish Cypriots to leave for a better life abroad. As before, most emigrants left for Australia and Britain, but some settled in Turkey. By 1972 the Turkish Cypriot population had declined to around 78,000, and prospects for the community's survival on the island looked bleak.

After the de facto partition of the island in 1974, Turkish Cypriots began to return to Cyprus, and the decline was reversed. In addition, some 20,000 Turkish guest workers moved to the island to revive the Turkish Cypriot economy. Many of these workers eventually decided to remain permanently and take "TRNC" citizenship. Some immigration from Turkey continued in subsequent years. Largely as a result of this dual immigration, the Turkish Cypriot population totaled 167,256 in 1988, according to the "TRNC" State Planning Organisation.

The average annual rate of population increase during the period 1978–87 was 1.3 percent. In 1987 the rate was 1.5 percent. Despite the smallness of most age cohorts (that is, those born in a particular year) born in the 1970s (a probable reflection of the decade's turbulence), more than half the population was less than twenty-five years of age (see fig. 6). The age-sex distribution matched standard patterns, with males in the majority in the first few decades, and women in the majority thereafter.

Ethnicity

Traditionally, both Cypriot communities were very conscious of their languages, cultures, and histories. Turkish Cypriots thought of themselves as Turks living on Cyprus and as members of the larger Turkish nation. Greek Cypriots believed that their language, history, culture and Orthodox religion made them part of the larger Greek nation. It is probably not an exaggeration to say that over the centuries, neither group accepted the equality of the other's language, culture, ethnicity, and religion. Despite the separate lives of the two communities, however, some degree of cross-cultural development did occur. Furthermore, both the Greek and Turkish Cypriots were strongly attached to their island, and they distinguished themselves from foreigners, including mainland Greeks and Turks.

One can observe a great irony in Cypriot self-identification. On the one hand, the two communities were proud to identify themselves with their respective greater nations. On the other hand, both shared the belief that they were socially more progressive (better educated and less conservative) and therefore distinct from the mainlanders. Thus, until the events of 1963, which led to a strict separation of the two communities, Greek and Turkish Cypriots lived side by side in a love-hate relationship. The two communities had borrowed some customs and ways of living from one another, and to some degree a recognizable "Cypriot feeling" had developed over the centuries, distinguishing Cypriots from their cousins in Greece and Turkey. Generally, one did not know to which community a Cypriot belonged until he or she spoke. Yet the two communities viewed each other with some suspicion and dislike. Tragically, however, a deepening of shared feelings was precluded by the events of late 1963. After these events, Greek and Turkish Cypriots lived separately, and their offspring grew up with no intercommunal contact.

Broadly, three main forces—education, British colonial practices, and secularization accompanying economic development—can be held responsible for transforming two ethnic communities into two national ones. Education was perhaps the most important, for it affected Cypriots during childhood and youth, the period of greatest susceptibility to outside influences. The two communities adopted the educational policies of Greece and Turkey, respectively, resulting in the nationalist indoctrination of their youth. The schools polarized Cypriots in at least two ways. The segregated school systems

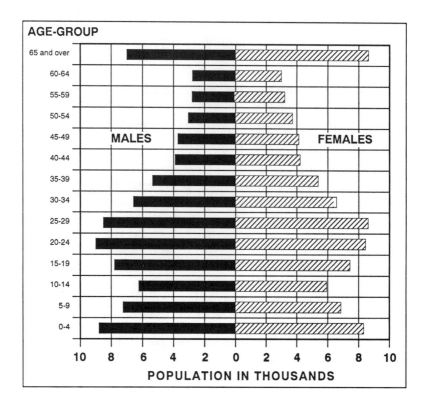

AGE-GROUP

Source: Based on information from "Turkish Republic of Northern Cyprus," State Planning Organisation, Statistics and Research Department, *Statistical Yearbook, 1988*, Nicosia, 1989, 12.

Figure 6. "Turkish Republic of Northern Cyprus": Population by Age and Sex, 1989

of the colonial and postindependence period socialized students into Greek and Turkish ethnicity, teaching mainland speech, culture, folklore, and nationalist myths. The texts used in these schools also included ethnic propaganda, often highly chauvinistic, with each community emphasizing its superiority over the other.

British colonial policies also promoted ethnic polarization. The British applied the principle of "divide and rule," setting the two groups against each other to prevent combined action against colonial rule. For example, when Greek Cypriots rebelled in the 1950s, the colonial administration established an all-Turkish police force, known as the Auxiliary Police, to combat Greek Cypriots. This and similar practices contributed to intercommunal animosity.

Secularization also fostered ethnic nationalism. Although economic development and increased education reduced the explicitly religious characteristics of the two communities, the growth of nationalism on the two mainlands increased the significance of other differences. Turkish nationalism was at the core of the revolutionary program promoted by the father of modern Turkey, Kemal Atatürk (1881–1938), and affected Turkish Cypriots who followed his principles. President of the Republic of Turkey from 1923 to 1938, Atatürk attempted to build a new nation on the ruins of the Ottoman Empire and elaborated a program of six principles (the ''Six Arrows'') to do so. His principles of secularism (laicism) and nationalism reduced Islam's role in the everyday life of individuals and emphasized Turkish identity as the main source of nationalism. Traditional education with a religious foundation was discarded and replaced with one that followed secular principles and, shorn of Arab and Persian influences, was purely Turkish. Turkish Cypriots quickly adopted the secular program of Turkish nationalism. Under Ottoman rule, Turkish Cypriots had been classified as Muslims, a distinction based on religion; Atatürk's program made their Turkishness paramount and further reinforced their division from their Greek Cypriot neighbors.

Ethnic Values and Attitudes

American sociologists Marvin Gerst and James H. Tenzel studied both ethnic communities in the early 1970s, after a decade of the postindependence struggle. Gerst and Tenzel focused mainly on the psychological grounds of ethnic conflict. One survey instrument used in their interviews with several hundred Cypriots measured perceptions of one's own and the opposing ethnic group; the results were then standardized in reference to a third group, American males. Although both Cypriot groups varied considerably from the American statistical norms, Greek and Turkish Cypriots had similar scores as regards their own behavior and perceptions of the other community as acting according to a shared list of generally negative behavior traits.

The Turkish Cypriots scored as patient, obliging, stability seeking, thorough, self-effacing, dependent, mannerly, tactful, less self-aggrandizing, and more open to reasonable argument. Tenzel and Gerst described the Turkish Cypriots as hierarchical, patriarchal, and authoritarian—characteristics of a society in which roles are clearly defined. Turkish Cypriots regarded public service as a more prestigious though ill-paying occupation than a successful business career. As psychologist Vamik Volkan also argued, these roles were instilled in childhood: Turkish Cypriot child care favored imitative, docile behavior and discouraged activity, curiosity, and talkativeness.

The psychological and behavioral differences between the two communities were perceived as extremely negative stereotypes by the other. Greek Cypriots, for example, scored as assertive in the survey done by Gerst and Tenzel. This quality appeared as impolite aggressiveness to Turkish Cypriots. Greek Cypriots, on the other hand, viewed the Turkish Cypriot attention to manners and procedures as dullness and lack of ambition. In the context of interethnic conflict, each group denied the goodness of the other and pointed to examples illustrating these differing norms to "prove" the identical charges of aggression, brutality, and stubbornness.

Language

The Turkish dialect spoken by Turkish Cypriots is closely related to other dialects of Anatolia, but distinct from the urban dialects of Istanbul, Ankara, and İzmir. Turkish Cypriots faced few difficulties communicating with mainland Turks. The differences that exist are much less significant than those found between Turkish and other Turkic languages of Central Asia. Atatürk's language and educational reforms brought sweeping changes in standard Turkish. A Latin alphabet was introduced in place of the Arabic script, and the heavily Arabicized and Persianized court dialect was rejected as the basis for standardization. The Turkish Cypriot community was the only Turkish minority in former Ottoman territories outside mainland Turkey to quickly adopt Atatürk's linguistic changes as well as the other revolutionary principles of his program.

Social Structure

The structure of Turkish Cypriot society changed dramatically during the twentieth century, especially after World War II. The main force for change was the growth of a modern and prosperous economy that required a variety of occupations, encouraged urbanization, made education more accessible, and permitted more contact with the outside world. The de facto partition of the island in 1974 also strongly changed how Turkish Cypriots lived. The evolution of a Western-style family out of the traditional family structure was perhaps the most socially significant of these changes.

Urban-Rural Composition

When the Republic of Cyprus was established in 1960, 60 percent of Turkish Cypriots lived in villages. The rest lived in the five urban centers of Nicosia (Lefkoşa), Famagusta (Gazimağusa), Larnaca,

Limassol, and Paphos. Few Turkish Cypriots lived in Kyrenia (Girne). During the period of intercommunal conflict, the urban-rural distribution of the Turkish Cypriot population was unclear because of the thousands of refugees living in tents and temporary shelters. After the de facto division of the island in 1974, however, there was a gradual change in the urban-rural ratio. By the late 1980s, 51 percent of the Turkish Cypriot population lived in urban areas. Given the small number of Turkish Cypriots, however, urban centers were not large. As of 1987, the Turkish Cypriot section of Nicosia had only about 38,000 inhabitants, Famagusta 20,000, and Kyrenia 7,100.

One reason for increased urbanization was the resettlement program after 1974, which placed refugees from territory controlled by the government of the Republic of Cyprus in houses previously occupied by Greek Cypriots in the urban areas of Kyrenia, Morphou (Güzelyurt), and Famagusta. Immigrants from Turkey were largely settled in villages.

Resettlement was an extensive process that directly involved about two-thirds of the Turkish Cypriot population. According to some estimates, about 60,000 Turkish Cypriots moved from their places of residence following the establishment of a cease-fire in 1974. Most managed to move behind Turkish military lines on their own. Others, however, required international agreements or diplomatic initiatives in order to join their ethnic community. About 9,400 Turkish Cypriots took refuge in the British base areas. Another 8,100 came to territory controlled by Turkish forces after negotiations between Greek Cypriot and Turkish Cypriot leaders under United Nations (UN) auspices resulted in an agreement to exchange populations. Although all Turkish Cypriots moved to areas controlled by their community, not all Greek Cypriots returned to areas controlled by the Republic of Cyprus. Most of these Greek Cypriots lived in the Karpas Peninsula.

The growth in the urban sector also reflected a changed Turkish Cypriot economy. In 1960 agriculture employed nearly half of all Turkish Cypriots. By 1990 this sector accounted for well under a third of the work force; about half of economically active Turkish Cypriots earned their livelihoods in the service sector and one-fifth in construction and industry. Except for agricultural work, most employment was in urban areas.

Despite the marked decline in agricultural employment, at the end of the 1980s, 49 percent of Turkish Cypriots still lived in areas classified as rural. Urbanization was not as extensive as suggested by employment figures. The discrepancy resulted from the small size of the "TRNC." Many of those who worked in urban areas were able to remain in their villages because the distance between most villages and urban centers was less than an hour's drive by car. Workers did not migrate to areas of employment, but instead commuted. As a result of such commuting, other urban developments, such as changes in attitudes toward education and social values, were more easily diffused than otherwise would have been the case.

Class Structure

The Turkish Cypriot class structure changed markedly after 1974. During the colonial and pre-1963 independence years, most Turkish Cypriots lived in rural areas and engaged in farming. Others living in urban areas were mostly employed by the civil service. Very few Turkish Cypriots engaged in business. Under these conditions, one found the following social classes in the Turkish Cypriot community: large landowners (descendants of the Ottoman administrators), bureaucrats, a small class of professionals, and peasants/farmers.

Once Turkish Cypriots had created their own government and economy, they began to enter new occupations, altering the class structure of their community. At the beginning of the 1990s, there were many more Turkish Cypriot businessmen than there had been a generation earlier, and many others were highly trained professionals because of the marked expansion of higher education. The old landed aristocracy no longer accounted for all wealthy Turkish Cypriots. This class was joined by the new rich, who had economic ties to the outside world. Although such developments should have contributed to the rise of middle-income groups among the Turkish Cypriots, the economic difficulties faced by the new state (most significantly high inflation) seriously eroded the real incomes of the middle class, most of whom were civil servants.

At the beginning of the 1990s, most Turkish Cypriots were neither wealthy nor had professional occupations. The majority were wage earners, working in small production units or at routine clerical and service jobs. About one-fourth of the work force was engaged in farming.

Marriage and Family

Turkish Cypriots were generally concerned with promoting the honor, prestige, and economic prosperity of their families. A major part of the thought, energy, and income of the family went to educating children, marrying them well, and helping them find good jobs. More than in most Western societies, Turkish Cypriots were conscious of their family as a whole and identified strongly with how its individual members fared as part of this whole. However, socio-economic changes in recent decades have led to the existence of two types of families in Turkish Cypriot society: traditional and largely rural, and modern and urban.

The traditional family maintained strong links between the nuclear or core family and the extended family. The extended family included the parents' siblings and their children, grandparents, and in many cases second and third cousins. Within this family network, financial and social support were key links among the members. When one of the extended family suffered economic hardship, that person could expect aid from able relatives. It was also common to help relatives in the field or on the farm.

The nuclear or core traditional family might include not only the husband and wife and their unmarried children, but also a newly married son and his family, and sometimes the mother's parents. The presence of the mother's parents in the core family was an important variation from the traditional Turkish family structure, in which the husband's parents lived with the family.

According to traditional Turkish family structure, the bride married into the groom's family and became virtually a servant to the household. The legitimation of the bride's lower status was found in the custom of *başlik parası* (bonnet money) practiced in traditional Turkish society and reintroduced into Cyprus by some Turkish settlers after 1974. According to this custom, money or valuable goods were paid to the bride's father by the bridegroom and his family. If the bridegroom was unable to meet the amount specified by the bride's father, the marriage could not occur. In this practice, the money paid to the father did not go toward helping the newlyweds in any form. Rather, the money stayed with the girl's father. Widely practiced in rural Turkey, the custom frequently results in the marriages of unwilling brides. The long absence of this custom among Turkish Cypriots was a sign of women's more secure and higher status on the island.

Turkish Cypriots employed a different form of financial arrangement in marriages, *drahoma,* a dowry custom of Greek Cypriot origin. It is probable that over the centuries the Turkish Cypriots recognized the advantages of this custom and adapted it to their own needs. *Drahoma,* as practiced by Greek Cypriots, required that the bride's family provide substantial assistance to the newlyweds. Turkish Cypriots modified it to include assistance from both families. Traditionally, the bride's family provided a house, some furniture, and money as part of their daughter's dowry. The bridegroom's family met the young couple's remaining housing needs. If the bride's family was unable to provide such assistance, the young couple lived with the bride's family until they saved enough money to set up their own separate household. Lastly, the bride brought to her new home the rest of her dowry, known as *cehiz,* making the new family financially more secure. The advantages of *drahoma* were so obvious to the Turkish Cypriot community that modern families also practiced it.

In the traditional Turkish Cypriot family, the father had the last word in his children's choice of spouses. Customarily, the bride and groom did not have a chance for individual visits prior to their engagement. Usually, an elderly member of the suitor's family went to the young woman's parents and asked for her hand in marriage. If her father agreed, gifts were exchanged between the two families and the engagement took place.

Originally, the wedding ceremonies for the bridegroom and bride occurred separately. Turkish Cypriots no longer practiced this custom. Only the Turkish rural migrants to Cyprus continued the tradition of separate ceremonies. In rural Turkish Cypriot society, the bride and bridegroom attended the same ceremony and the festivities lasted for several days.

Women of traditional families generally did not work outside the home. It was their responsibility to tend to the traditional domestic tasks, while husbands and sons dealt with business and other concerns outside the home.

In contrast to the traditional family, the modern family structure revolved around the nuclear family and had a distinctly urban character. Although maintaining close social ties with the extended family, members of the nuclear family remained economically isolated from other relatives. There were joint economic relations among nuclear and extended family members, but they were far less common than with the traditional family.

Another important difference between traditional and modern families was that marriage was not under the strict control of the father. Young couples often decided on marriage themselves. Although dating, as practiced in the United States, was not common even at the beginning of the 1990s, couples met together in small groups of friends. Once a couple decided to marry, both sets of parents were consulted. The families then arranged the engagement and marriage. As noted, *drahoma* was also practiced by modern urban families.

The modern family usually consisted of only the husband, wife, and unmarried children. Large multigenerational extended families were unusual. Although the husband continued even in the 1980s to have a strong decision-making role, the wife became increasingly involved in the family's economic and social choices.

A major factor in the wife's changing family role was the fact that she also worked outside the home to support the family.

Working wives and mothers were a relatively new phenomenon in Turkish Cypriot society. Until the post-1974 period, few women worked outside the home and even fewer had professional educations. Men's earnings had to be sufficient to satisfy the needs of their families, and women typically remained home and focused their efforts on raising their children.

After the 1974 war, this traditional arrangement lost its predominance. Once Turkish Cypriots established a government of their own, they faced immense difficulties in managing its institutions and creating a functioning economy. Adding to the intrinsic difficulties of these tasks were the lack of international recognition of their state and the Greek Cypriot economic blockade. Under these circumstances, women's participation in the work force became essential to meet both their state's and their families' needs. Building a new state required officials to hire trained personnel of both sexes to fill positions in the bureaucracy. As a result, Turkish Cypriot women came to be employed outside the home to a much greater extent than previously.

Women's absence from home worked a hardship on families with children. For the first time, child care became a serious issue in Turkish Cypriot society. Day-care centers were established in many cases, but when centers were unavailable, grandparents frequently helped care for their children's offspring. The emergence of the child-care problem was an unfortunate result of women's employment. It was an indication, however, that the structure of many Turkish Cypriot families in urban areas had become Westernized.

Divorce was legal in the "TRNC." During the first eight years of the 1980s, the number of divorces increased from 149 in 1980 to 177 in 1987. The increase was slightly higher than the increase in marriages, which went from 1,058 in 1981, to 1,162 in 1987. Incompatibility was the cause given for about 90 percent of divorces. The highest frequency of divorce occurred in the first year of marriage.

Religion

Nearly all Turkish Cypriots were followers of Islam, but, unlike most predominantly Muslim societies, the "TRNC" was a secular state, as specified in the first article of the 1985 constitution. There was no state religion, and Turkish Cypriots were free to choose their own religion. Religious leaders had little influence in politics, and religious instruction, although available in schools, was not obligatory. The few Greek Cypriots who lived in the

Kyrenia (Girne)
Courtesy Office of the ''Turkish Republic of Northern Cyprus,'' Washington

"TRNC" were free to follow their Greek Orthodox faith. The tiny Maronite community had its Christian Maronite Church. In addition, there were Anglican and Roman Catholic churches.

The position of Islam and Islamic institutions in the Turkish Cypriot community differed from the position of Greek Orthodoxy among Greek Cypriots. In contrast to the Greek Cypriot *millet's* ethnarch, there was no Islamic religious figure with political power. Whereas the Church of Cyprus was intimately identified with Greek nationalism and the campaign for enosis, Islam played virtually no role in Turkish Cypriot nationalism. The great figure of this latter movement was Atatürk, a man famous for secularism, and in many respects the polar opposite of Archbishop Makarios III, who was both a religious and political leader. It was Atatürk who established the secular Turkish state, which has generally adhered to his doctrines ever since. Although Atatürk had no jurisdiction over Cyprus, Turkish Cypriots adopted most of his program voluntarily and with little controversy. Turkish Cypriots were among the first to adopt Atatürk's prohibition of Arabic in religious services and to use the Quran in Turkish translation. Since Atatürk's death, Turkish Cypriots have usually followed the religious practices of Turkey. When in 1951, for example, Turkish authorities once again allowed the use of the Quran in Arabic and directed that the call to prayers also be in Arabic, Turkish Cypriots followed suit. Despite these lapses from Atatürk's policies, both Turkey and the "TRNC" remained fundamentally secular.

The Islamic faith arose from the teachings of the Prophet Muhammad in Arabia in the seventh century. It is based on a monotheistic belief in God (Allah) as all-powerful in the universe and in human subservience to God's will. All devout persons should submit to the divinely willed plan; the word Muslim means one who has surrendered to God's will. This will has been made known through the prophets, including those of the Old Testament and Jesus, with Muhammad being the last of them. The Quran, held to have been revealed by God to Muhammad and dictated by him to scribes, is thus a guide to practical living and the basis for law covering all spheres of life.

The principal religious observances, often known as the five pillars of Islam, are the profession of faith that "there is no God but God and Muhammad is his messenger"; daily prayer; fasting during the month of Ramadan when the Quran was revealed; almsgiving; and once in one's lifetime, if feasible, the pilgrimage to Mecca, the birthplace of Muhammad and eventual home of his community of disciples. The daily prayers are called from the minaret of the mosque at dawn, noon, midafternoon, sunset, and early evening. Devout Muslim males also attend community prayer services at the mosque on Friday, the weekly holy day.

Turkish Cypriots, like most Turkish nationals, are followers of Sunni Islam. After the Prophet's death, his followers split over the question of the method of choosing his successors. The Sunnis (from *sunnah,* tradition) argued that Muhammad had prescribed no definitive procedure; the Shias (from Shiat Ali, party of Ali) insisted that his designation of his cousin and son-in-law Ali established a hereditary succession. Basic questions of theology and practice deepened the split. Sunnis consider the Quran and the *hadith,* a separate collection of the sayings and deeds of Muhmamad, to be a complete, comprehensive, and eternally correct source of religious guidance requiring only deductive elaboration by scholars. Shias accept an additional body of esoteric lore handed down by Muhammad to Ali, which may be revealed and expanded by divinely inspired Imams who were descendants of Ali. Within Sunni Islam, Turkish Cypriots have traditionally followed the Hanafi school of legal interpretation, a rather austere variety of Islam.

Evkaf Idaresi (Turkish Religious Trust, usually known as Evkaf) was the prime institutional representative of the Turkish Cypriot community. Until 1915 it was governed by delegates chosen by the sultan and the British, with the Turkish delegate generally exercising wide discretion; after formal annexation of the island, the British appointed both delegates. The Evkaf functioned during the colonial period as a government department. However, in the intensely nationalistic period before independence, control was given to a new elective council, and the constitution of 1960 assigned religious matters as one of the major powers of the new Turkish Cypriot Communal Chamber. Since 1973, the Evkaf has been an independent foundation with its own budget, insulated to some extent from the political leadership of the Turkish Cypriot community. Whereas the Evkaf operated Muslim schools in the past, in recent decades it has simply provided funds for the salary of the mufti, the highest religious figure, and for the construction, repair, and maintenance of the mosques. The Evkak's revenues were derived from its large landholdings and other property placed in trust for religious purposes. Before 1974 it was the second largest landowner in Cyprus, surpassed only by the Church of Cyprus. Because much of its property was located in territory occupied by the Republic of Cyprus, however, the de facto partition of the island cost the Evkaf half of its agricultural property and nearly all of its building sites.

The mufti was the spiritual head of the Turkish Cypriot Islamic community. His office underwent dramatic changes after the Ottoman period, when religion and administration were fused under the sultan as God's representative ruling over the Islamic community. The mufti's role was essentially that of supreme authority in religious law rather than high priest or administrator. He was appointed by the sultan until Atatürk abolished the caliphate. The British abolished the position in 1928 and transferred its duties to a new official in the Evkaf. The office was revived in 1956 as part of the reforms that gave Turkish Cypriots control over the Evkaf; the new mufti was elected by the island's Muslims and his retirement age set at seventy-five. Because of the secularization of the Turkish Cypriot society, however, the mufti lost his jurisdiction over such matters as law, marriage, and education.

Turkish Cypriots were among the most secular of Islamic peoples. Wedding ceremonies were civil, rather than religious, for example. The eight decades of British rule contributed to this secularization. More significant was the Turkish Cypriots' close adherence to Atatürk's reforms in Turkey. Religion came to be a personal matter among Turkish Cypriots, and they did not attempt to impose their religious beliefs on others. Although there was some fasting during the month of Ramadan, moderate attendance at the Friday prayers, and widespread observation of the holy days, few Turkish Cypriots were orthodox Muslims. Most of those who fasted during Ramadan, for example, lived an unorthodox life the rest of the year, and Turkish Cypriots generally did not abstain from alcohol as standard Muslim teaching requires, but followed traditional Mediterranean drinking customs.

There were groups and organizations in the "TRNC" that opposed traditional Turkish Cypriot secularism and religious tolerance. Some Saudi Arabian and Libyan aid came from groups that wished to see an upsurge of Islamism (sometimes seen as fundamentalism) on the island. Some of the aid funded new mosques and Quran schools around the island and the new Islamic university in Lefka (Lefke).

The Cyprus Turkish Islam Society (CTIS) was one of the organizations working for an expanded role for Islam in the "TRNC." The group's program, the Turkish-Islamic Synthesis (Türk-Islam Sentezi), called for the union of Turkish nationalism and Islam, a coalition between government and military, and a society built on Islamic foundations and the rule of religious law, sharia (*şeriat* in Turkish). The Turkish-Islamic Synthesis also identified enemies to be controlled or eliminated, including atheists, communists, Western humanists, members of other religions, and those who blame Islam for the collapse of the Ottoman Empire. It maintained close ties to Sheyh Nazım Adil Kıbrıslı, a Cypriot living in London, who was a leading member of the Nakşibendi order of Sunni Islam in Europe. The Nakşibendi order also advocated a return to sharia and openly opposed Atatürk's reforms.

Given the secular traditions of Turkish Cypriots, these and other like-minded groups have an uphill task to realize their aims. Nevertheless, some Turkish Cypriots would certainly find these aims attractive. This fact and the access of Islamic groups to the financial resources of oil-producing nations made it likely that their presence would continue to be felt in the "TRNC."

Education

Although the "TRNC" was by most standards still a so-called "developing society" at the beginning of the 1990s, with a per capita income and other social indicators similar to those of Greece, Turkey, and Chile, the Turkish Cypriot educational level was that of more advanced countries. The Turkish Cypriot literacy rate stood at 97 percent, and there was a high number of university students. These educational attainments stemmed in part from relatively enlightened British rule in the colonial period and the close adherence of Turkish Cypriots to Atatürk's educational reforms. These reforms entailed the adoption of the Latin alphabet and an emphasis on secular values. Also contributing to the educational successes were the easily manageable size of Turkish Cypriot society and the fact that a well-trained work force was necessary if the "TRNC" were to prosper.

Few Turkish Cypriots received a university education in the period before the island became independent in 1960, and those who did frequently did not return to Cyprus upon completion of their studies. The fact that a high-school graduate in the 1940s and 1950s immediately attained a respectable position in the bureaucracy indicated the scarcity of university graduates.

The small number of university-educated Turkish Cypriots created a serious problem when government agencies were staffed according to the 70 to 30 Greek Cypriot to Turkish Cypriot ratio agreed upon when the Republic of Cyprus was established in 1960. To overcome this problem, Turkish Cypriots began a massive education training program that involved sending their high-school graduates to universities in Turkey. To facilitate this process, the Turkish authorities provided special quotas for Turkish Cypriot students. Thus, Cypriot Turks obtained easier access to university education in Turkey than did mainland Turks. This procedure ended in the late 1970s. Since then, Turkish Cypriots have participated in the general university entrance examination set by the Turkish Ministry of Education.

Turkish Cypriots set up their own education system after the de facto partition of the island in 1974. By the beginning of the 1990s, they had schools and universities that taught their youth from age four up to the graduate level. A preprimary school system was not yet run by the state, but private kindergartens were in operation in many areas. The public school system, under the direction of the Ministry of Education, Sports, and Youth, began with primary school, which was free and compulsory for all children between the ages of six and fifteen. Primary school was divided into two stages: the first for children aged six to twelve, and the second for children between thirteen and fifteen. Three years of secondary education for youth sixteen to eighteen took place at lycées (high schools) offering general academic courses and at technical and vocational schools providing specialized training.

The Turkish Cypriot education system expanded rapidly, with regard to both numbers and types of schools and students (see table 9, Appendix). The number of preprimary and elementary schools increased significantly. In these institutions, the student-teacher ratio also improved, from thirty in 1976–77 to twenty-seven in preprimary and twenty-three in elementary schools in 1988–89. At the junior high-school level, the student/teacher ratio improved from twenty in 1976–77 to twenty-two in 1988–89. The figures in 1986–87 for the lycées and colleges were 20 and 15.6, respectively. In the vocational and technical schools, the 1988–89 figures indicated a student/teacher ratio of eight to one, a tremendous advantage for individual student training. In terms of literacy, state statistics show important improvements. The rate of those attending school in 1987 was seven to twelve years of age, 98 percent; thirteen to fifteen, 66 percent; and fifteen to eighteen, 50 percent.

Turkish Cypriot teachers often studied abroad, but they could also receive their training from a domestic teacher training college. The Higher Technical Institute and the Eastern Mediterranean University (EMU) at Famagusta provided education at the university level, as did the private University College of North Cyprus and the religious institution Lefke University. EMU, the largest of these schools, offered courses in engineering, business, and economics. The medium of teaching at this university was English, a considerable attraction, and most of its students were foreigners, mainly Turks. Enrollment grew rapidly. During the 1984–85 academic year, EMU had 458 students. Enrollment nearly tripled the following year, and in the 1990–91 academic year amounted to 3,585. Two-thirds of the students were Turkish, 715 were Turkish Cypriots, and most of the remainder came from other Middle Eastern countries. In addition to those enrolled at the EMU,

Dr. Burhan Nalbantoğlu General Hospital in Nicosia
Courtesy Office of the ''Turkish Republic of Northern Cyprus,'' Washington

1,875 Turkish Cypriots attended foreign universities in 1988, 1,580 of them in Turkey. The United States and Britain each had more than 100 Turkish Cypriot university students.

The growing emphasis on university education among Turkish Cypriots was not without its drawbacks. Because the available jobs for university graduates were limited in such a small state, many graduates chose to remain outside Cyprus. This fact was especially true of those with advanced degrees. The resulting brain drain might be reduced by the continued expansion of faculty and staff at EMU.

Lefke University was founded in 1990 by the Cyprus Science Wakf (a religious foundation) with US$2 million in funds from the Islamic Development Bank. The university had as its goal the combining of Islamic principles with advanced education for the benefit of students of the Middle East. It was thus a departure from the Turkish Cypriot tradition of secular education. At its founding, however, the new university had strong links not with Turkish Cypriots, but rather with Saudi Arabian groups and Turkish Islamists who wished to establish a university according to their ideals in Turkey. Strong opposition from Turkey's academic institutions forced them to settle on Lefka as a suitable site. The new university's closeness to Turkey and the fact that Turkish and Turkish

101

Cypriot citizens enjoyed preferential treatment in each other's state meant that Turkish students of an Islamist bent would be able to study there. Some observers feared that Lefke University would have a negative effect on the Turkish Cypriot tradition of secularism. Others welcomed the establishment of a center of sharia in the "TRNC."

Health and Welfare

In the late 1980s, the Turkish Cypriot health care system consisted of two general hospitals, two district hospitals, one psychiatric hospital—all of which were operated by the state—and four private specialized hospitals. There were also ten public health centers that treated less serious medical problems. Between 1963 and 1989, the number of doctors serving in the public sector increased from 76 to 116. This increase was seen in the numbers of both general practitioners and specialists. During the same period, the number of nurses increased from 225 to 315, and the number of public hospital beds rose from 497 to 833. The number of hospital beds in private hospitals was 193 in 1989. With these improvements, the ratio of persons per physician declined from 1,908 in 1963 to 685 in 1989. The number of dentists also increased. In 1989 there were eighteen dentists in state hospitals and eighty-two in private practice.

Health care services were administered by two directorates under the Ministry of Health and Social Welfare, the Directorate of Medicine and Health and the State Laboratories Directorate, and by the Social Assistance Services Office.

Health care was socialized in the "TRNC," although there remained a substantial private component. The main objective of the Ministry of Health and Social Welfare was to guarantee basic health care services for all citizens. In addition, the ministry assumed the responsibility of facilitating the satisfactory social use of these services. Such socialized health care required much capital—in short supply in the "TRNC." As a result of financial problems, the state faced great difficulties in providing major health care services quickly. In addition, the state sought to send patients to medical centers abroad, mostly to Turkey and Britain, when medical care for major health problems was not available domestically. All expenses including transportation were paid by the government.

The regional welfare offices in larger population centers operated under the Directorate of Social Welfare. The main duties of the directorate were child and family welfare, rehabilitation of juvenile delinquents, care of senior citizens, general community services, and provision of services for the families of the victims of intercommunal strife and the disabled. The three main towns contained housing centers for rural and/or poor children attending schools there.

The government also provided generous welfare and retirement benefits. The foundations for this system were laid by the British colonial administration. At the beginning of the 1990s, Turkish Cypriot social welfare policies compared favorably with those of advanced West European countries.

The Social Insurance Fund covered 75,000 citizens in 1989. In addition to paying for health care costs, the fund provided retirement benefits and financial aid to the needy, and assisted those disabled and survivors of those killed during intercommunal conflict. In October 1989, about 9,000 persons received monthly payments from the fund.

* * *

Statistical reports of the Republic of Cyprus are the most current source of information about Greek Cypriot society. Publications of the Social Research Center in Nicosia also cover a range of social topics. *The Cyprus Review,* also published in Nicosia, frequently contains articles dealing with recent social developments in Cyprus. There are a number of excellent books about Greek Cypriot society, but they treat only developments of the 1960s and 1970s. *The Greek Gift* and *The Heart Grown Bitter,* both by Peter Loizos, contain detailed treatments of the lives of the inhabitants of a village before and after the events of 1974. Kyriacos C. Markides and others deal with a larger village in *Lysi: Social Change in a Cypriot Village,* and Michael A. Attalides examines the capital in *Social Change and Urbanization in Cyprus.*

Readers wishing to learn more of Turkish Cypriot society will find their choice of sources restricted to a few books and publications. The *North Cyprus Almanack* published in London by K. Rüstem and Brother covers many social topics. Vamik Volkan has written numerous articles and books that treat, sometimes only in passing, the psychology and way of life of Turkish Cypriots. *The Cyprus Review* is also informative about Turkish Cypriot society. The journal attempts to bridge the gap between the island's two communities and contains scholarly articles that deal with a great variety of subjects. Statistics published by the "TRNC" State Planning Organisation can help a researcher learn much about the structure of Turkish Cypriot society. Finally, Lawrence Durrel's *Bitter Lemons,* written in the 1950s, provides glimpses of Cypriots of both communities before independence. (For further information and complete citations, see Bibliography.)

Chapter 3. The Economy

*Ruins of ancient aqueduct at Salamis near
the contemporary village of Ayios Seryios*

CYPRIOTS HAVE EXPERIENCED A SUBSTANTIAL improvement in their living standards since World War II. Cyprus benefited from the war, and in succeeding decades its economy grew at rates that matched those of other countries that profited from the general West European boom that began in the 1950s and lasted up to the first oil price increase of 1973. Cypriot per capita income increased steadily through this period; the economy diversified and ceased to be that of a Third World colony. This success was achieved despite widespread turmoil stemming from shaking off British rule in the 1950s and intercommunal warfare during the 1960s.

Cyprus was affected in 1973 and 1979 by the first and second oil price increases, for it was almost completely lacking in domestic sources of energy. However, energy-related economic disruption was negligible compared with the effects of the Turkish invasion of 1974, which ended in the de facto partition of the Republic of Cyprus. The island's economy disintegrated as a third of its inhabitants fled their homes and livelihoods and many farming, manufacturing, and commercial relationships were shattered. Thereafter, the island's Greek Cypriot and Turkish Cypriot communities lived separated from one another. Each sought to re-create a functioning economy.

Greeks Cypriots were the more successful. Republic of Cyprus planners adopted an aggressive program of constructive deficit spending, economic incentives, and targeted investments that led the Greek Cypriot economy to reach pre-1974 levels within a few years. This was an astonishing accomplishment in that the island's partition had cost the republic much of its agricultural and manufacturing assets.

The 1980s saw healthy growth and low unemployment. Tourism swelled, and by 1990 more than a million tourists, mostly from Western Europe, visited the republic each year. Housing them caused much construction and an explosion in the value of property along the coast. Manufacturing and trade were encouraged and grew. The destruction of Beirut permitted the republic to become a regional center for services and finance. As the 1990s began, Greek Cypriots were upgrading their tourist trade and aiming at a more diversified and sophisticated manufacturing sector. Leaders of the republic's economy hoped to take advantage of the republic's able and motivated work force and a strong and flexible commercial tradition.

The Turkish Cypriot economy also grew. Facing many obstacles and beginning at a lower point, however, its successes were smaller, and at the beginning of the 1990s Turkish Cypriots enjoyed a per capita income about one-third that of Greek Cypriots. Economic obstacles included the lack of a commercial tradition, a less well-trained work force, and rampant inflation largely imported from Turkey. However, perhaps the most serious economic hurdle Turkish Cypriots had to surmount was their state's lack of international recognition. Its absence deprived them of some international aid and made foreign connections difficult. Despite these difficulties, however, Turkish Cypriots could look with some optimism toward the future. Tourism expanded rapidly in the late 1980s and brought in vital foreign exchange. The overall economy had diversified to some extent. Agriculture was more efficient and employed a smaller share of the work force. The service sector had increased in importance. Analysts expected, however, that the Turkish Cypriot economy would likely continue to need Turkish assistance for the foreseeable future.

Republic of Cyprus

From independence in 1960 until the Turkish occupation of the north in 1974, the economy of Cyprus performed well overall, and the gross domestic product (GDP—see Glossary) increased at an average annual rate of about 7 percent in real terms. However, the Turkish Cypriot community did not share in this growth, living in its scattered agricultural enclaves under conditions like those of less developed countries (see The Republic of Cyprus, ch. 1).

The Turkish invasion and occupation of the northern 37 percent of the island severely disrupted the economy of the Republic of Cyprus. Fragmentation of the market, a massive displacement of people (about a third of the island's population), and loss of important natural resources had devastating effects. The government responded with the first and second emergency economic action plans, for 1975–76 and 1977–78. The pre-1974 policy of balanced budgets was replaced by expansionary fiscal and monetary policies aimed at stimulating economic activity. Incentive plans to encourage private economic activity were implemented, as were housing and employment programs for refugees who had fled areas seized by the Turks.

These efforts proved phenomenally successful. The economy expanded at a 6 percent rate in real terms between 1974 and 1978, and by 1978 unemployment stood at about 2 percent, compared with 30 percent at the end of 1974. This growth continued through the 1980s. In 1988 the per capita gross national product (GNP—see

Glossary) in current prices was about US$7,200 or C£3,597 (for value of the Cyprus pound—see Glossary), compared with C£537.9 in 1973.

The economy of the Republic of Cyprus changed as it grew in size and complexity. The primary sector lost ground, as it had in the decades before the Turkish invasion. Agriculture declined from more than 20 percent of GDP at the end of the 1960s to only about 7 percent by the end of the 1980s, although it employed about 15 percent of the labor force. Mining, vital in the 1950s as a source of exports, became insignificant.

Manufacturing increased at double-digit rates during much of the 1980s. At the end of the decade, it accounted for 15.2 percent of GDP, the second largest share, after the service sector's, and was the second largest source of employment. Manufacturing depended on exports, most to the Middle East and the European Economic Community (EEC—see Glossary). However, rising labor costs and relatively low-quality products stood in the way of future industrial growth. Construction provided just under 10 percent of GDP in 1989 and was the fourth largest private employer. Construction had declined in importance since the second half of the 1970s, when much housing for refugees was built and work began on constructing the tourist facilities that were important to the south's economy.

The service, or tertiary, sector was the dominant sector in the Greek Cypriot economy after the late 1970s. In 1988 it accounted for 50.2 percent of GDP. The sector's most dynamic component was trade, restaurants, and hotels (or tourism), which supplied 20.8 percent of the GDP and employed 22.3 percent of the labor force in 1988. The gigantic increase in the number of tourists—from 165,000 in 1976 to 1,376,000 in 1989—was the main cause of this subsector's growth. Tourism was also an important source of foreign exchange, exceeding the income from the export of domestic goods from 1985 through 1988.

The other branches of the service sector—transportation, storage, telecommunications, finance, insurance, real estate, and business services—also experienced steady growth and improvement. Another dynamic component of the sector, important to Cyprus's future economic growth, was offshore enterprises, which conducted diverse businesses abroad from a base in southern Cyprus. Attracted by generous tax concessions, the island's strategic location between Europe and the Middle East, and stable political conditions, many foreign businesses established themselves in the republic. By 1990 more than 5,000 permits for offshore enterprises had been issued.

The government played an active and successful role in planning after 1974. This planning was indicative in nature. That is, the government set goals for the economy and limited its direct participation to improving the nation's infrastructure and supporting and guiding the private sector. These activities were costly, however, and resulted in large and expanding budget deficits. By the end of 1987, the total deficit of the 1975–87 period amounted to C£640.6 million.

Another problem was a consistently unfavorable trade balance. In most years, however, expanding surpluses in the invisibles account, mainly from tourist receipts, nearly offset the trade deficits. At the beginning of the 1990s, it was not yet clear what effect the 1988 Customs Union Agreement with the EEC would have on this deficit. Many Cypriots saw the agreement as an opportunity. Access to the community's market of 320 million people might prove beneficial, provided that the manufacturing sector, consisting of small, labor-intensive firms, was restructured and modernized. Undoubtedly, the economy would face more intense competition in the 1990s, but its main asset, a versatile and educated human capital, could make the difference again as it had often done in the past.

Development of the Economy since Independence

Cyprus faced a number of structural problems when it gained independence in 1960. Agriculture, the dominant sector, was subject to fluctuating weather conditions and characterized by low productivity. The island's small manufacturing sector centered on small family firms specializing in handicrafts. Tourism was limited to a few hill resorts. The main exports were minerals. The country's infrastructure was that of a Third World country.

These problems and the prevailing view that the market system alone would not be able to provide the basis for major structural changes and for intensive infrastructure building led to the conclusion that economic planning was necessary. The government adopted a system of indicative planning, setting goals for the economy and seeking to encourage and support the private sector's efforts to reach those goals through legislation and monetary and fiscal policies. In addition, the state spent substantial resources to improve the country's physical and institutional infrastructure. Planners believed such measures would be sufficient for the island's dynamic private sector to function well and reach by itself the selected goals, with minimal government participation in the day-to-day operations of the economy. Indicative planning was managed by the Planning Bureau under the Ministry of Finance. The bureau, aided by expert advice from abroad, formulated three five-year development plans before the Turkish invasion in 1974, four emergency economic action plans after 1974, and a revised five-year plan for 1989 to 1993.

The first five-year plan, for 1962 to 1966, aimed at achieving higher incomes, full employment, price stability, an improved balance of payments, and greater economic equality between rural and urban areas. The plan provided for a sizeable public investment expenditure, C£62 million, on development projects for roads, ports, airport facilities, irrigation projects, and telecommunications and electricity systems. The Agricultural Research Institute was established in 1962 to improve the quality of agriculture, and the Central Bank of Cyprus was created in 1963 to ensure that an appropriate volume of credit was available to the private sector. This first plan achieved remarkable success, most obviously in agricultural production.

The second five-year plan, for 1967 to 1971, moved beyond the fundamental approach of the first plan, seeking to provide the social and legal structures needed by a more advanced economy. It also gave the business community a more active role in planning. The third five-year plan, for 1972 to 1976, stressed regional planning, to promote more even economic growth throughout the island. This plan also concerned itself with the social and cultural aspects of development. The Cyprus Development Bank was established to provide medium- and long-term loans for development projects, as well as technical and administrative assistance. The Higher Technical Institute and the Hotel and Catering Institute were established to provide specialized training.

The success of these plans was shown by the great gains the Cypriot economy made in the first fourteen years of independence. Although agriculture had become much more productive, the secondary and tertiary sectors had shown even greater productivity as Cyprus became a more developed nation. The primary sector's share of GDP declined from 26.3 percent in 1960 to 17 percent in 1973, while the secondary and tertiary sectors' shares expanded, respectively, from 19.5 to 25 percent and from 54.2 to 58 percent. In addition, the productivity of these two latter sectors was considerably higher than that of the primary sector.

The economy was devastated by the 1974 Turkish invasion and the subsequent occupation of the northern 37 percent of the island. Serious problems included a large number of refugees (about a third of the populations of both communities), fragmentation of the island's market, and the loss by the government-controlled area of land containing raw materials, agricultural resources, and important infrastructure facilities such as the Nicosia International Airport and Famagusta, the island's largest port. The need for reconstruction and development was critical. To meet this challenge, a series of emergency economic action plans for two-year periods was instituted.

The first and second emergency economic action plans, covering the period from 1975 to 1978, aimed mainly at aiding the refugees, then living in camps, by establishing a housing program for them. The plans also directed the government to stimulate the economy by adopting expansionary fiscal and monetary policies. The results were positive. The economy expanded by about 6 percent per year, and the unemployment rate declined to about 2 percent in 1978. Increased domestic consumption and rising oil prices, however, produced some overheating of the economy; the inflation rate reached 7.4 percent in 1978. Despite this problem, the achievement of housing the refugees and getting the economy going again with fewer resources in such a brief period of time was considered almost miraculous.

The third Emergency Economic Action Plan, covering 1979 to 1981 (the last of the two-year plans), aimed at countering the overheating of the economy by adopting a restrictive monetary policy. The main goal of the fourth Emergency Economic Action Plan, covering 1982 to 1986, was to balance economic expansion with monetary stability. These goals were reached. Retail price inflation fell from 13.5 percent in 1980 and 10.8 percent in 1981 to 5 or 6 percent in the next few years and 1.2 percent in 1986. High growth rates with low unemployment continued.

Overall, the economy of Cyprus performed relatively well in the three areas of economic growth, full employment, and monetary stability between 1976 and the late 1980s. Between 1976 and 1986, GDP grew at an average annual rate of 8.4 percent in real terms. Per capita GNP in current prices increased from C£537.9 in 1973 to C£3,597 in 1988, or US$7,200, one of the highest in the Mediterranean area. Unemployment averaged 3.2 percent per year, and price increases 6.3 percent per year, during the 1976–88 period. The price increases of 1980 and 1981 pushed the average up, and the increases of the late 1980s were substantially lower (2.8 percent in 1987 and 3.8 percent in 1989). Government support of the private sector, through tax incentives, loan guarantees for export-oriented industries, grants and loans to agriculture and small industries, training programs for the manufacturing sector, and the substantial improvement of the infrastructure, contributed greatly to this success.

Analysts believed that the 1990s would challenge the economy. The Customs Union Agreement with the EEC could be disastrous if manufacturing were not fundamentally restructured. The high tariffs that had protected manufacturing for decades would be dismantled in the 1990s under the terms of the agreement. The republic's seemingly permanent trade deficit would have to be substantially reduced if it were not to damage the economy in the long term. Agriculture would also be affected; some of its branches, mainly cereals and livestock, which enjoyed direct or indirect subsidies, might fall to foreign competition. The service sector would grow in importance. Tourism, which could not expect further growth in quantity, would have to bring in more receipts by improving the quality of its product. Financial services and offshore enterprises would likely increase in importance.

The Government Sector

The government accounted for about 12 to 13 percent of GDP during the 1980s (see table 10, Appendix). The need to stimulate the economy after the division of the island in 1974 caused the government to abandon the old policy of balanced budgets and to adopt expansionary fiscal and monetary policies. The results were large and widening budget deficits paid for by borrowing at home and abroad. Domestic public debt rose from C£7.5 million in 1976 to C£161.5 million in 1988. Public and publicly guaranteed foreign debt increased from C£61.8 million in 1976 to C£602.5 million in 1988. The total public and publicly guaranteed domestic and foreign debt rose from C£760.8 million in 1987 to C£764 million (38.7 percent of GDP) in 1988. The foreign debt service ratio (total service payments as a percentage of exports of goods and services) was 11.8 in 1987 and 10.8 in 1988. Domestic borrowing only was used to cover the budget deficit in 1988. Thus, there was a decline in government foreign borrowing in 1988 to C£602.5 million, compared to C£617.5 million in 1987. Still, the burden of servicing the foreign debt continued to be significant. For instance, servicing the external debt was more than half the revenue from exports of domestically produced goods in 1987.

Furthermore, it was anticipated that the tariff reductions that would result from the Customs Union Agreement with the EEC would produce revenue losses, raising the fiscal deficit to C£126 million in 1992, compared with C£73.5 million in 1987. As a consequence, both public and foreign debts were expected to increase. The president of Cyprus, George Vassiliou, forecast a rise in the per capita public debt from C£2,107 in 1987 to C£3,563 in 1992 and a rise in the total foreign debt to C£1,082 million in 1992.

Given the government's ever-present fiscal deficit, there were concrete proposals at the beginning of the 1990s for the introduction of a value-added tax (VAT—see Glossary) to improve the state's finances. The Republic of Cyprus lacked a broad-based consumption tax, and a VAT would generate much revenue. The income tax system was also to be overhauled, to reduce tax evasion.

A specific look at government public finances shows that the Republic of Cyprus maintained three types of budgets: the Ordinary Budget, which included expenditures for government operations and other current expenses; the Development Budget, which included development programs; and the Special Relief Fund, which covered state aid for the housing and care of refugees.

The Ordinary Budget

The major sources of revenue of the Ordinary Budget included direct taxes; indirect taxes; loan proceeds; sales of goods and services; interest, dividends, rents, and royalties; and foreign grants. Revenue in 1987 from direct taxes was C£107 million, or 27 percent of the total revenue for the Ordinary Budget; revenue from indirect taxes was C£151.3 million, or 38.2 percent; and proceeds from loans were C£68 million, or 17.2 percent. These three main sources of revenue brought in 82.4 percent of the total revenue of the Ordinary Budget.

The major expenditures of the Ordinary Budget were salaries, fees, and allowances; public debt charges; and subventions and contributions and subsidies. Salaries, fees, and allowances accounted for 33.9 percent of total expenditures in 1987; public debt charges, 30.7 percent; subventions and contributions, 9.4 percent; and subsidies, 6.1 percent. The Ordinary Budget showed deficits of C£17.9 million in 1985, C£12.5 million in 1986, C£32.1 million in 1987, and C£28.7 million in 1988.

The Development Budget

There was no revenue in the Development Budget during the period 1976–87. If there had been public savings (i.e., excesses of current revenues over current expenditures) in the Ordinary Budget, they could have provided the means to finance all or a part of the investment and other development expenditures. However, for most of the years of the 1976–87 period, there were no public savings. Thus, the Development Budget had to rely on domestic and foreign borrowing to cover its expenditures. The major expenditure items of the Development Budget were investment, capital transfers, and land acquisition. Another sizeable item was expenditures for wages and salaries. Investment expenditures amounted to C£46 million in 1988. Investment expenditures in the period 1985–88 were mainly to finance the Southern Conveyor Project, the Khrysokhou Irrigation Project, the Nicosia-Limassol Highway, several other major roads, and Larnaca Airport. For this reason, construction activity absorbed most of the investment expenditures between 1985 and 1988. Investment's share of the total development expenditures was 60.22 percent in 1985, 76.19 percent in 1986, 75.1 percent in 1987, and 67.74 in 1988.

The Special Relief Fund

The revenues of the Special Relief Fund were C£21.5 million in 1987. Expenditures were C£21.5 million. The fund showed a surplus in the period 1985–88. The main sources of revenue were direct taxes (a special contribution), indirect taxes (a temporary refugee levy on imports), and foreign grants. The main expenditures of the fund in 1988 included investment, C£10 million; current transfers, C£7.6 million; capital transfers, C£4.2 million; and wages and salaries, C£1.4 million.

Employment and Labor Relations

The south's successful economy kept unemployment rates low. During the 1980s, unemployment rose above 3.3 percent only once, in 1987, when it reached 3.7 percent. In 1988 unemployment was 2.8 percent. Unemployment rates were also low in the years just before the Turkish invasion of 1974, averaging about 1 percent. The invasion and division of the island disrupted the economy, and in the government-controlled area unemployment averaged 16.2 percent in 1975 and 8.5 percent in 1976. During 1977 the rate fell to 3 percent, a rate typical for the south's economy during the 1980s.

The south's economy frequently had to contend with a shortage of workers and in some years was forced to import workers from abroad to meet the needs of various sectors, especially the tourist industry. This shortfall reflected the changing employment patterns of the economy as a whole (see table 11, Appendix). The only population group that consistently had difficulty finding employment was composed of university graduates. Their discontent sometimes resulted in demonstrations and demands that the civil service be expanded.

In 1973 about 37.5 percent of those gainfully employed were members of labor unions. Union membership increased greatly between 1974 and 1977, reaching 62 percent at the end of 1977. This trend continued, and in 1988 labor unions represented more than 80 percent of the work force.

The most prominent unions in the government-controlled area were the left-wing Pan-Cyprian Federation of Labor (Pankypria

Ergatiki Omospondia—PEO) with about 70,000 members at the end of the 1980s, and the right-wing Cyprus Workers' Confederation (Synomospondia Ergaton Kyprou—SEK) with about 50,000 members. Third in importance was the civil servants' labor union, with a membership of about 13,000. Employers were organized in various associations represented in the Cyprus Employers' and Industrialists' Federation.

Terms and conditions of employment were negotiated either directly between employee and employer or through collective bargaining between trade unions and employers' organizations. The government's policy was to remain largely uninvolved in these negotiations unless a deadlock had been reached or its participation had been requested, when it acted through its Industrial Relations Section, a part of the Ministry of Labor and Social Insurance. This section routinely acted to prevent labor-employer discord by providing both groups with guidance and information about good industrial relations. As a result, the number of working days lost to strikes was among the lowest in the Western world relative to the size of the work force.

In the 1980s, wages rose faster than prices. A part of the wage increase was brought about through wage indexation, with automatic quarterly wage increases equal to about half the inflation rate. Even at this rate, however, wage increases could be troublesome for the economy. In 1988, for example, average wages and salaries increased 4.5 percent in real terms, but exceeded the productivity gain of 3.5 percent. The relative scarcity of labor and rising labor costs affected the economy in the 1980s and were expected to continue to do in the 1990s.

Primary Sector

At the beginning of the 1990s, the primary sector was no longer as important as it had been. Agriculture's contribution to GDP had declined from about 20 percent at the end of the 1960s to about 7 percent at the end of the 1980s. Mining's importance had fallen so much that it was no longer significant. Forestry and fishing were also of little importance. Nevertheless, agriculture would remain a stable element in the Republic of Cyprus for both economic and social reasons. Vast irrigation projects were underway for agriculture's benefit; government programs for a continuing reform of land tenure patterns were in place; and the cooperative movement was a significant force in the banking industry.

Agriculture

When Cyprus achieved independence in 1960, the backbone of

its economy was agriculture, mostly small farms, and sometimes even subsistence farms. During the 1960s, irrigation projects made possible vegetable and fruit exports; increasingly, commercialized farming was able to meet the demands for meat, dairy products, and wine from the British and United Nations troops stationed on the island and from the growing number of tourists.

In the early 1970s, Cypriot farms, still overwhelmingly small, owner-run units, furnished about 70 percent of commodity exports and employed about 95,000 people, or one-third of the island's economically active population. Given the expansion of the manufacturing and service sectors, however, agriculture's importance was declining, and in the first half of the 1970s its share of GDP amounted to 18 percent.

The de facto division of the island in 1974 left the Turkish Cypriot community in the north in possession of agricultural resources that produced about four-fifths of the citrus and cereal crops, two-thirds of the green fodder, and all of the tobacco (see fig. 7). The south retained nearly all of the island's grape-growing areas and deciduous fruit orchards. The south also possessed lands producing roughly three-fourths of the valuable potato crop and other vegetables (excluding carrots), half the island's olive trees, and two-thirds of its carob trees. In addition, the south retained two-thirds of the livestock population.

The Turkish occupation caused a large-scale uncoordinated exchange of the agricultural work force between the northern and southern zones. The resulting substantial agricultural unemployment was countered by government actions that included financial assistance on easy terms to farmers. By 1978 the number of persons working in agriculture in the government-controlled area amounted to about 47,000, or 23 percent of the working population. Thereafter, however, agriculture's portion of the work force declined to 20.7 percent in 1979 and 15.8 percent in 1987. Its contribution to the economy also declined; from 17.3 percent of GDP in 1976 to 10.7 percent in 1979 and 7.7 percent in 1988. This share was important to the south's economy, however, and in 1988 value added in agriculture, at constant 1985 prices, was C£112.7 million.

Agriculture's share of the national economy could be expected to decline still further in the 1990s, as the Greek Cypriot economy became even more dominated by the service sector. The island's favorable climate and its location near its leading market, Western Europe, however, meant that farming would remain an important and stable part of the overall economy. Government irrigation projects, subsidies, and tax policies encouraged farming's existence,

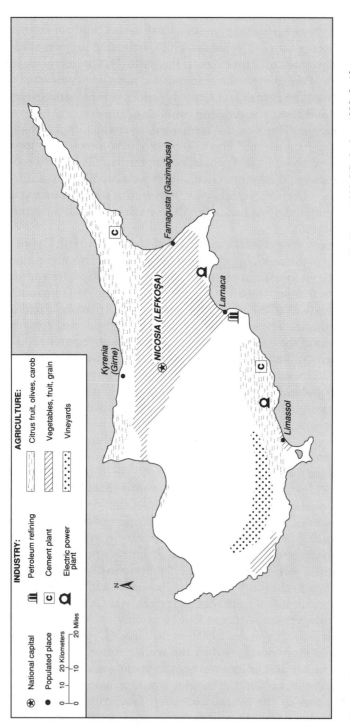

Source: Based on information from Federal Republic of Germany, Statistisches Bundesamt, *Länderbericht Zypern, 1986*, Wiesbaden, 1986, 9, 10.

Figure 7. Economic Activity, 1990

as did research in new crops and new varieties of ones already in cultivation.

The Ministry of Agriculture and Natural Resources oversaw efforts to improve agriculture, fishing, and forestry. Subordinate to this ministry and assisting it were, among others, the Agricultural Research Institute, the Veterinary Service, the Meteorological Service, the Department of Water Development, the Department of Forests, and the Department of Geological Survey.

In addition to macroeconomic considerations, the government encouraged agriculture because it provided rural employment, which maintained village life and relieved urban crowding. Small-scale agricultural activity prevented some regions from losing much of their population. Part-time agricultural work also permitted urban residents to keep in contact with their villages and gave them supplemental income.

Water Resources

Cyprus's water supply was both inadequate and irregular. The average rainfall of 500 millimeters, mostly in the winter, left the island quite dry much of the rest of the time because no rivers flowed year round. During the colonial period, a dam and reservoir construction program was begun, and by independence Cyprus had sixteen dams with a storage capacity of 6 million cubic meters, or 1 percent of the island's estimated 600 million cubic meters of usable runoff from annual rainfall.

After independence a number of large projects were mounted to increase reservoir storage capacity, which reached 300 million cubic meters by 1990. The most important of these projects, and the largest development project in Cyprus since independence, was the Southern Conveyor Project, which collected surplus water from the southwestern part of the island and conveyed it by a 110-kilometer-long water carrier to the central and eastern areas. When the project reached completion in 1993, it, and a number of other large projects, would guarantee farmers and the inhabitants of Nicosia and other towns adequate amounts of water into the next century.

Land Use and Tenure

Three categories of landownership existed in Cyprus during the Ottoman period: private, state, and communal. This division continued to characterize landholding in the Greek Cypriot area in 1990. Most land was privately owned. The largest private landowner was the Church of Cyprus, whose holdings before the Turkish invasion included an estimated 5.8 percent of the island's arable land.

Unrestricted legal ownership of private land dated only from 1946, when the British administration enacted a new land law that superseded the land code in effect under the Ottomans, in which all agricultural land belonged to the state. Those who worked the land were in effect hereditary tenants, whose right to the land was usufructuary. Land could be transmitted from father to son, but could not be disposed of otherwise without official permission.

The Immovable Property (Tenure, Registration, and Valuation) Law of 1946 established the present-day legal basis for landholding. All former state lands that had been properly acquired by individuals were declared to be private property; private property as defined in the former Ottoman land code also continued to be private property. Communal land remained the property of villages or towns, and all unoccupied and vacant land not lawfully held (most forest land, for example) became state land.

Both Greek and Turkish inheritance practices required the division of an estate among the surviving heirs. At the time of the 1946 law, fragmentation of land was already great, many holdings did not have access roads, and owners frequently possessed varying numbers of plots that might be separated by distances of several kilometers.

Despite the 1946 law, however, fragmentation of plots continued. The 1946 census showed 60,179 holdings averaging 7.2 hectares. By 1960 the number of holdings had risen to 69,445, an increase of 15.4 percent, and the average holding had decreased to 6.2 hectares. By 1974 the average holding was an estimated 5 hectares. Holdings were seldom a single piece of land; most consisted of small plots, an average of ten per holding in 1960. In some villages, the average number of plots was 40, and extremes of 100 plots held by a single farmer were reported.

The government enacted the Land Consolidation Law of 1969 to resolve the problem of land tenure. The law established the Central Land Consolidation Authority, with the power to buy and also acquire compulsorily land and other property, which it could sell or use for land consolidation. The authority's board included members of several ministries and departments and also representatives of the farmers. At the village level, committees of government representatives and local farmers coordinated and supervised the local program.

Land consolidation consisted of merging fragmented holdings. Dual and multiple holdings were to be eliminated, and plots smaller than the minimums listed in the 1946 land law were to be expropriated. Government-owned land could be used to enlarge holdings; recipients could purchase the land at current market prices, paying

Grape harvest
Courtesy Embassy of Cyprus, Washington

in installments at low interest rates. A farmer-owner who lost land in the redistribution process was to receive land having the same value as his former holding. The land consolidation program also involved the construction of a service road network to connect all plots to larger roads.

By the end of 1988, twenty-eight land consolidation projects had been completed, and thirty-one projects were underway. Where projects had been completed, minute plots were almost completely eliminated, the average size of plots increased by 100 percent, and the number of plots declined by about 70 percent.

Agricultural Cooperatives

The agricultural cooperative movement in Cyprus was founded in 1909 by a village society of farmers who had returned from an inspection tour of Britain and Germany. The cooperative movement's development was slow, largely because few villagers were qualified to manage cooperatives. The Agricultural Bank, established in 1925 to furnish medium- and long-term loans to farmers, functioned through the cooperative societies. In 1937 a new impetus was given to the movement by the establishment of the Cooperative Central Bank (CCB), with membership limited to the cooperative societies.

The bank's initial function was to furnish the societies with funds for short-term loans to members. This function was expanded in 1960 (when the CCB absorbed the Agricultural Bank) to include medium- and long-term loans. By the late 1980s, the CCB was the third largest bank in the government-controlled area in terms of deposits. The cooperative movement's banking activity was especially strong in the countryside, but also competed with conventional banks in urban areas and had about a 30 percent share of the banking business as a whole.

In addition to banking and credit activities, the cooperative movement maintained retail stores. Cooperatives also marketed agricultural products and exported large amounts of citrus fruits, other fruits, table grapes, and vegetables. The largest winery on the island was the Cooperative Winery SODAP Ltd.

Crops

Crop production was by far the most important component of agriculture. In 1988 it contributed 71 percent of total value added in agriculture, compared with 19 percent for livestock. Ancillary production contributed 6 percent; the shares of fishing and forestry were 3 and 1 percent, respectively.

A wide range of crops were grown on Cyprus. Cereals (wheat and barley), legumes, vegetables (carrots, potatoes, and tomatoes), and fruit and other tree crops (almonds, apples, bananas, carobs, grapes, grapefruit, lemons, melons, olives, oranges, and peaches) (see table 12, Appendix).

Crops were rainfed or irrigated. Wheat and barley were rainfed or dryland crops, as were carobs, olives, fodder, and wine grapes. Crops that required irrigation included vegetables, citrus fruits, deciduous fruits, bananas, and table grapes. These irrigated crops accounted for half of agricultural production.

Cereals, mainly wheat and barley, grew mostly on the Mesaoria, the island's central plain. Production fluctuated widely, depending on rainfall. Wheat's importance relative to barley declined steadily during the 1980s, the result of greater subsidies paid for the raising of barley. Despite the subsidies and a doubling of barley production, only part of the domestic need for cereals was met, and substantial imports were necessary.

Market vegetables grew in many areas around the island. The potato was the most important of these crops, far outstripping tomatoes, carrots, watermelons and sweet melons, cucumbers, and others in both weight and value. In fact, the potato was the most important agricultural product in the late 1980s, during which more than 80 percent of its production was exported (see table 13, Appendix). In 1987 the potato earned 10 percent of the total value of domestic exports, more than any other item except clothing. Because the Cypriot potato was harvested twice, in winter and in early spring, it had a competitive advantage in the European market. Britain was the largest consumer. A shortage of suitable land and a need for irrigation meant that the potato's importance for Cypriot agriculture would likely decline in the 1990s, but it would remain one of the sector's main supports.

Citrus production was another irrigated crop that was important for exports; about 75 percent of production was consumed abroad. Groves of oranges, lemons, grapefruit, and tangerines were located along the coasts. Unlike potato production, that of citrus fruits was expected to expand greatly in the 1990s, and one estimate foresaw a yield of 350,000 tons by the turn of the century, compared with 169,000 tons in 1989.

Viniculture and the production of wine have been major economic activities for centuries in Cyprus. Most vineyards are located in the southwestern part of the island on the slopes of the Troodos Mountains in the Paphos district and in hilly areas in the Limassol district. Some grapes were grown for table consumption, but about four-fifths of the harvest was used for wine, two-thirds of it exported. In 1989 the grape harvest amounted to 212,000 tons, and wine production was 34.1 million liters. The most commonly grown grapes were the xymisteria and mavro varieties. Systematic efforts were undertaken by the government to improve the quality of Cypriot grapes, and different kinds of wine were manufactured to increase exports, mainly to Europe.

Deciduous tree crops common to temperate climates, including olives, apples, pears, peaches, carobs, and cherries, were also grown. These crops required some cool weather during the year, and the orchards were almost entirely in mountainous areas. Almond trees, which do not need cool weather, were widespread on the plains. Olives were easily the most important export item of these tree crops.

Livestock and Poultry

Livestock products, including poultry and milk, made up a significant part of the gross output by value of the agricultural sector. In 1989 there were 49,000 cattle, 325,000 sheep, 208,000 goats, 281,000 pigs, and 2,475,000 chickens in the government-controlled area. During the 1980s, livestock production roughly doubled, as a result of subsidies, strict import regulations, and government-sponsored research that improved both the quality of livestock and its management. Although Greek Cypriots had become self-sufficient with regard to pork and poultry, it was necessary to import beef, veal, and mutton to meet domestic needs. Specialists believed that the gradual lifting of import restrictions, as required by the EEC Customs Union Agreement, would put many inefficient breeders of livestock out of business.

Fishing and Forestry

Fishing has been of small importance to Cyprus throughout history. The intermittent nature of the rivers inhibits natural propagation of freshwater fish, and the surrounding waters are generally deficient in the nutrients and associated plankton essential to the growth of a large marine fish population.

The Turkish invasion resulted in the loss of some of the better fishing areas. By the second half of the 1980s, loans and subsidies from the Department of Fisheries had secured the existence of a fishing fleet of several hundred small vessels, and annual catches exceeded those preceding 1974. In 1989 the catch totaled 2,600 tons at live weight.

The 1980s also saw saltwater and freshwater fish farms come into operation. Much of their production was exported. An experimental fish farm was scheduled to open in the 1990s at Meneou, near Larnaca.

Forestry played a very small role in the Greek Cypriot economy. In the period 1986-1988, its value added was 0.01 percent of the agricultural total in all three years.

Nearly all of the south's forests were owned by the state, which had long managed an active and sophisticated program for their care and improvement. The Turkish invasion of 1974 damaged the island's forests extensively, but by the 1980s reforestation projects had repaired much of the harm. The College of Forestry, established by the British in the colonial period, enjoyed an international reputation for excellence.

Mining and Quarrying

For several millennia, Cyprus was an important source of copper ores (mainly cuprous pyrite) and other ores and minerals, including chromite, iron pyrite (mined for its sulphur content), asbestos, gypsum, and umber (see fig. 8). In addition to these minerals, exploited mainly for export, limestone, sand, and aggregates were quarried in substantial quantities for the domestic cement and construction industries. In the 1950s, minerals accounted for three-fifths of exports and employed 6,700 persons. By 1963 minerals' share of exports had fallen to 34 percent, owing to both a changing world market and the growth of other sectors of the Cypriot economy. The Turkish invasion of 1974 disrupted or ended much mining activity. Many deposits in the government-controlled territory were nearing exhaustion. In 1981 minerals supplied only 4.5 percent of exports, and by the end of the 1980s less than 1 percent. Mining and quarrying also employed fewer persons: 1,800 in 1979 and half that in 1987. The subsector's contribution to GDP had also become quite small: 0.5 percent to GDP in 1985 and in 1986 and 0.4 percent in 1987 and 1988. With the closure of the asbestos mine in 1988, the industry's contribution to GDP declined still further. In 1989 the principal minerals mined were flotation pyrites (57,455 tons), copper concentrates (1,752 tons), and copper precipitates (1,080 tons). The quarrying of sand, gravel, and road aggregate depended on construction demands. In the late 1980s, demand was generally good. In 1982 a port was constructed at Vasilikos on the south central coast to handle the mining and cement production of the Hellenic Mining Company.

Secondary Sector

Manufacturing, the largest component of the secondary sector, consisted mainly of light manufacturing. Government policies, especially since the events of 1974, had long aimed at strengthening light manufacturing and increasing its export production. The trade

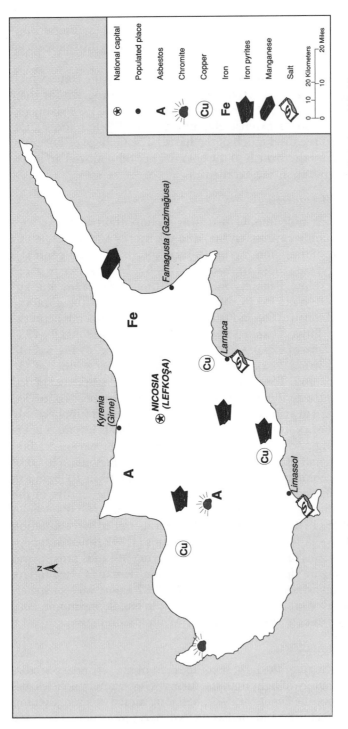

Source: Based on information from Federal Republic of Germany, Statistisches Bundesamt, *Länderbericht Zypern, 1986*, Wiesbaden, 1986, 10.

Figure 8. Minerals, 1990

agreement with the EEC that went into effect in 1988 could have momentous effects on this subsector, most obviously in removing the tariffs that had protected Cypriot manufacturing from foreign competition. Energy production and construction were also significant components of this sector.

Manufacturing

At independence the manufacturing sector consisted almost entirely of small, family-owned enterprises, most with fewer than five workers. Production consisted mainly of consumer goods and items for the construction industry, all for the local market. Obstacles to the development of larger establishments were the limited domestic market, a generally low level of income, a lack of available capital, and a shortage of skilled labor.

During the period of the second five-year plan (1967-71), steps were taken by the government to encourage industrial development. Import duties on raw materials were reduced or abolished, and tariffs were imposed to protect domestic industry. Generous depreciation allowances and tax remissions were granted. In addition, training centers were set up for management, technical personnel, and workers. Industrial parks were established in Nicosia, Limassol, and Larnaca. Government policy generally left manufacturing to private enterprise, but in some cases, such as the petroleum refinery at Larnaca, the government made direct investments.

During the plan period, some seventy larger manufacturing plants were constructed. These plants included a petroleum refinery, biscuit and margarine factories, fruit- and meat-canning plants, a brewery, an edible oil plant, paper products factories, textile and hosiery mills, pharmaceutical plants, and metal fabricating plants. A 1972 census of industrial production, covering Greek Cypriot establishments plus estimates for the Turkish Cypriot community, showed that more than four-fifths of the 7,612 plants in manufacturing (excluding cottage industries) still had 1 to 4 employees; only about thirty establishments had more than 100. These larger establishments, however, accounted for 81.4 percent of the value added by manufacturing. Despite this change, manufacturing as a whole remained largely geared to the local market, the principal exception being canned goods, most of which were exported.

The Turkish occupation resulted in a major division of the island's manufacturing sector, because one-third of the larger enterprises were located in the north. Another immediate effect was disruption of the domestic market. The division also cut off the sources of some raw materials and intermediate goods.

The sharp general drop in incomes in the south after mid-1974 forced the manufacturing industry to reorient production toward exports. A principal objective of the first Emergency Economic Action Plan (1975–76) was the reactivation of manufacturing with emphasis on the development of such labor-intensive industries as clothing and footwear aimed at the export market. This effort also included measures to reestablish in the Greek Cypriot area the operations of entrepreneurs who had fled the Turkish Cypriot zone. During this plan period, 200 new or reopened plants went into production, and at the end of the period more than 130 additional ones were under construction.

The Greek Cypriot government took other steps to create an export climate attractive to industrial entrepreneurs. Raw material and machinery imports were duty-free, a guarantee scheme was established for bank credits for exports, and a tax allowance was granted on foreign exchange earnings from exports. Trade centers were also set up abroad, and there was participation in foreign trade exhibitions. Some indication of the success of the overall effort was seen in the tripling of exports of manufactured goods from C£22.5 million in 1975 to C£66.5 million in 1978. By the late 1970s, manufacturing was very close to wholesale and retail trade in its contribution to GDP, and there were some 1,320 manufacturing enterprises covering a broad range of industrial activity.

During the decade of 1979–88, the contribution of manufacturing to GDP at current prices nearly tripled (see table 14, Appendix). Manufacturing's share of GDP, however, declined slightly during this period, beginning in 1984. The decline moved manufacturing into second place, after the category of wholesale and retail trade, restaurants, and hotels.

The principal industrial products were food, beverages, and tobacco; textiles, wearing apparel, and leather; wood and wood products; paper and paper products; printing and publishing; chemicals and toiletries, petroleum, rubber, and plastic products; nonmetallic mineral products, such as cement; and metal products, machinery, and equipment.

The three subsectors of food, beverages, and tobacco; textiles, wearing apparel, and leather; and chemicals and toiletries, petroleum, rubber, and plastic products represented 65.4 percent of the total gross industrial output in 1979, and in 1987 they represented 64.7 percent. In 1987 the relative share in industrial output of food, beverages, and tobacco was 27.4 percent; of textiles, wearing apparel, and leather, 23.2 percent; and of chemicals and toiletries, petroleum, rubber, and plastic products, 14 percent. During the period 1979–87, the two most important subsectors for exports were food, beverages, and tobacco and textiles, wearing apparel, and leather. In 1987 they accounted for 21.6 and 54.2 percent of total industrial exports, respectively.

Industrial output came to depend on exports. The Arab Middle East was a key market for industrial production, but the EEC purchased 39.3 percent of exported manufactures in 1987. These two markets and the protected domestic market absorbed about 90 percent of manufactured products.

The traditional markets for Cypriot manufactured goods could not be regarded as secure at the beginning of the 1990s. The Arab Middle East markets were often highly volatile, for both political and economic reasons, and the European market had also become increasingly competitive. A main threat to Cypriot exports in these areas were Asian manufacturers with lower labor costs and higher-quality goods. The domestic market was also increasingly threatened because the terms of the Customs Union Agreement with the EEC required the country to gradually dismantle its highly protective tariff system. (In the late 1980s, for example, Cypriot tariffs on clothing imports from the EEC were over 80 percent.)

In meeting these mounting challenges, Cypriot manufacturers were striving to raise the quality of their production, improve marketing, and contain labor costs through productivity gains as tariffs came down. The government continued its longstanding policy of encouraging manufacturing by improving the infrastructure and creating industrial parks and free industrial zones. It also identified new industries and products suitable for future development. Because of the number of small, labor-intensive plants with well-qualified workers adept at learning new technologies, the government recommended that these plants adopt the principle of "flexible specialization," with modern design techniques, quick turn-around times, and computer-controlled machinery, to meet the rigors of the global market of the 1990s.

Energy Resources

Cyprus had an unfortunate energy situation. The island had no known deposits of mineral fuels, and the lack of rivers that flowed year-round made significant generation of hydroelectric power impossible. The island did have a great amount of sunlight, however, and in the government-controlled sector about 35 percent of houses were fitted with rooftop solar panels for heating water. By 1990 Cyprus was one of the world's foremost users of solar energy. The only other domestic source of energy was firewood.

Petroleum, all of it imported, supplied about 95 percent of the island's energy. Oil imports consumed about 50 percent of foreign exchange earnings in some years. Imported crude was processed by the Larnaca refinery of the Cyprus Petroleum Refinery Ltd. In 1989 this refinery had a capacity of 17,000 barrels a day, or 800,000 tons a year. Major users imported their own heavy fuel oil directly via oil terminals at Larnaca, Dhekelia, to the east of Larnaca, and Moni, near Limassol.

The largest single user of petroleum, consuming about 35 percent of the total, was the Electricity Authority of Cyprus (EAC), a public corporation founded in 1952. The EAC was responsible for nearly all of the island's generation, transmission, and distribution of electric power. The "Turkish Republic of Northern Cyprus" ("TRNC") had no significant power plants and received its electricity from the EAC. As of 1990, it had not paid for any of this power.

In 1989 the EAC produced 1.84 gigawatt-hours from three oil-fired thermal stations, two at Dhekelia (one old plant with a capacity of 42 megawatts, used only in emergencies, and a new plant with a capacity of 240 megawatts), and one at Moni, near Limassol, with a capacity of 180 megawatts. The EAC also had a few small standby diesel plants. A number of industrial operations had their own generating facilities. At the beginning of the 1990s, there were plans to construct a coal-fired power plant at Vasilikos to reduce petroleum dependency, but environmental concerns may prevent its being built.

Construction

Increased economic activity from the late 1960s, stimulated in part by the second five-year plan, resulted in a rapid growth of construction, including new urban and rural housing, commercial establishments, industrial facilities, tourist accommodations, and government infrastructure projects. The sector's growth rate averaged 17.5 percent per year in current terms between 1968 and 1972 and rose to 24.8 percent in 1973. Construction workers numbered 25,000 to 28,600 in the 1968-73 period and constituted about one-tenth of the island's gainfully employed work force.

The construction industry was hard hit by the Turkish invasion and occupation; construction by the private sector ceased almost completely. In 1975 the construction work force numbered only about 8,900, or 6.2 percent of persons gainfully employed in the south.

Commercial construction revived in 1976, when the industry, in response to government policy decisions and actions, began to build housing for nearly 200,000 refugees, many of whom were living in tents and makeshift shacks. This construction boom lasted

Clothing plant, an example of Cypriot light industry
Courtesy Embassy of Cyprus, Washington

until 1981. The boom was further energized by events in the Middle East, which caused many businesses to move their headquarters or offices from Lebanon to Cyprus. Rapidly expanding tourism also stimulated construction of new facilities, as did industrial plant construction. After the refugees were housed, the government began its program of building housing for low-income groups as part of a new, wider concept of government social responsibility. An especially strong year in the boom period was 1979, when the construction industry expanded 36.3 percent and made up 13.4 percent of the GDP in 1979.

The construction industry experienced much lower growth rates in the 1980s. In the 1985–87 period, it actually shrank in real terms, and some Cypriot contractors were obliged to go abroad to find work. The industry remained an important part of the economy, however, with regard to both its contribution to the GDP and the employment it provided. In 1987, a representative year, dwellings absorbed about half of total construction investment, nonresidential buildings about a quarter, and infrastructure (such as roads, bridges, dams, irrigation works, and telecommunication and electrical transmissions lines) the rest.

Important spurs to the construction industry were the Housing Finance Corporation and the Land Development Corporation, government entities created to enable middle- and low-income people to acquire their own houses. During the late 1980s, these organizations provided low-cost loans and managed the construction of several hundred houses a year (in 1989 eighty-two housing units in Nicosia alone). The goal for 1990 was to construct 575 units in the whole of the Republic of Cyprus.

Tertiary Sector

By the beginning of the 1990s, the service, or tertiary, sector had become the most important part of the economy of the Republic of Cyprus and accounted for more than half the country's GDP. It was also the economy's fastest growing component and through this growth was gradually transforming the economy into a postindustrial and information one. Tourism had long been the most important subsector, but in the future financial and transport services and offshore enterprises were thought likely to take the leading role, favored by the island's fortunate location between Europe and the Middle East and its stable social and economic conditions.

Trade, Restaurants, and Hotels

Since the late 1970s, the largest and most dynamic component of the service sector has been that of wholesale and retail trade, restaurants, and hotels (tourism). It grew at double-digit rates between 1979 and 1988, except for 1986 (see table 15, Appendix). Its contribution to the GDP in current terms quadrupled between 1979 and 1988. By the late 1980s, with about 50,000 workers, it had also become the largest source of employment.

Tourism gained importance in this subsector during the 1980s, but had not overtaken trade. Trade (wholesale and retail) contributed C£76.7 million, in current terms, to GDP in 1979 (79.56 percent of the sector) and C£217.3 million (55.4 percent) in 1988. Restaurants and hotels (tourism) contributed C£19.7 million in 1979 (20.43 percent of the total sector) and C£174.6 million (44.55 percent) in 1988. The value added to GDP by trade nearly tripled in current prices between 1979 and 1988, and that of restaurants and hotels (tourism) increased about nine times.

Tourism was seriously disrupted by the Turkish invasion of 1974. Only 47,000 tourists came to the island in 1975, down from 264,000 in 1973. However, under the influence of the emergency economic action plans of 1976–78, 1979–81, and 1982–86, earnings from tourism increased at least 20 percent for eleven straight years, and the number of tourists who visited the Republic of Cyprus went from 165,000 in 1976 to 1,376,000 in 1989. Foreign currency earnings from tourism amounted to almost C£500 million in 1989.

Earnings were so significant that tourism was a greater source of foreign exchange than the export of domestic goods from 1986 through 1989.

Most of the tourists who came to the government-controlled areas were middle-income Europeans. For many years, British visitors were the most numerous and made up about one-third of the total. Swedes were the second largest group in the late 1980s, closely followed by Germans. Most tourists came for stays of about ten days and arrived during the warm months, despite efforts by the Cyprus Tourism Organisation (CTO) to achieve a more even seasonal distribution of visits. In the late 1980s, the CTO began to be successful in increasing conference tourism as a step toward this goal.

By the late 1980s, efforts were underway to raise the quality rather than quantity of tourism because the south's ability to receive more tourists had reached a saturation point. A one-year ban on licenses for new hotels in coastal areas was announced in March 1989 to check unplanned development. The volume of demand had surpassed the available infrastructure to support it, with resulting problems of traffic congestion, water shortages, and inadequate sewerage capacity.

Future growth was to depend on attracting wealthier tourists, who would spend more money during their stays. This aim was to be accomplished by turning away from simple sun-and-sea tourism and developing higher-quality hotels with facilities such as golf courses, marinas for yachting, and casinos. Emphasis was also to be placed on building mountain resorts and developing the island's archaeological sites for sightseeing.

Transportation, Storage, and Telecommunications

Transportation, storage, and telecommunications contributed in current prices 8.1 percent of GDP in 1979 and 9.4 percent in 1988. The subsector accounted for 5.5 percent of the gainfully employed in 1979 and 6 percent in 1987. The value contributed by the subsector to GDP was C£48.7 million in 1979 and C£178 million in 1988. Transportation and storage alone represented 74.7 percent of the subsector's value in 1979 and 72 percent in 1988. The subsector could be considered to some extent trade because of large components in transshipment trade, warehousing services, and air passenger services connected with tourism.

Transportation

The transportation system in the government-controlled area was well developed (see fig. 9). The road network was satisfactory for passenger and freight traffic. In 1989 the government-controlled area had 9,824 kilometers of roads, of which 5,240 kilometers were asphalted or tarred and 4,584 kilometers were dirt or gravel. An expressway linked the major port town of Limassol with the capital, and in 1990 work was underway on a highway to Paphos and Larnaca from this road. There were no railroads in Cyprus.

At the time of the Turkish invasion, the country's main airport was the Nicosia International Airport. It was closed after the Turkish invasion of 1974, however, because it was located on the Attila Line that divided the island. It was replaced by international airports at Larnaca and Paphos. Passenger arrivals at these two airports totaled 2,900,000 in 1989. In 1990 about thirty airlines offered more than 100 scheduled flights per week from Larnaca to Western and Eastern Europe, Africa, the Middle East, and the Persian Gulf. A number of charter passenger and freight flights were also available. Cyprus Airways, the country's national airline, was both publicly and privately owned. It operated about a dozen large aircraft at the beginning of the 1990s.

The de facto division of Cyprus closed Famagusta, then the island's main port. Larnaca and Limassol took its place. Both ports were modernized and fitted with late-design container and break-bulk facilities that permitted them to warehouse goods and function as major container transshipment centers in the eastern

Mediterranean. Transit cargoes enjoyed special treatment, including minimal customs formalities, free trade facilities, and special rates for long-term storage. In addition to these two ports, the island had the smaller ports of Paphos and Vasilikos and three oil terminals for importing petroleum. About 100 shipping lines included Cyprus in their regular schedules. In 1989, 5,678 ships, totaling 14.8 million net registered tons, called at Cypriot ports. During the 1980s, Cyprus became a major shipping nation, moving from twenty-ninth place in the early 1980s, in terms of registered tonnage, to seventh place, with close to 2,000 ships totaling 18.5 million gross tons. Most were foreign-owned.

Telecommunications

Telecommunications in the Republic of Cyprus were excellent. In 1990 the island had 210,000 telephones, or 30 per 100 population. All telephones were connected to automatic exchanges, and international direct dialing was available throughout the island. International facsimile (fax), data transmission, and telex services were also available. The domestic transmission system consisted of a mix of coaxial cables and analog radio links, along with the latest technologies of digital radio-relay and fiber optics cables. There were 234,000 television sets (color and black and white) in the nation at the beginning of the 1990s. The state Cyprus Broadcasting Corporation had two radio stations and one television station. There was also a private radio station, and, in addition, the British forces had both radio and television broadcasting facilities. International communications were via three submarine cables, two to Europe and one to Lebanon; tropospheric-scatter radio links to Greece and Turkey; and three satellite ground stations, two working with the International Telecommunications Satellite Organization (Intelsat) Atlantic Ocean and Indian Ocean satellites and the third linked to the European Telecommunications Satellite Organisation (Eutelsat) system.

Finance, Insurance, Real Estate, and Business Services

Economic activity by this subsector expanded substantially after 1976. Some of the forces contributing to this expansion were the housing boom, which stemmed from the need to accommodate refugees from the Turkish-occupied north; the offshore business and banking activities, which began in the late 1970s; and other business services, such as accounting, computer programming, and consultancy services. Many of these services proved to be a dynamic component of the economy. This subsector was not

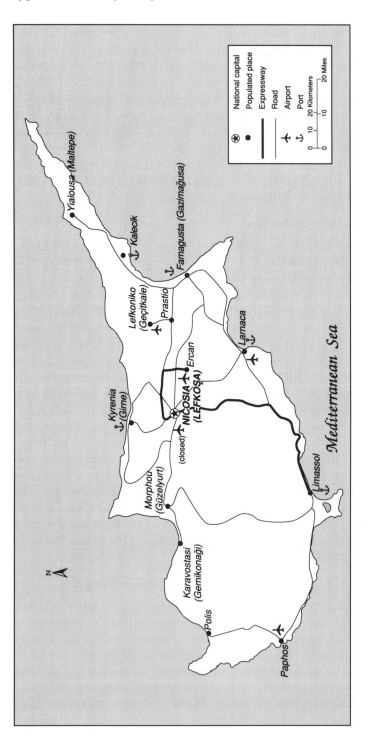

Figure 9. Transportation System, 1990

a large employer, but many of those it employed were among the best trained in the country.

Banking services in Cyprus were relatively well developed. In 1989 Cyprus had a central bank, eight commercial banks, nineteen offshore banks, and four specialized financial institutions. About 320 branches of the commercial banks were located throughout the republic.

The Central Bank of Cyprus had the exclusive right to issue notes and coins, regulate the supply of money and credit, and act as banker, financial agent, and economic adviser to the government. It supervised all banks and designated financial institutions, managed the international reserves of the country, administered the exchange control legislation, and determined the exchange rate of the Cyprus pound.

Commercial banks were the main source of funds for working capital and capital investment. They provided about 80 percent of the loan funds flowing into the private sector, and also provided housing, professional, and personal loans. In addition to providing these conventional banking services, the banks had entered the fields of installment-plan financing, general insurance, data processing, and trustee services. Commercial banks had strong networks of correspondent relationships with many foreign banks, and some Cypriot banks were connected to the Society of Worldwide Interbank Financial Telecommunications (SWIFT), an international system of telecommunications for the computerized transmission of commercial and financial messages among 1,500 banks worldwide.

Offshore banks had become an important subsector since the first offshore banking license was granted in 1982. The guidelines governing the establishment and operation of these units were clearly laid out by the Central Bank of Cyprus. Offshore banks could only transact business abroad and with nonresidents of Cyprus.

In addition to offshore banks, offshore businesses as a whole were a dynamic element in Cyprus's growth. Between 1975 and the end of the 1980s, more than 5,000 permits were issued by the Central Bank of Cyprus for the establishment of these enterprises. The island's central geographic location, English legal system, low cost of living, and generous tax incentives made it a major center for offshore businesses. Many kinds of activities were conducted, including marketing of consumer goods, transit and storage trade, holding of property and securities, business consulting and services, distribution and repair of equipment, architecture and town planning, road and airport construction, maintenance of computer hardware, ship management, and insurance.

Foreign exchange earnings from offshore enterprises were C£44.5 million in 1988. In that year, 555 new permits were issued.

At the end of the 1980s, about 700 offshore enterprises maintained fully staffed administrative offices in the Republic of Cyprus, employing about 3,000 persons, 1,800 of them foreigners.

More than fifty insurance companies operated in Cyprus. Many were incorporated abroad and represented well-known multinational insurance companies. The industry was regulated by the government to safeguard the interests of the insured and to prevent the uncontrolled flow of capital from the island.

Community, Social, and Personal Services

The principal activities of this subsector were personal and household services, social and related community services, and recreational and cultural services rendered by the private sector. As the Republic of Cyprus became a wealthier and more diverse society, this branch's share of GDP grew, from 3.4 percent in 1979 to 5.5 percent in 1988 (increasing fivefold in current prices). Its share of the work force grew even more, from 4.7 percent of the gainfully employed in 1979 to 7.2 percent in 1987.

Foreign Trade and the Balance of Payments

Cyprus's trade balance has been consistently unfavorable since before independence. Given its large and expanding trade deficit, the Republic of Cyprus was fortunate to have a large and growing surplus in its invisibles account, enough even to offset the trade deficit in 1987 and 1988 (see table 16, Appendix). The major factors contributing to this surplus were tourist receipts, receipts from transfers, and income from other goods and services (such as foreign military expenditures in Cyprus, embassy expenditures, and foreign exchange from offshore enterprises). Tourist receipts expanded from C£232 million in 1985 to C£386 million in 1988. Income from other goods and services increased from C£173.3 million in 1985 to C£208.2 million in 1988.

Cyprus experienced its first overall balance-of-payments deficit after independence in 1973. During the 1980s, the influx of capital in the form of loans and investments was sufficient to give the country a positive balance of payments in all years except 1985 and 1988, despite the usually negative current account balance.

The foreign exchange reserves of the Republic of Cyprus at the end of 1988 reached C£571.8 million, an improvement over the reserves of C£501.2 million at the end of 1987. These reserves were estimated to be sufficient to cover about nine months of imports.

Even though the trade balance was chronically unfavorable, exports had greatly increased since the Turkish occupation in 1974. Exports of goods and services rose by an average of 20.7 percent

Limassol, an important port and tourist center
Courtesy Embassy of Cyprus, Washington

annually (in current prices) during the 1975–86 period; they increased 16.5 percent in 1987 and 10.5 percent in 1988.

The main domestic exports had been agricultural exports, especially citrus fruits and potatoes, and manufactured products, most importantly clothing, footwear, chemicals, and machinery. Agricultural exports amounted to 24.7 percent of total domestic exports in 1985 but declined to 20.5 percent in 1988; manufactured exports were 71.7 percent of the total in 1985 and rose to 77.4 percent in 1988.

The European Economic Community (EEC) continued to be the main market for the republic's exports, absorbing 42.7 percent of total domestic exports in 1986, some 45 percent in 1987, and 47 percent in 1988. Among the EEC countries, the top customer continued to be Britain, with a share of 50.4 percent in 1988, followed by Greece with a share of 19.5 percent. The other major block of countries to which the republic's exports continued to do well were the Arab countries. In 1986 this group took 42.2 percent of total domestic exports, in 1987 38.6 percent, and in 1988 36.7 percent.

The Republic of Cyprus was dependent on imports for many raw materials, consumer goods, transportation equipment, capital goods, and fuels. Total imports increased from C£177.8 million in 1976 to C£1.130 billion in 1989. The seemingly permanent trade deficits amounted to C£365.8 million in 1987, C£476.6 million in 1988, and C£668.6 million in 1989. In 1989 consumer goods were 18.8 percent of total imports; intermediate goods (raw materials), 41.6 percent; capital goods, 9.5 percent; transport equipment, 20.4 percent; and fuels, 9.6 percent.

Most of the republic's imports came from the EEC: 60.7 percent in 1986 and 54.5 percent in 1988. Britain was the largest source of imports among the EEC countries, accounting for 22.1 percent of imports from the group in 1986 and 25.5 percent in 1988. Italy, the Federal Republic of Germany (West Germany), and Greece had the next three largest shares. Other major trading areas that provided imports to the republic were Eastern Europe (5.2 percent of total imports in 1986 and 7.1 percent in 1988) and the Arab countries (7.2 percent in 1986 and 4.8 percent in 1988). The rest of the world provided 26.8 percent of imports in 1986 and 33.5 percent in 1988; Japan accounted for 34.7 percent of this group's exports in 1988, and the United States, 13.6 percent.

The balance of payments record of the Republic of Cyprus indicated the economy's vulnerability in the early 1990s. Imports continued to outpace exports, resulting in ever-expanding trade deficits. This situation would have been worse if it were not for the high protection afforded the domestic market. Although the Customs Union Agreement with the EEC, which became effective in January 1988, abolished all import duties on Cypriot industrial exports to the EEC countries, the real test for Cypriot manufacturing was expected in the second half of the 1990s, when all tariffs on EEC industrial and agricultural exports to Cyprus were to be phased out. EEC duties on Cyprus's agricultural exports to the EEC will also be phased out by then. Although some exceptions were allowed, the agreement would require free trade with the main Cypriot export market.

The Customs Union Agreement was the outcome of long negotiations. After Britain's entry into the EEC, Cyprus signed an association agreement, to become effective in June 1973 and to cover a ten-year period. According to the terms of the agreement, Cyprus received preferential access to the British market in return for a 35 percent reduction of tariffs on EEC goods, phased in over five years. A follow-up phase of the agreement, covering 1978 to 1983, would have led to a full customs union. The Turkish occupation interrupted the natural progress of this agreement. Cyprus was still allowed to export most of its industrial goods to the EEC without tariffs, but rules of origin restrictions applied, as did some restrictions on agricultural exports.

The Customs Union Agreement posed a major challenge to the highly protected manufacturing sector of Cyprus, revealing its competitive weaknesses. Only a restructuring of the sector by increasing the size of its units, reducing its labor-unit costs, improving its productivity, and strengthening the marketing of products to new markets would allow it to prosper. At the beginning of the 1990s, the sector's restructuring was under way, and the government had established the Council for the Promotion of Exports to make Cypriot products better known abroad.

"Turkish Republic of Northern Cyprus"

Between 1963 and 1974, the economy of the Turkish Cypriot community was that of an underdeveloped society. Much of this backwardness resulted from the economic blockade imposed by Greek Cypriots on the Turkish Cypriot enclaves, which largely cut them off from the outside world. The geographical separation of the enclaves from one another only worsened their plight. In addition to external obstacles, Turkish Cypriots were not a notably commercial people or much involved in the island's limited manufacturing sector. Most Turkish Cypriots earned their livelihood from farming or government employment. By the early 1970s, Turkish Cypriots accounted for only 6 percent of the island's gross domestic product (GDP—see Glossary), although they constituted about 20 percent of its population.

The harsh economic conditions began to change after the Turkish intervention of 1974 and the subsequent de facto partition of Cyprus. The Turkish Cypriots formed their own "state" in 1975, and in 1983 declared the area they occupied in northern Cyprus to be the "Turkish Republic of Northern Cyprus" ("TRNC"). Once they had their own contiguous territory and government, Turkish Cypriots began to work toward economic development. Their efforts were aided by significant financial and technical assistance from Turkey and an influx of workers from that country. Some of these workers came as settlers. Others were Turkish Cypriots who had left the island during the violent and uncertain 1963–74 period.

The Turkish Cypriots had some success in fashioning a working economy. The GDP of the "TRNC" nearly doubled in real terms between 1977 and 1990 (see table 17, Appendix). According to Turkish Cypriot statistics, the GDP of the "TRNC" grew at an average annual rate of 6.4 percent between 1977 and 1988. The rate of growth was 7.5 percent in 1988 and 7.1 percent in 1989, and similar growth was expected in 1990.

In addition to healthy growth rates, the economy was becoming more modern in structure. In 1989 industry's share of GDP was 14 percent and surpassed for the first time agriculture's share of 10.9 percent (see table 18, Appendix). Services represented nearly half of GDP, although an unhealthy proportion of this share stemmed from government services and employment.

Turkish Cypriots still lagged far behind Greek Cypriots economically. For example, per capita income increased from US$586 in 1974 to US$2,245 in 1989, but was only a third of the level achieved in the Republic of Cyprus. Turkish Cypriots often contended that many of their economic difficulties stemmed from the Greek Cypriot effort to impose an economic blockade, cutting them off from the rest of the world except Turkey. There was another cause of difficulties: because the "TRNC" was recognized only by Turkey, most international economic assistance to Cyprus from international organizations such as the World Bank (see Glossary) and the European Community (EC—see Glossary) went to the Republic of Cyprus. In short, although the Turkish Cypriots had achieved a measure of political independence and economic success, by late 1990 the "TRNC" still lacked the external recognition necessary for greater economic development.

The State and Economic Development

In the first years after the de facto partition of the island, the

Turkish Cypriot community had sought by any means possible to establish a viable economy. Faced with the problem of creating an economy from a very small base, the government became the employer of first resort. Numerous semipublic economic enterprises were set up with Turkish aid, and a functioning economy was put in place. The Cyprus Turkish Industrial Enterprises Holding Company, the Cyprus Turkish Tourism Management Company, and the Cyprus Turkish Maritime Company were examples of these state-sponsored entities. They were nonprofit and service-oriented and staffed by state-appointed managers. State planners created them to meet economic needs the private sector was unable to satisfy.

The State Planning Organisation (SPO) was the agency responsible for planning. The SPO was subordinate to the prime minister, but its daily activities were conducted in cooperation with the Ministry of Economy and Finance. The SPO helped establish long-term economic goals and coordinated the planning activities of ministries. The two main components of the SPO were the State Planning Section and the Coordination, Executive, and Technical Assistance Section.

The State Planning Section was responsible for preparing economic and social development plans. Such plans required research, analysis, and project evaluation. The section also monitored the implementation of plans and cooperated in preparing the government's Annual Development Budget.

The Coordination, Executive, and Technical Assistance Section prepared the Annual Development Budget and supervised its implementation. It also implemented development plans, provided technical data for the working committees of the National Assembly, and prepared requests for technical and economic assistance. In addition, the section published statistical reports on all sectors of the economy.

The Turkish Cypriot economy was mixed, neither wholly state-managed, nor privately owned. Although the state economic enterprises were significant actors, and the state set the overall direction of the economy, the state did not generally interfere in the private sector beyond legislation that set wage rates and taxation. The state supported and encouraged the private sector through investments in the national infrastructure and other measures. For example, it set up "free economic zones" to attract foreign investment. By the late 1980s, about fifty foreign investors had taken advantage of these zones' generous tax provisions.

In the second half of the 1980s, however, the government changed its policy in response to persistent economic dependence on Turkey.

In late 1986, the "TRNC" signed an economic agreement with Turkey, and in 1987 a development plan was formulated. Both the agreement and the plan aimed at transforming the Turkish Cypriot economy into one based on liberal economic doctrines. The long-term result, it was hoped, would be a stronger economy less dependent on Turkish aid and one that in time would become self-sustaining.

The movement toward a liberal, market-oriented economy was to be realized by making tourism the driving force. Tourism would pull the rest of the economy into growth and reduce the importance of state-owned and state-managed enterprises. Turkey increased its aid, much of which went toward improving the infrastructure, and promised to guarantee all foreign investments in the "TRNC." The government offered tax concessions, long-term, low-cost leases, and reduced controls on transfers of foreign exchange. These and other measures were successful. Tourism's earnings tripled between 1986 and 1989. Manufacturing also increased its share of GDP, as did nongovernment services, and the size of the state sector and agriculture began to fall. The ratio of the public sector to the private sector in fixed capital investments gradually changed from two to one to the reverse.

A key aim of the new liberal policies was to reduce the burden of a swollen government sector. Although some reduction was achieved, serious problems in this area remained at the beginning of the 1990s. Expenditures for wages and pensions, for example, made up two-thirds of the government's budget. Reforms of very generous pension plans for civil servants were needed, as was a streamlining of the government's cumbersome bureaucratic procedures.

Chronic inflation was another problem that needed to be addressed. Inflation rates ranged from lows of 33 percent in 1982 and 1983, to a high of over 100 percent in 1979. The year 1988 saw a rate of 62 percent. The most serious cause of inflation was the use of the Turkish lira (TL; for value of the lira—see Glossary) as legal tender. This currency's persistently high inflation rate was imported into the "TRNC." There were from time to time discussions of the desirability and practicality of the Turkish Cypriots' having their own currency, but as of 1990 no steps in this direction had been taken. Some inflation, however, was domestic in origin, stemming from excessive state spending.

Although the government's share of GDP declined somewhat as the economy grew and modernized, at the beginning of the 1990s the "TRNC" still relied on Turkish aid. Turkey's aid to Turkish Cypriots in 1990, in both loans and grants, was expected to amount to TL140 billion (US$60.5 million), a sizeable increase over the TL88 billion provided in 1989. An indication of the increasing health of the Turkish Cypriot economy, however, was that in 1988, for the first time, local government revenues substantially exceeded Turkish aid. The figures for 1989 also reflected this change.

A potentially serious problem for the Turkish Cypriot economy at the end of 1990 was the apparent collapse of the economic empire of Asil Nadir, the only major foreign investor in the "TRNC." Nadir was a native-born Turkish Cypriot long resident in London. As chairman of a large multinational company, Polly Peck International, Nadir had taken advantage of the government's "free economic zone" policy and invested heavily in industry, citrus production, and tourism. He was surpassed only by the state as an employer in the "TRNC," with as many as 8,000 people, by some estimates, earning their livings from his varied enterprises. Late in 1990, however, Nadir's international empire suffered reverses and faced possible bankruptcy and liquidation. The long-term effects of Nadir's legal and financial difficulties on his investments in the "TRNC" were not known, but the short-term effects were painful.

The Work Force and Labor Unions

Nearly 70,000 Turkish Cypriots were economically active in 1989. Unemployment was measured at about 1 percent. A shortage of skilled workers in some areas required the immigration of some foreign labor. According to government statistics, agriculture accounted for the largest share of employment, followed by government (see table 19, Appendix). These two branches of the economy accounted for just under half the work force. Some Turkish Cypriot economists have noted that both these sectors were relatively inefficient and contained some hidden unemployment. Agriculture's share of the work force had slowly declined during the 1980s, and government's share declined by a fraction. The shares of other sectors rose slowly as the economy modernized.

Turkish Cypriots enjoyed a higher standard of living than citizens of Turkey. The minimum wage, for example, was higher than on the mainland. In addition, wages rose steadily. The chronic high inflation led the government to use a cost of living adjustment (COLA) mechanism that increased all wages every three months in step with inflation. This policy limited or prevented real reductions in wages. In addition, annual merit raises were typical.

As of 1986, the last year for which figures were available, one-third of the work force was unionized, a large proportion for a developing country with a large agricultural sector. The establishment of labor unions was free from government interference. According to Articles 70 and 71 of the constitution and the Trade Unions Law, no prior permission from the state was necessary for the formation of trade unions. The only legal requirement was that a minimum of twenty persons should come together to establish a union. However, in cases in which the total number of persons active in a field was less than twenty, but more than three, a trade union could also be formed.

In the second half of the 1980s, there were two main trade union federations in the "TRNC." In addition, seventeen independent unions represented about one-third of the unionized workers. The oldest federation, the Turkish Cypriot Trade Union Federation (Kıbrıs Türk İşçi Sendikaları Federasyonu—TÜRK–SEN) was founded in 1954 and by the mid-1980s had about 9,300 members belonging to fifteen unions. This federation emphasized practical issues as opposed to ideology and was a member of the International Confederation of Free Trade Unions (ICFTU) and the European Trade Union Confederation. It also maintained close ties with the American Federation of Labor-Congress of Industrial Organizations (AFL–CIO). TÜRK–SEN was closely affiliated with the Confederation of Turkish Trade Unions, from which it received financial and technical assistance to promote job unionism in the "TRNC." The other major labor organization was the Revolutionary Trade Unions' Federation (Devrimci İşçi Sendikaları Federasyonu—DEV–İŞ). Founded in 1976, DEV–İŞ had about 4,500 members in two unions in 1986. It was a member of the World Federation of Trade Unions (WFTU) and maintained close relations with similar foreign trade unions. A strong rival to TÜRK–SEN, DEV–İŞ emphasized "ideological unionism" and propagated leftist political ideas. DEV–İŞ operated freely in the "TRNC," although its sister union in Turkey was declared illegal after the 1980 military coup (and as of 1990, despite the return to civilian rule in 1983 in Turkey, was still banned). To some observers, the freedom of DEV–İŞ was a clear indication that politics in the "TRNC" was not controlled by Turkish authorities, despite the obvious economic and military dependence of Turkish Cypriots on the Turkish state.

Primary Sector

The primary sector of the Turkish Cypriot economy accounted for about one-tenth of the total GDP at the beginning of the 1990s, but its share was in decline, indicating that the economy was modernizing. Agriculture made up virtually all of the primary sector;

fishing and forestry together accounted for less than 1 percent of Turkish Cypriot GDP in 1990.

Agriculture

Although there was a sharp rise in the urban population in the 1980s, the "TRNC" still had a significant rural element. Close to three-fourths of its land was used for farming or forestry, and almost a third of its work force was employed in this sector. Even in the second half of the 1980s, agricultural products made up well over half of all exports. The economy of the "TRNC" was becoming more developed, however, and by 1990 agriculture's share of GDP was only about 9 percent, half of its share in 1980.

Turkish Cypriot farming became increasingly mechanized during the 1980s. At the end of the decade there were 4,500 tractors in the "TRNC," compared with 975 in 1975, and 220 combines. Modernization also brought extensive use of fertilizers, insecticides, and feeds. In some areas, however, where modern methods were not practical, traditional farming methods were still to be seen.

The government attempted to ensure a steady rise in agricultural production by participating directly in this sector. It established the necessary infrastructure by carrying out irrigation projects, promoting land consolidation, and constructing farm roads. The state also oversaw broad research and education programs to inform farmers of the latest agricultural methods. A quasigovernmental agency, Tarım Sigortası, provided insurance against crop failures. In addition, the government helped farmers to organize the marketing of their produce. Finally, the state provided agricultural credits and subsidies to farmers to help them improve their production and increase their incomes.

Water Resources

Despite government support of agriculture, the future of Turkish Cypriot farming was threatened by an insufficient supply of water. Rainfall, long inadequate, in the 1980s was more meager than usual. In addition to the problem of scarcity was the difficulty of providing an adequate supply of water throughout the year because of the high costs of containment and distribution. Extremely irregular river flow necessitated large storage capacities, the terrain required unusually high dams, and high erosion rates in the watersheds required extra storage space to allow for siltation of reservoirs. Cost factors deterred significant construction by the British administration until the 1950s, when a modest program was initiated. After independence was gained in 1960, construction of dams and supply systems accelerated. In the 1980s, the Republic of Cyprus undertook extensive water development projects. These Greek Cypriot projects sometimes had unfavorable effects on Turkish Cypriots, because many of the projects trapped water in the Troodos Mountains, where most of the island's rainfall and snow fell, and prevented the flow of water downstream into the "TRNC."

Turkish Cypriots sought to alleviate their water shortage by building dams and a series of irrigation networks. In 1989 a dam was completed at Geçitköy, at the western end of the Kyrenia Range, and seven more dams were under construction, with another dozen or so in the planning stage. As of the late 1980s, however, only about 5 percent of agricultural land was irrigable throughout the growing season. In 1976 Turkish Cypriots initiated a massive reforestation project in the Kyrenia Range in the hope of attracting more rainfall into this region. The success of all of these projects depended ultimately, however, on the level of rainfall, which declined during much of the 1980s.

Land Use and Tenure

At the end of the 1980s, the total area of the "TRNC" was measured at 2,496,370 hectares. Of this area, 56.7 percent was agricultural land, 19.5 percent forest, 4.96 percent uncultivated, 10.68 percent occupied by towns, villages, and roads, and 8.16 percent unusable. In 1975, of the agricultural land, 50 percent was cultivated; by 1987, some 68.7 percent was cultivated.

The "TRNC" recognized three categories of land ownership: private, state, and communal. The greatest amount of land was privately owned. Unrestricted legal ownership of private land in Cyprus dated only from 1946, when the British administration enacted a new land law, the Immovable Property (Tenure, Registration, and Valuation) Law, which superseded the land code in effect under the Ottomans. Under the Ottoman code, all land belonged to the state, and those who worked the land were in effect hereditary tenants whose right to the land was usufructuary. Land could be transmitted from father to son, but could not otherwise be disposed of without official permission. The 1946 British law ended this tradition, stipulating that all state land properly acquired by individuals became their private property. Communal land remained as before, but all unoccupied and vacant land not lawfully held became the property of the state. As a result, virtually all forests become state property.

The Muslim religious foundation Evkaf Idaresi (Turkish Religious Trust, usually known as Evkaf) was the largest private owner of property in the "TRNC." Before the events of 1974, Evkaf owned 1 to 2 percent of the island's total farmland. These holdings dated back to Ottoman times and were mainly donations in perpetuity from members of the Turkish Cypriot community. Much of Evkaf's land was located in parts of the island that remained under the control of the Republic of Cyprus.

Agricultural Cooperatives

The cooperative movement was established in Cyprus during the period of British rule to better the economic conditions of farmers and villagers. As of 1987, there were 257 active cooperative societies in the "TRNC." Most villages and towns had cooperative credit unions that provided savings and loan services for members. Loans were made both in cash and in kind (items needed for farming) to assist cooperative society members. One of the banks operating in the "TRNC" was the cooperative societies' own bank, the Turkish Cypriot Cooperative Central Bank. The government oversaw the activities of the societies through the Office of the Registrar of Cooperative Societies.

Crops

Crops made up about 70 percent of the primary sector's contribution to the GDP of the "TRNC." Animal husbandry supplied nearly all the rest, with fishing and forestry accounting for a very small share (less than 1 percent between them). As in the Republic of Cyprus, agriculture in the "TRNC" was rainfed or irrigated. Rainfed, or dryland, agriculture produced cereals, fodder, tobacco, olives, carobs, almonds, and wine grapes. Irrigated agriculture yielded citrus fruits, deciduous fruits, potatoes, vegetables, table grapes, and bananas.

Cereal cultivation in the "TRNC" occupied one-third of all cultivated land. Barley production exceeded domestic consumption requirements, and the surplus was exported. Wheat production met two-thirds of domestic demand. Mechanized farming had significantly improved cereal production. In 1975 total cereal production stood at 59,913 tons. By 1987 production had nearly doubled, to 111,867 tons.

Citrus fruits (oranges, lemons, and grapefruit) were by far the most valuable agricultural products. These fruits usually accounted for at least two-thirds of the total agricultural exports of the "TRNC," and until the very end of the 1980s they were a more important export than manufactured goods. Citrus fruits were grown on irrigated land in areas with mild winter weather near Famagusta (Gazimağusa), Morphou (Güzelyurt), Lefka (Lefke), and Lapithos (Lapta).

Other important tree crops were carobs and olives, frequently grown intermixed on hillsides and mountain slopes. Only a few of the 1.5 million olive trees in the "TRNC" were grown in groves. The carob tree, a member of the pulse family, is a native of the eastern Mediterranean whose seeds are used mainly for cattle fodder. Most exports went to Britain. Deciduous tree crops common to temperate climates, including apples, pears, plums, apricots, pomegranates, and figs, were also grown in the "TRNC," but to a much lesser extent than in the Republic of Cyprus.

Industrial crops included fibers (cotton, flax, and hemp), spices (cumin and aniseed), and tobacco. Tobacco grew in the northeast corner of the island. At the end of the 1980s, tobacco was not an important crop, but it did yield some exports.

The diverse topography and climate of Cyprus permit the cultivation of a great variety of other crops. An important crop was the potato. Two potato crops a year permitted substantial exports, mainly to Britain. In the second half of the 1980s, potatoes accounted for about 5 percent of Turkish Cypriot exports. Potato farming developed during the post-1974 years as a result of an improved irrigation system. Other vegetables and fruits grown included cabbage, cauliflower, carrots, cucumbers, onions, squash, strawberries, tomatoes, artichokes, avocados, bananas, leeks, and okra. Most were grown not only for domestic consumption but also for export. Vines occupied the largest area in the Karpas Peninsula, and some groves were also found in the Kyrenia (Girne) region. Some fresh grapes were exported. Because of water shortages, however, grape production fell to only about 100 tons a year in the late 1980s.

Livestock and Poultry

Livestock was an important part of Turkish Cypriot agriculture. Beginning in the mid-1970s, the number of animals raised increased significantly. The number of cattle increased 40 percent, from 8,600 in 1975 to 12,038 in 1987, and the number of sheep rose from 147,609 in 1975 to 185,238 in 1987. The goat population was reduced by 3.3 percent in this period because of the damage goats did to vegetation. During this same period, milk production increased by 50 percent, from 20,000 to 29,937 tons a year; meat production increased by 166 percent, from 1,891 to 5,320 tons; and poultry production increased by 265 percent, from 800 to 2,920 tons. In 1985, 1986, and 1987, live animal exports to Arab countries were an important Turkish Cypriot export. For example, government statistics indicated that 20,596 sheep and 11,104 goats, worth TL1.6 billion, were exported to Arab countries in 1987. Live

Citrus grove near Lefka (Lefke)
Courtesy Office of the "Turkish Republic of Northern Cyprus," Washington

animal exports fell in the next two years; it was not certain what future trends would be.

A large and modern meat and poultry factory, financed by Turkey, was built in the second half of the 1980s to meet long-term consumer needs for these products. Completed in 1989, with an annual processing capacity of 6,000 tons of sheep meat, 2,600 tons of cattle meat, 1,000 tons of goat meat, and 3,000 tons of poultry, the plant could also use bones, leather, and other substances for food and other purposes. Despite its sanitary advantages and highly economic production costs, the plant's opening was prevented by local agricultural interests.

Forestry and Fishing

The main forests of the "TRNC" were in the areas of Lapithos, Bellapais, Buffavento, Kantara, and Kartal—all located along the Kyrenia (Girne) Range. Forests located on the northern slopes of the Kyrenia Range were a mixture of pine and Mediterranean cypress. Forests on the southern slopes of the Kyrenia Range and in the Karpas Peninsula were mostly olive brush and tamarisk. Cedar and golden oak (both endemic to Cyprus), plane, and alder were also found in the "TRNC," as were species of eucalyptus and acacia. The Muslim religious foundation Evkaf had some forest holdings, but most forests were state owned and managed by the Department of Forestry, under the Ministry of Agriculture and Natural Resources. One of the department's aims was reforestation of the barren slopes of Pentadaktylos Mountain (Beşparmak Mountain) in the Kyrenia Range and other forest areas burned during fighting in 1974, estimated at forty-eight square kilometers of "TRNC" territory. Forestry provided some employment but was of almost no significance to the economy as a whole, accounting for only 0.1 percent of GDP in the late 1980s.

The fishing industry met about 60 percent of domestic demand and was a significant source of employment in Boghaz (Boğaz) on the southern coast of the Karpas Peninsula and Kyrenia. Deep-sea fishing was done by trawlers. Most Turkish Cypriot fishermen, however, used small boats with fishing nets. Foreign vessels were not permitted to fish within the six-mile territorial limit of the "TRNC." In the late 1980s, fishing accounted for only about 0.6 percent of GDP.

Secondary Sector

The secondary sector of the Turkish Cypriot economy, consisting of manufacturing, energy, mining, and construction, had shown strong growth since 1977. In 1977 the secondary sector made up

13.8 percent of the "TRNC's" GDP, and by 1990, it had grown to 21 percent. In 1990 manufacturing was the sector's most important branch, accounting for 12.3 percent of GDP; construction's share was 7.3 percent; mining's share was a negligible 0.3 percent; and energy-related activities accounted for 1.7 percent.

Manufacturing

Manufacturing showed steady progress after the late 1970s, and by 1990 was an important component of the Turkish Cypriot economy. In 1989 it surpassed for the first time agriculture's contribution to GDP. Only government services and trade were more important. Manufactured products were important exports. Their share of exports expanded rapidly in the 1980s, from 19 percent in 1981 to 45 percent in 1989. Manufacturing's share of employment increased only slightly, however.

Except for a cement factory at Boghaz, manufacturing in the "TRNC" consisted entirely of light industry. About 600 firms, mostly small and family-owned, were active at the end of the 1980s. Clothing and textiles were the most important products, and clothing came to account for about 30 percent of exports in the late 1980s, exceeded only by citrus exports. A number of foreign companies were active in the clothing industry. Other manufactured products included footwear, leather goods, furniture, chemicals, paper, and some metal items.

Energy Resources and Mining

Turkish Cypriot manufacturing faced frequent power shortages because virtually all electricity consumed in the "TRNC" came from power plants in the Republic of Cyprus. Until the second half of the 1980s, the "TRNC" received electricity in exchange for water it supplied to the republic. By the late 1980s, however, the republic had made extensive investments in water management facilities and no longer needed water from the "TRNC." A result of this independence, Turkish Cypriots contended, was that the provision of electricity to them was frequently, even daily, interrupted for short periods beginning in the late 1980s. To counter the uncertain supply of electric power, Turkish Cypriots began constructing an oil-fired power plant near Kyrenia. Financed by Turkey, the plant was scheduled to go into production by 1993 with a capacity of 120 megawatts and an annual production of 750 million kilowatt-hours. Greek Cypriot opinion about the power plant was mixed. Its construction would mean that the Republic of Cyprus would no longer need to supply the "TRNC" with electricity. The resulting energy independence of Turkish Cypriots

153

would, however, make them less susceptible to Greek Cypriot pressure.

Like Greek Cypriots, Turkish Cypriots were entirely dependent on imports for petroleum. All petroleum imports were in the form of finished products because the "TRNC" had no refineries.

Mining was once quite important for the Cypriot economy, but by the late 1980s it represented only 0.3 percent of the GDP of the "TRNC." There was some mining in the area around Lefka, but about 90 percent of mineral deposits of value were in the Republic of Cyprus. Minerals in the "TRNC" that could be exported included cuprous and iron pyrites, chrome iron ore, manganese ore, gypsum, earth colors, and lime.

Construction

The construction industry was an important segment of the Turkish Cypriot economy and provided about 10 percent of employment and about 7 percent of GDP in the late 1980s. Demand for housing, especially for the refugees displaced by the events of 1974, extensive work on the infrastructure, and a rapidly expanding tourist industry accounted for much of this activity. Government-financed housing programs for civil servants also helped maintain the construction industry. The cost of government-financed housing of this kind was cheaper than in the private sector and permitted ordinary wage-earners to become homeowners.

Tertiary Sector

The tertiary, or service, sector of the Turkish Cypriot economy grew in importance during the 1980s as part of the economy's modernization. The greatest expansion was in trade and tourism; earnings from tourism tripled between 1986 and 1989. Financial, business, and personal services also grew more important to the economy in the 1980s. Government still accounted for too large a share of the Turkish Cypriot economy at the end of the 1980s, but its share was declining. A new development in the late 1980s was the founding of Eastern Mediterranean University in Famagusta. With an enrollment of 3,500 students (2,800 of whom were foreign), it was a valuable new source of employment and foreign exchange, and an example of how the Turkish Cypriot service sector might grow in the future.

Banking

The Central Bank of North Cyprus, the central bank of the "TRNC," was established by law in 1983 and began operation the next year. It performed the usual functions of a central bank,

Famagusta (Gazimağusa) port
Courtesy Office of the "Turkish Republic of Northern Cyprus," Washington

but did not issue a national currency. The Turkish lira was used instead. Establishment of a separate "TRNC" currency was occasionally discussed, but concrete action for this purpose had not been undertaken as of 1990. Foreign exchange was traded freely in the "TRNC," with no restrictions on transactions. A free currency exchange market was seen as part of a liberal economy. The government set interest rates as high as 40 percent for one-year deposits and 48 percent for some other deposits to prevent capital flight and shield deposits against the effects of chronic high inflation.

The central bank monitored the activities of about a dozen Turkish Cypriot banks and the branches of several Turkish banks active in the "TRNC." By the late 1980s, the largest commercial bank was the Türk Bankası, followed by the Cyprus Credit Bank and the Cyprus Commercial Bank. The cooperative movement's bank, the Turkish Cypriot Cooperative Central Bank, was important to cooperative members throughout the "TRNC." The Muslim religious foundation Evkaf had its own bank, Kıbrıs Vakıflar Bankası, which managed the foundation's financial assets and the revenue accruing to it from its widespread and varied real estate holdings.

Transportation

According to government statistics, the Turkish Cypriot road network in the mid-1980s consisted of 5,280 kilometers of paved and 800 kilometers of unpaved roads. In an effort to support farming, the government constructed many service roads. The Department of Public Works was responsible for about 2,720 kilometers of paved roads, and the rest came under the jurisdiction of municipal administrations. After 1974, major highways were built between Nicosia and Morphou, Nicosia and Kyrenia, and Nicosia and Ercan Airport. Another highway to Geçitkale Airport was under consideration in the late 1980s.

The two major international airports in the "TRNC," Ercan and Geçitkale, were both administered by the Department of Civil Aviation. Ercan Airport was equipped with navigational aids and equipment and was capable of handling all types of aircraft (including the DC–10 and Airbus 300). About 120,000 passengers traveled through Ercan Airport each year. The national airline of the "TRNC," Turkish Cypriot Airlines, operated a small fleet of large, modern aircraft.

The major ports of the "TRNC" were Famagusta, Kyrenia, and Kalecik, located on the southwestern coast of the Karpas Peninsula. Famagusta was the main multipurpose port, capable of receiving in its inner harbor vessels up to 131 meters in length and with a draft of up to 6.7 meters. Part of Famagusta's outer harbor was a free port. Famagusta's port was equipped with tugboats, mobile and floating cranes, forklifts, warehouses, and a quay-connected modern silo with a storage capacity of 20,000 tons. In 1975, 608 ships sailed into the port. In 1987 this number increased to 1,042. The number of passengers increased from 65,403 to 91,986, and the total tonnage of goods entering the port from 72,755 to 290,736 tons.

The port of Kalecik consisted of two privately owned sections. One was equipped with a conveyor belt for bulk and/or bagged cargo and a pier 42 meters in length. The other section was a tanker terminal with submerged pipelines.

Kyrenia's small port had a maximum depth of 3.2 meters and was used mainly as a yacht harbor. Newer facilities to the east of the old port served as loading docks for ferries between the island and Turkey. The new port's total quay length in the mid-1980s was 409 meters; the main quay was 150 meters long, with an average depth of 8 meters. In 1987 more than 400 ships visited the port, bringing 37,000 passengers and 1,500 vehicles.

Telecommunications

Telephone, telex, fax, and telegraph communications between the "TRNC" and the outside world were carried out via fully automatic exchange services. All villages and towns were connected to this system, and 40,000 households had telephones. Substantial assistance from Turkey financed the modernization of the telecommunications system. A further modernization of this system, planned in the late 1980s, included the installation of a fully computerized digital exchange system with fiber optic lines. By early 1990, some fiber optics were already in use. At the beginning of the 1990s, there were 75,000 television sets (color and black and white) in the ''TRNC.'' The state Bayrak Radio and Television Corporation had eight radio and three television stations.

Tourism

Tourism was the most important source of foreign currency in the late 1980s, earning US$118 million in 1988 and US$126.8 million in 1989. The ''TRNC'' had direct air and sea links only to Turkey because this country alone recognized it as an independent nation. Despite this handicap, the number of foreign tourists from countries other than Turkey increased substantially in the late 1980s, as did the foreign exchange they brought with them.

The number of tourists coming to the ''TRNC'' tripled during the 1980s, from 87,000 in 1981 to 310,000 in 1990. About 20 percent of the tourists were from countries other than Turkey. The number of tourist beds approximately doubled during the 1980s, to more than 7,000 by 1990. Tourism became a year-round business, with a professional staff trained at the Hotel and Catering Training Center at Kyrenia. This facility was under the Ministry of Tourism and Culture. A range of accommodations was available, from campsites to luxury hotels. Tourism was expected to continue to grow in the 1990s.

The expansion of tourism was especially noticeable in the late 1980s. Earnings more than tripled between 1986 and 1989. This increase was a result of the government's decision in late 1986 to make tourism the locomotive that would pull the entire economy. To promote the tourism industry and attract foreign investment in it, the government introduced a number of incentives, including long-term, low-cost leases on government-owned land and buildings, exemption of many goods serving tourism from import duties, and exemption or moderation of some taxes.

Foreign Trade

At the beginning of the 1990s, the ''TRNC'' traded with more than sixty countries around the world. Among these trading partners were members of the EC, countries of the Middle East, the United States, Japan, and numerous other countries in Africa and

Asia. Lack of recognition of the "TRNC" and the economic and political blockade imposed by the Republic of Cyprus made it difficult for the "TRNC" to establish direct and regular sea and air links with countries other than Turkey. The blockade could be circumvented, however, by trading through international companies.

The Turkish Cypriot economy suffered from a chronic trade deficit. During the 1980s, imports often exceeded imports by margins of three and four to one, and in some years, 1989 for example, the ratio was even worse (see table 20, Appendix). More than half the imports were of manufactured goods; the Turkish Cypriot economy had a small manufacturing sector. Foods, fuels, and chemicals accounted for most of the remaining imports.

Turkey was by far the main source of imports (see table 21, Appendix). In the late 1980s, Turkey supplied roughly two-fifths of total imports. Countries of the EC supplied one-third, half of which came from Britain. The Far East was the source of most of the remainder.

The most important customer for Turkish Cypriot goods in the late 1980s was Britain, which took about two-thirds notably citrus fruits and vegetables. The other EC countries bought a much smaller share, and Turkey accounted for 12 to 17 percent between 1986 and 1989. The Middle East fluctuated widely in its share of Turkish Cypriot exports, buying 10.2 percent in 1986 and 3.6 percent in 1988. The Far East purchased virtually no Turkish Cypriot goods.

The government attempted to stimulate trade by various means, including liberal tax concessions and the free exchange of foreign currency. The establishment of a free port and zone at Famagusta in late 1977 was another government initiative to boost foreign trade. To make business in the free port attractive to investors, the government exempted income from activities there from corporate and income taxes. Imports into the free port and zone were also exempt from duties and tolls. Import duties elsewhere in the "TRNC" could be onerous. Furthermore, profits and capital from the free port and zone could be repatriated without limit. In addition to these highly competitive concessions, the area's infrastructure was suitable for all kinds of manufacturing, processing, and construction activities.

*   *   *

The Republic of Cyprus and its ministries, departments, and banks publish a variety of statistical reports that provide useful economic information, usually with a one- to two-year time lag. Particularly relevant are the *Annual Reports* of the Central Bank of Cyprus, the *Economic Reports* of the Department of Statistics and Research, Ministry of Finance; the *Annual Reports* of the Cyprus Telecommunications Authority and of the Cyprus Electricity Authority; and the special reports of the Cyprus Development Bank on issues such as "Consumption Expenditures in Cyprus" and "The Cyprus Economy."

Other noteworthy reports and studies include reports from the International Trade Administration of the United States Department of Commerce (prepared by the American Embassy in Nicosia), which summarize major economic trends, especially those pertinent to the United States economy. The Economist Intelligence Unit's *Country Report: Lebanon, Cyprus* and *Country Profile: Lebanon, Cyprus* offer quarterly and annual analyses, respectively, of economic and political trends in Cyprus. A monograph by John Hudson and Marina Dymiotou-Jensen, *Modelling a Developing Country,* gives, among other things, a brief and expert account of the government's planning process.

The sources most readily available for those wishing to know more of the economy of the "TRNC" are published by Europa Publications Ltd. *The Europe World Year Book* and *The Middle East and North Africa,* for example, will provide much basic information. *North Cyprus Almanack,* published by K. Rüstem and Brother in London, treats a number of aspects of the Turkish Cypriot economy. The State Planning Organisation of the "TRNC" publishes annual comprehensive economic statistics. These are available at "TRNC" offices around the world. (For further information and complete citations, see Bibliography.)

Chapter 4. Government and Politics

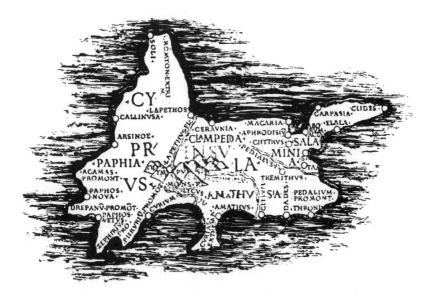

Artist's rendition of early map of Cyprus

THE SHAPE, STRUCTURE, AND STATUS of Cyprus's government have been sources of bitter controversy since independence in 1960, and have become the "national" question for both Greek Cypriots and Turkish Cypriots. Politics in both communities, governed separately since 1964 and physically separated since 1974, have been dominated by the lack of consensus, both between and within the two communities, over the very identity of the state and the structure of its government and political institutions.

The original political arrangements outlined in the 1960 constitution were in effect for only three years. By 1963, after proposals by President Archbishop Makarios III (1960–77) to amend the constitution in ways widely viewed as favoring the majority Greek Cypriot population, Turkish Cypriots withdrew from many national institutions and began self-government in the Turkish quarters of the island's towns and cities and in Turkish Cypriot villages.

A more significant change occurred after the 1974 Turkish intervention. Following the dislocation and resettlement of large segments of both communities, the current situation emerged: two separate governments—only one of which enjoys international recognition as the legitimate government—functioning in two discrete geographic zones. In February 1975, the provisional Turkish Cypriot administration declared itself the "Turkish Federated State of Cyprus" ("TFSC"), although it stated its intention to move toward a federal solution with the Greek Cypriots and pledged not to seek recognition as an independent state. In October 1983, after continued stalemate of United Nations (UN) efforts toward a settlement, Turkish Cypriots renamed their "state" the "Turkish Republic of Northern Cyprus" ("TRNC"). While restating their commitment to working toward a federal solution, Turkish Cypriot authorities launched an international campaign for recognition of their state, arguing that recognition would facilitate a solution by according the island's two political entities equal status. As of the early 1990s, however, only Turkey had recognized the "TRNC."

Greek Cypriots maintained that the Republic of Cyprus established in 1960 continued to exist, with functioning institutions, absent Turkish Cypriot participation. The status of the 1959 treaties that established the republic in 1960 remained in dispute, posing a challenge to the Greek Cypriot claim of legal authority and sovereignty over the whole island (except for the 256 square kilometers that are sovereign British base areas). The Greek Cypriot position on the legal status of the 1959 agreements is not completely clear. The late president Makarios attempted to invalidate the Treaty of Guarantee, and later Greek Cypriot leaders claimed it violated their sovereignty, but on occasion they have tried to invoke it. For example, after the 1983 Turkish Cypriot declaration of statehood, the republic's president tried to persuade the British government to intervene under the terms of that treaty's Article IV.

Since the 1974 crisis and the emergence of the Cyprus question as an international political problem, the Republic of Cyprus has had three presidents. Makarios, the dominant political and religious figure for Greek Cypriots, died of a heart attack in the summer of 1977 at age sixty-three. He was succeeded by Spyros Kyprianou, leader of the ruling Democratic Front, and Makarios's ecclesiastical responsibilities were assumed by Bishop Chrysostomos of Paphos. Kyprianou was reelected unopposed in January 1978 and was reelected in contested elections in 1983. In February 1988, Kyprianou was ousted in an upset by newcomer George Vassiliou, a successful businessman with no party affiliation, who campaigned on a promise to bring fresh ideas and energy to the settlement process.

Leadership of the Turkish Cypriot community has remained since 1974 in the hands of Rauf Denktaş, elected president of the "Turkish Federated State of Cyprus" ("TFSC") in July 1975 and reelected in 1981. In 1985, under a new constitution in the newly formed "Turkish Republic of Northern Cyprus" ("TRNC"), Denktaş again won at the polls, by a vote of 70.4 percent, and in April 1990 received 67.1 percent of the vote, defeating two opponents.

The search for a settlement through creation of a new federal republic continued in the late 1980s and in 1990. Talks intensified after Vassiliou's election, and the UN-sponsored negotiations between Greek and Turkish Cypriots in 1988–90 aimed at outlining a framework for establishing a federal republic that would be bicommunal with respect to constitutional issues and bizonal with respect to territorial concerns. Early optimism that Vassiliou would be the catalytic force to bring the talks to a successful conclusion was dampened when talks broke down in early 1990. Despite tentative progress on closing the gap between Greek Cypriot demands for freedom of movement, property, and settlement and the Turkish Cypriot demand for strict bizonality with considerable authority to the two provinces or states, the process was encumbered by deep mistrust between the two sides and a growing conviction that the Turkish Cypriot side was more inclined to work for its separate status than for power sharing in a unitary state with Greek Cypriots.

Background

The Republic of Cyprus was created in 1960 through international agreements reached in Zurich and London in February 1959, with a constitution that went into effect in August 1960. The constitution recognized the strong bicommunal character of the new state, with elaborate safeguards for the minority Turkish Cypriot community. In the preindependence debate over the governmental structure of the new state, neither Britain nor the Turkish Cypriot community accepted the concept of "minority rights" as an organizing principle. Rather, the Turkish Cypriots were recognized as one of two "communities" with certain rights; the legitimacy of the state would derive from the partnership between the two communities. The Cypriot consociational experiment had some unique features designed to achieve a delicate balance between the prevailing Greek Cypriot preference for a unitary state and the Turkish Cypriot desire for as much recognition as a separate political entity as possible. The tension between these two communal priorities proved insurmountable.

Since 1964, the constitution of 1960 has not been the legal document governing relations between the two communities, although it remains the basis of government and law for the 80 percent of the population that are Greek Cypriot and residing in the two-thirds of the island controlled by the authorities of the Republic of Cyprus. The "TRNC" approved a new constitution in 1985, which established a parliamentary system in the north.

1960 Constitution

At independence, Cyprus's constitution called for a government divided into executive, legislative, and judicial branches, headed by a president, with strong guarantees for the Turkish Cypriot community. The constitution arranged for a Greek Cypriot president and Turkish Cypriot vice president, elected by their respective communities for five-year terms of office. Members of the island's other minorities—Armenians, Maronites, and Roman Catholics—were given the option of joining one of the communities for voting purposes. All chose to be identified as Greek, although some have continued to live in the Turkish zone since the 1974 division of the island. Greek and Turkish were designated as official languages, and the two communities were given the right to celebrate, respectively, Greek and Turkish national holidays.

The constitution further provided that executive power in all but communal matters be vested in the president and vice president. The two executives had the right of veto, separately or jointly, over certain laws or decisions of both the Council of Ministers and the House of Representatives, the legislative body. The constitution spelled out in detail their powers and duties.

The Council of Ministers was to be composed of seven Greek Cypriots and three Turkish Cypriots, with the former appointed by the president and the latter by the vice president. Decisions of the council were to be taken by absolute majority. Of three key portfolios—defense, finance, and foreign affairs—one was to be held by a Turkish Cypriot.

The unicameral House of Representatives was designed to legislate for the republic in all matters except those expressly reserved to separate communal chambers. The constitution provided that thirty-five of its members be Greek Cypriots and fifteen Turkish Cypriots. (Representation in proportion to communal strength would have resulted in a forty-to-ten ratio.) Members, elected from separate communal rolls, were to serve for terms of five years. The president of the House of Representatives was to be a Greek Cypriot and its vice president, a Turkish Cypriot.

Voting in the House of Representatives was to be by majority, except that separate majorities in the two communities were required for imposition of taxes or duties, modification of the electoral law, or laws relating to the separate municipalities in the five main towns. The establishment of these municipalities became one of the most controversial intercommunal issues. Although the constitution called for their establishment, implementing legislation was never passed because the Greeks were convinced that such laws could lead to partition. Turkish Cypriots have long cited this issue as evidence of the Greek Cypriots' intention to undermine the Turkish Cypriots' separate communal identity.

The constitution also called for the creation of two communal chambers, composed of representatives elected by each community. These chambers were empowered to deal with religious, educational, and cultural matters, questions of personal status, and the supervision of cooperatives and credit societies. To supplement an annual provision to the chambers from the government budget, the constitution enabled the communal chambers to impose taxes and fees of their own to support their activities.

The judicial system broadly outlined in the Zurich-London accords and stipulated in detail in the constitution included the Supreme Constitutional Court, the High Court of Justice, district and assize courts, and communal courts. At the summit was the Supreme Constitutional Court, composed of three judges: a Greek Cypriot, a Turkish Cypriot, and a contracted judge from a neutral country who would serve as president of the court. The president, who was entitled to two votes, would serve for six years, while the Greek Cypriot and Turkish Cypriot judges would serve until age sixty-eight. The court was to have final jurisdiction on matters of constitutional interpretation and adjudication of disputes centering on alleged discrimination in law against either of the two communities.

This bicommunal structure was duplicated in the High Court of Justice, which exercised appellate jurisdiction over lower courts in civil and criminal matters. The lower courts were assize courts, with criminal jurisdiction, and district courts, with civil jurisdiction except in questions of personal status and religious matters. Disputes between plaintiffs and the defendants belonging to the same community were to be tried by tribunals composed of judges belonging to the appropriate community. Disputes between members of different communities were to be tried by mixed tribunals whose compositions were to be determined by the High Court of Justice.

Civil disputes relating to questions of personal status and religious matters were to be tried in communal courts. These courts were rigidly limited in jurisdiction and could not impose restraint, detention, or imprisonment.

The constitution set forth other safeguards for the Turkish Cypriot minority in sections dealing with the civil service and the armed forces of the republic. According to the 1960 census, Greek Cypriots composed 77 percent of the population, Turkish Cypriots 18.3 percent, and other minorities the remainder. The constitution required that the two groups be represented in the civil service at a ratio of 70 to 30 percent. In addition, the republic was to have an army of 2,000 members, 60 percent Greek Cypriot and 40 percent Turkish Cypriot. After an initial period, a 2,000-member security force consisting of police and gendarmerie was to be 70 percent Greek Cypriot and 30 percent Turkish Cypriot.

The organizational structure and qualifications of the civil service were laid down on the model of the British civil service, with provisions for tenure, career status, and promotion through a grade-level system. The ten-member Public Service Commission determined the rules of conduct and qualifications for the various positions.

1963 Constitutional Breakdown

The 1960 constitution did not succeed in providing the framework for a lasting compromise between Greek and Turkish Cypriots. Rather, its bicommunal features impeded administration and gave rise to continuing dissension, which culminated finally in armed violence between members of the two communities. Beginning in late 1963, Turkish Cypriots withdrew from the government, and by 1965 the Greek Cypriots were in full charge.

The constitution failed to allay the suspicion and distrust that had increasingly divided the two communities, especially since the eruption of intercommunal violence in 1958. Many Greek Cypriots viewed the Zurich-London agreements as imposed on Cyprus from outside and therefore illegitimate. Their main objection to the agreements, however, was that they barred the unification, or enosis, of Cyprus with Greece. Greek Cypriots also viewed the constitutional provisions drafted to safeguard minority rights as granting the Turkish Cypriots disproportionate privileges that the Turkish Cypriots abused. Therefore, some politically active elements of the Greek Cypriot community were motivated to undermine the constitution, or at least press for modifications.

Turkish Cypriots, some of whom also would have preferred different arrangements than those contained in the independence documents, such as *taksim,* or partition, of the island and union of its two parts with the respective motherlands (so-called double enosis), nonetheless maintained that the separative provisions of the constitution were essential to their security and identity as a separate national community.

A number of quarrels broke out over the balance of representation of the two communities in the government and over foreign policy, taxation by communal chambers, and other matters. The disputes brought the government to a virtual standstill. The leading cause of disagreements was the ratio of Greek Cypriots to Turkish Cypriots in the civil service. Turkish Cypriots complained that the seventy-to-thirty ratio was not enforced. Greek Cypriots felt that the provisions discriminated against them because they constituted almost 80 percent of the population. Another major point of contention concerned the composition of units under the sixty-to-forty ratio decreed for the Cypriot army. President Makarios favored complete integration; Vice President Fazıl Küçük accepted a mixed force at the battalion level but insisted on segregated companies. On October 20, 1961, Küçük used his constitutional veto power for the first and only time to halt the development of a fully integrated force. Makarios then stated that the country could not afford an army anyway. Planning and development of the national army ceased, and paramilitary forces arose in each community.

From the start, Greek Cypriots had been uneasy about the idea of separate municipalities, which Turkish Cypriots were determined to preserve. The Greek Cypriot Communal Chamber also failed to set up a communal court system, whereas Turkish Cypriot communal courts were established.

Still another issue that provoked strong Greek Cypriot criticism was the right of the veto held by the Turkish Cypriot vice president and what amounted to final veto power held by the Turkish Cypriot representatives in the House of Representatives with respect to laws and decisions affecting the entire population. Turkish Cypriot representatives had exercised this veto power with respect to income tax legislation, seriously limiting government revenues.

In late 1963, after three years' experience of unsteady self-government, Makarios declared that certain constitutional provisions "threatened to paralyze the State machinery." Revisions were necessary, he said, to remove obstacles that prevented Greek and Turkish Cypriots from "cooperating in the spirit of understanding and friendship." On November 30, 1963, Makarios proposed thirteen amendments to be considered immediately by the leaders of the Turkish Cypriot community.

These proposals, outlined in a presidential memorandum entitled "Suggested Measures for Facilitating the Smooth Functioning of the State and for the Removal of Certain Causes of Intercommunal Friction," reflected all the constitutional problems that had arisen. The president's action had far-reaching implications. Most important, it deeply eroded Turkish Cypriot confidence in the fragile power-sharing arrangement. The proposals also automatically involved Greece, Turkey, and Britain, which as signatories to the Treaties of Guarantee and Alliance had pledged to guarantee the status quo under the constitution.

The proposed amendments would have eliminated most of the special rights of Turkish Cypriots. For instance, they would have abolished many of the provisions for separate communal institutions, substituting an integrated state with limited guarantees for the minority community. The administration of justice was to be unified. Instead of having separate municipalities in the five largest towns, a provision originally called for in the constitution, municipalities were to be unified. The veto powers of the president and vice president were to be abandoned, as were the provisions for separate parliamentary majorities in certain areas of legislation. Turkish Cypriot representation in the civil service was to be proportionate to the size of the community. By way of compensation, the Turkish Cypriot vice president was to be given the right to deputize for the Greek Cypriot president in case of his absence, and the vice president of the House of Representatives was to be acting president of the body during the temporary absence or incapacity of the president.

Küçük reportedly had agreed to consider these proposals. The Turkish government, however, rejected the entire list. In any case, intercommunal fighting erupted in December 1963, and in March 1964 the UN Security Council authorized the establishment of an international peace-keeping force to control the violence and act as a buffer between the two communities.

1964–74 Situation: Separate Communal Life

By the spring of 1964, the legislature was effectively a Greek Cypriot body. Turkish Cypriot representatives, like their counterparts in the civil service, feared for their safety in the Greek-dominated parts of Nicosia and did not participate.

Turkish Cypriots have argued that what they considered their involuntary nonparticipation rendered any acts of that parliament unconstitutional. Greek Cypriots have maintained that the institutions continued to function under the constitution, despite Turkish Cypriot absence.

In 1964 the Greek Cypriot-controlled House of Representatives passed a number of important pieces of legislation, including laws providing for the establishment of an armed force, the National Guard, and for the restoration to the government of its rights to impose an income tax. Other laws altered the government structure and some of the bicommunal arrangements, including abolishing separate electoral rolls for Greek and Turkish Cypriots, abolishing the Greek Cypriot Communal Chamber, and amalgamating the Supreme Constitutional Court and the High Court of Justice into the Supreme Court.

Reaction of the Turkish Cypriot judiciary to this judicial change was apparently not unfavorable, since a Turkish Cypriot was named president of the Supreme Court. He assumed his post, and other Turkish Cypriot judges returned to the bench. For about two years, Turkish Cypriot judges participated in the revised court system, dealing with both Greek and Turkish Cypriots. In June 1966, however, the Turkish Cypriot judges withdrew from the system, claiming harassment. The Turkish Cypriot leadership directed its community not to use the courts of the republic, to which, however, they continued to be legally entitled, according to the Greek Cypriots. In turn, the Greek Cypriot government considered the judicial processes set up in the Turkish Cypriot community to be without legal foundation.

The establishment of a separate Turkish Cypriot administration evolved in late 1967, in the wake of renewed intercommunal hostilities (see Intercommunal Violence, ch. 1). Turkish Cypriot leaders, on December 29, 1967, announced the formation of a "transitional administration" to oversee the affairs of the Turkish Cypriot community "until such time as provisions of the 1960 constitution have been fully implemented.'' The administration was to be headed by Küçük as president and Rauf Denktaş (the former president of the Turkish Cypriot Communal Chamber, who had been living in exile in Turkey) as vice president.

The fifteen Turkish Cypriot former members of the republic's House of Representatives joined the members of the Turkish Cypriot Communal Chamber to constitute a Turkish Cypriot legislative assembly. Nine of the members were to function as an executive council to carry out ministerial duties. President Makarios declared the administration illegal and its actions devoid of any legal effect.

On February 25, 1968, Greek Cypriots reelected Makarios to office, in the first presidential election since 1960, by an overwhelming majority. Running against a single opponent campaigning for enosis, Makarios won about 96 percent of the votes cast.

Intercommunal talks for a solution to the constitutional crisis began on June 24, 1968, and reached a deadlock on September 20, 1971. Talks resumed in July 1972, in the presence of UN Secretary General Kurt Waldheim and one constitutional adviser each from Greece and Turkey. Both sides realized that the basic articles of the constitution, intended to balance the rights and interests of both communities, had become moot and that new constitutional arrangements had to be found.

At the same time, extralegal political activities were proliferating, some based on preindependence clandestine movements. The emergence of these groups, namely, the National Organization of Cypriot Fighters B (Ethniki Organosis Kyprion Agoniston B— EOKA B) and its Turkish Cypriot response, the Turkish Resistance Organization (Türk Mukavemet Teşkilâtı—TMT), was eroding the authority of conventional politicians. There were mounting calls for enosis from forces no longer supportive of Makarios, notably the National Guard, and there was a radical Turkish Cypriot reaction (see Conflict Within the Greek Cypriot Community, 1967–74, ch. 5).

The 1974 Crisis and Division of the Island

Pressures mounting within the Cypriot communities and within the military junta ruling Greece converged in the summer of 1974. Greek military officials, angered by Makarios's independence from Greece and his policy of nonalignment, backed a coup d'état by Greek Cypriot National Guard officers intent on enosis. The coup imposed Nicos Sampson as provisional president.

The Turkish response was swift. On July 20, Turkish troops reached the island and established a beachhead in the north. A ceasefire was reached two days later, with the North Atlantic Treaty

Organization (NATO) allies of Greece and Turkey working urgently to avoid an intra-alliance confrontation. Peace talks were hastily convened in Geneva, but those talks did not satisfy Turkish concerns. On August 14, the Turks began a second offensive that resulted in their control of over 36 percent of the island. The ceasefire lines achieved after the extension of Turkish control formed the basis for the buffer zone manned by the United Nations Peacekeeping Force in Cyprus (UNFICYP), which has been in place since 1964 (see United Nations Peace-keeping Force in Cyprus, ch. 5).

The events of 1974 dramatically altered the internal balance of power between the two Cypriot communities and coupled their prevailing political and institutional separation with stark physical and geographical separation. In a grim historical echo of the widely praised 1930 Greek-Turkish exchange-of-population agreements, roughly a third of each community, displaced by the war, was transferred to the side of the island that its community controlled. As a consequence, in 1990 nearly a third of the people of Cyprus lived outside their birthplaces or places of residence in 1974.

Institutionally, Turkish Cypriots simply consolidated what had been a separate administration run out of Turkish Cypriot enclaves across the island into the northern third, made secure by Turkish troops. That presence altered the political life of the Turkish Cypriots, however. Many decisions affecting the life of the community had a security dimension, and the economy of the small entity has been dependent on Turkish subsidies and trade. Thus, the extent of the real autonomy of Turkish Cypriot authorities from their mainland protectors and benefactors was the subject of continued speculation and uncertainty.

Search for a New Political Formula

Clearly, the debate over government and politics on the island of Cyprus is more fundamental than in many other countries. The lack of consensus between the two major communities over how to govern and administer the island shapes daily life in each community and dominates the island's relations with the outside world. At issue is whether the island should have one government or two, whether the two communities in fact constitute two distinct political entities and "nations," and whether some form of cooperation and power sharing between the two communities is possible.

After 1974, the debate over these issues resumed, mainly in a formal process under the auspices of the UN secretary general. Political leaders in each community asserted that there was general agreement on how to proceed with the settlement negotiations, and

The Archbishopric in Nicosia as it appeared
after the violent summer of 1974
The Archbishopric after its restoration, with a statue of Archbishop
Markarios III, president of the Republic of Cyprus, 1960–77
Courtesy Embassy of Cyprus, Washington

that both sides had minimum requirements that had to be recognized. These mainstream positions fell along a continuum from a concept of federalism, in which major powers and functions would be retained at the federal level and residual powers at the level of the province or state, to something more like confederalism, with emphasis placed on maximum authority in the constituent states and more symbolic power for the overarching apparatus.

The interests of the two communities diverged over this range, with Greek Cypriots seeking to maximize prospects for functional reunification of the island and internal mobility of people and goods, and Turkish Cypriots arguing that separation of the communities and their authority best served their security interests. As a consequence, the two sides did not share the same sense of urgency about settlement. Greek Cypriots believed that time was not on their side, and that continued division of the island favored the separation preferred by Turkish Cypriots. Greek Cypriots thus felt a greater sense of urgency than Turkish Cypriots, who were more satisfied with the status quo.

At the same time, dissident voices, with little political significance, argued for options other than the federal solution, including returning to preindependence proposals such as enosis, possibly with certain rights provided to Turkey, or double enosis, in which the two parts of the divided island would become states or provinces of their respective motherlands.

As of 1990, the governments of the Greek Cypriots and Turkish Cypriots and the world community had embraced the idea that settlement of the Cyprus question was possible through negotiations aiming to reestablish a single government, bizonal with respect to territory and bicommunal with respect to constitutional aspects. This process continued to dominate national life and political debate in both communities.

Milestones in the United Nations Settlement Process

In the immediate aftermath of the 1974 crisis, acting Greek Cypriot president Glafkos Clerides met with Rauf Denktaş in September. These intercommunal talks were initially limited to humanitarian issues, such as the exchange of population between the two sides of the island. Later, at the urging of the United States, the two men, with Clerides the intercommunal negotiator in a restored Makarios government, resumed a substantive agenda and met in Vienna in January 1975. They both declared their support for the principle of an independent, nonaligned, and demilitarized Cyprus. Beyond these broad concepts, however, there were serious differences over the form of government, the size of the area to be retained by Turkish Cypriots, the return of refugees and compensation for property losses, and the timing of the withdrawal of Turkish troops.

By February 1976, the two sides, according to statements, had discussed territorial and constitutional issues and had agreed to exchange written proposals before May. Before the May meeting, however, difficulties arose within the Greek Cypriot camp. Clerides resigned as negotiator because of differences of view with Makarios and allegations that he was willing to accept a bizonal federation, an idea that Makarios opposed at the time.

Makarios appointed Tassos Papadopoulos, deputy president of the House of Representatives, to replace Clerides. Denktaş, who declined to deal face to face with Papadopoulos because he had been an active member of the EOKA, appointed Ümit Süleyman Onan to serve as negotiator.

1977 Makarios-Denktaş Accords

After intensive efforts by Waldheim, Makarios and Denktaş met on January 27, 1977, the first meeting between the two men since the Turkish Cypriots had withdrawn from the government of the republic in 1964. By then Makarios was leaning toward negotiation on the basis of a bizonal federation, provided that there be some Turkish Cypriot territorial concessions. He continued to insist on a strong central government and freedom of movement for all Cypriots. He demanded 80 percent of the territory, proportionate to the size of the Greek Cypriot population, but indicated that he might accept 75 percent if it included Varosha, the formerly prosperous tourist area of Famagusta to which 35,000 Greek Cypriots wanted to return. Denktaş apparently indicated readiness to consider about 68 percent.

On February 12, 1977, the two men met and agreed on four guidelines. The first was that Cyprus would be an independent, nonaligned, bicommunal federal republic. Second, the territory under the administration of each community was to be discussed in light of economic viability, productivity, and property rights. Third, questions of principle such as freedom of movement and settlement, rights of ownership, and certain special matters were to be open for discussion, taking into consideration the fundamental decision for a bicommunal federal system and certain practical difficulties. Finally, the powers and functions of a central government would be such as to safeguard the unity of the country.

This achievement raised hopes among Cyprus's foreign friends that a settlement could be reached. These hopes were dashed when President Makarios, the central figure in the Greek Cypriot community, died of a heart attack in August 1977. Spyros Kyprianou, his successor, pledged to adhere to positions he believed Makarios would have taken.

Over time, it became clear that Kyprianou enjoyed less political room to maneuver than his predecessor, partly because of the growing political strength of the refugees and displaced persons. Kyprianou found in this group a ready-made constituency, and he embraced their advocacy of their right to return to homes and property and their call for a permeable border and unimpeded free movement and unrestricted settlement. This position sharpened differences with the Turkish Cypriot advocacy of a tightly controlled border and guarantees that the ethnic balance established by the de facto partition would remain undisturbed.

In April 1978, a new set of Turkish Cypriot proposals was made public, but was quickly rejected by the Greek Cypriot negotiator, Papadopoulos, who objected to both the constitutional and the territorial aspects of the proposals. Kyprianou dismissed Papadopoulos in June over disagreements.

Later in 1978, external powers tried their hand at a Cyprus proposal. President Jimmy Carter had convinced a slim majority in the United States Congress to lift the arms embargo imposed against Turkey because of its intervention on Cyprus; Carter pledged to renew diplomatic efforts to resolve the Cyprus problem. The United States then worked with Britain and Canada to launch a new settlement plan. The twelve-point plan (often called the ABC plan because of its American, British, and Canadian sponsorship) proposed a biregional, independent federal republic. The state's constitutional structure would conform to the Makarios-Denktaş guidelines of February 1977, as well as to pertinent clauses of the 1960 constitution. There would be two constituent regions. The federal government would be responsible for foreign affairs, defense, currency and central banking, trade, communications, federal finance, customs, immigration and emigration, and civil aviation. Residual functions would rest with the two regions. A bicameral legislature would be established, with the upper chamber evenly divided between the two communities and the lower one divided on a population-ratio basis. The Council of Ministers would be jointly selected by the president and vice president, one of whom would be a Greek Cypriot and the other a Turkish Cypriot. On territorial issues, the plan envisioned significant Turkish Cypriot geographic concessions, although the size and locale of the two regions would take into account factors such as economic viability, security, population distribution, and history. The plan addressed the refugee issue and called for essentially a demilitarized republic and withdrawal of all foreign forces except for an agreed-upon contingent.

The Republic of Cyprus government objected to many points in the plan, largely because it preempted various positions of the two sides. The Greek Cypriot foreign minister said he would have preferred an agenda that did not go into so much detail. Other Greek Cypriot forces, including the church and some political parties, also opposed the plan. In the Greek community, only Glafkos Clerides urged its acceptance as a basis for talks. Turkish Cypriots also formally rejected the plan as an overall settlement package.

However, the ABC plan stimulated further efforts toward a settlement. The UN Security Council acted quickly to resume intercommunal talks, on the basis of an agenda that combined the Makarios-Denktaş guidelines with some aspects of the allied plan.

Two other effects of the American initiative should be noted. The plan was the last American-drafted proposal for Cyprus and convinced some in the Western policy community that even a fair-minded effort had little chance of winning Cypriot acceptance. Second, it reinforced Cypriot anxiety about having solutions imposed from outside. By the early 1990s, many features of the initiative remained part of the UN-brokered negotiating effort, but Cypriots remained committed to writing their own plan.

1979 Kyprianou-Denktaş Communiqué

In early 1979, President Kyprianou was persuaded by his political advisers to resume talks with Denktaş, and Javier Pérez de Cuéllar, then undersecretary general of the UN, called the two to a meeting in Nicosia in June. The two intercommunal negotiators, Minister to the President George Ioannides for the Greek Cypriots and Ümit Süleyman Onan for the Turkish Cypriots, pursued talks aiming at a communiqué stating the broad agenda for further talks. This process stalled temporarily when Greek Cypriots sought to give the Varosha issue priority above all other issues. On May 18 and 19, the two leaders held a second summit that led to the successful conclusion of a ten-point agreement that called for a resumption of talks on all territorial and constitutional issues; placed priority on reaching agreement on the resettlement of Varosha; stated the commitment of the parties to abstain from actions that could jeopardize the talks; and envisaged the demilitarization of Cyprus. The agreement also repeated past statements about guarantees against union with any other country, partition, or secession. The ten points were largely a tactical means to secure further negotiations and did not resolve any substantive issues.

177

One more meeting was held in June 1979, but the talks were then suspended until August 1980.

The UN-established common ground on which the talks resumed was a four-part agenda addressing, on a rotating basis, the resettlement of Varosha under UN auspices, initial practical measures to promote good will, constitutional issues, and territorial issues. The talks, conducted in Cyprus under the chairmanship of the UN secretary general's Special Representative on Cyprus, Ambassador Hugo Gobbi, continued without a major breakthrough and were temporarily suspended for the spring 1981 parliamentary elections on both sides of the island. In August and October 1981, the two sides made substantive presentations, which were welcomed as signs of commitment to compromise, but which also revealed the serious gap in the two sides' concepts of a solution.

The Turkish Cypriot proposal, submitted in August 1981, named four fundamental principles: a bicommunal and bizonal federal republic shall be established, but the two federated states will not form a unitary state; the Turkish Cypriot community will be regarded as an equal cofounder with the Greek Cypriot community, and all government institutions will be staffed on a fifty-fifty ratio; the federal or central government will not be so strong as to imperil the independence of its component states; and the three freedoms of movement, property, and settlement will be restricted as set out by the 1977 guidelines. The proposal identified as "federal matters" six functions, including foreign affairs; foreign financial affairs; tourism and information; posts and telecommunications; federal health and veterinarian services; and standards of weights and measures, patents, copyrights, and trademarks. The Turkish Cypriots also submitted two maps, one defining a proposed boundary line between the two federated states and one focused on Varosha in particular. The Turkish Cypriot proposal treated the federal concept narrowly, limiting federal authority.

The Greek Cypriots submitted their proposal on October 1, 1981. It contrasted sharply with the Turkish Cypriot proposal, with a heavy emphasis on the unity of the island and the powers of the federal republic. The plan's six principles included the indivisibility of the territory of the federal republic; the federal republic as sole subject of international law, to the exclusion of the provinces; and the use of the federal legislative and executive powers to ensure Cyprus's economic reintegration. The Turkish Cypriots considered this proposal merely an elaboration of a 1977 Greek Cypriot plan.

Despite the failure to make headway on the core political issues, this phase had one notable achievement: the agreement on terms of reference for a Committee on Missing Persons, consisting of representatives of the two communities and an international participant designated by the International Committee of the Red Cross. The committee's first meeting was held on July 14, 1981. The committee met sporadically throughout the 1980s, and new proposals to invigorate its work were discussed in early 1990. The work of the committee was hampered by sensitivity about exchanges of dossiers and information. Sensitive areas included security matters and religious questions, such as whether graves should be disturbed.

By late 1981, UN officials and other supporters of the settlement process had concluded that the talks needed new stimulus. Secretary General Waldheim issued an evaluation of the negotiations in November, in what he called a ''determined effort to lend structure and substance'' to the negotiating process. The evaluation identified major points of ''coincidence and equidistance'' in the positions held by the two sides and proposed that the contemplated republic's executive authority be exercised by a federal council having six ministerial functions, corresponding roughly to the narrow Turkish Cypriot concept. Waldheim also suggested a bicameral legislature, provincial chambers, and a territorial compromise in which the Greek Cypriot side would administer at least 70 percent of the island.

The settlement process in the early 1980s was affected by the need for President Kyprianou to establish his credibility and demonstrate his loyalty to the national cause after the death of the charismatic Makarios. To many observers, it appeared that Kyprianou had less room for maneuver and was less inclined, by political preference or capability, to put forth new strategic positions. The election of a socialist government in Athens in October 1981 may also have affected the attitudes of the parties; Greek Cypriots welcomed Greek prime minister Andreas Papandreou's desire to ''internationalize'' the Cyprus problem, which effectively gave Greek Cypriots some breathing room in the intercommunal process. Meanwhile, the Turkish Cypriot leaders were developing new formulas and concepts of their own and generally disapproved of efforts to internationalize the issue.

On November 15, 1983, after months of speculation, Rauf Denktaş declared Turkish Cypriot statehood, on the basis of the universal right to self-determination. His proclamation, which cited the United States Declaration of Independence, declared the establishment of the ''Turkish Republic of Northern Cyprus'' (''TRNC''). The move was not intended to block progress toward creating a federal republic, Denktaş said. Rather, the assertion of the political identity and equality of the Turkish Cypriots would, in his view, enhance prospects for a new relationship between the two sides of the island. He also pledged that the new state would not join any other state, meaning Turkey.

The move was widely condemned by Western powers and the UN. The secretary general considered the declaration contrary to past Security Council resolutions and at odds with the high-level agreements of 1977 and 1979. The United States urged nonrecognition of the entity and voted for a nearly unanimous Security Council resolution (541) that called for reversal of the declaration. (Jordan voted no; Pakistan abstained.)

1984 Proximity Talks

The statehood declaration did not end the negotiation process. In August 1984, the two sides met UN Secretary General Pérez de Cuéllar in Vienna. They agreed to proximity talks, that is, talks in which the parties do not meet directly, but communicate through an intermediary. These talks began in New York in September. After three months, Pérez de Cuéllar determined that the differences between the two sides had narrowed enough to allow for a direct summit between the two leaders. That meeting took place in New York on January 17, 1985.

The 1985 summit was in some ways a watershed in Cypriot settlement efforts because it altered, at least temporarily, external observers' perceptions of the sources of the stalemate, and because it represented the beginning of a phase of settlement efforts. But that phase would come to an end in early 1990.

1985–86 Draft Framework Exercise

At the January 1985 summit, UN officials presented a draft framework agreement for the establishment of a bizonal, bicommunal federal republic. The parties, according to many accounts, had been briefed on its contents but not directly involved in its drafting. Denktaş indicated his willingness to sign the draft, on the understanding that details would be worked out in separate talks. However, Kyprianou declined to sign, saying he considered the draft a basis for negotiations but that such a commitment was premature.

The collapse of the summit redounded to Turkish Cypriot favor, in the reactions of the news media and Cyprus's Western friends. By 1990, however, Turkish Cypriots referred to the 1985 summit as a regrettable Turkish Cypriot acquiescence to external pressure, from Turkey and the United States in particular.

The UN worked intensively with the two parties after the summit, on the assumption that a tactical misstep need not undermine the considerable achievement of drafting an outline reflecting broad areas of agreement. Yet UN efforts in the months that followed showed the near-impossibility of bridging the gaps; drafts proved acceptable to one side or the other, but never both. In April 1985, a draft framework agreement won acceptance by Greek Cypriots and was rejected by the Turkish Cypriot side. After extensive consultations, a new draft was promulgated; it was embraced by the Turkish Cypriots and rejected by the Greek Cypriots.

1988–90 Vassiliou-Denktaş Meetings

The politics of the settlement process appeared to change significantly when Greek Cypriots elected George Vassiliou president in February 1988. Vassiliou was a successful businessman with no important political party base (although his parents were founding members of the island's communist party, the Progressive Party of the Working People (Anorthotikon Komma Ergazomenou Laou—AKEL). He campaigned on a pledge to solve the Cyprus problem with new vigor and creativity. His upset victory over Spyros Kyprianou seemed to indicate popular support for a new approach and for more rapid progress on a settlement. The UN and Cyprus's Western partners welcomed Vassiliou's election and his statements about the settlement process.

The UN arranged for informal meetings between Vassiliou and Denktaş at the Nicosia home of the UN special representative, Oscar Camillion. The first round of these meetings took place between August and November 1988. A second round occurred between December 1988 and April 1989, but the talks faltered when the two sides began submitting papers and drafts that began to dominate the discussions. These two rounds raised new concerns that the UN had lost control of the process, and that reaching agreement on a fixed agenda or schedule might prove difficult.

In May 1989, a more formal process began, after Secretary General Pérez de Cuéllar assigned his two aides, Camillion and Gustave Feissel, to meet separately and jointly with the parties to draft an outline, which could be based on an "ideas paper" that the UN had circulated on a noncommittal basis to the parties. This third round was stalled for the second half of 1989, over procedural and substantive difficulties, with the Turkish Cypriots' objecting to the "ideas paper." The parties met in New York with the secretary general to report on their progress in February and March 1990.

The secretary general reported that the gap between the two sides remained wide and that he was not convinced there was an agreed-upon basis on which to proceed. He turned to the Security Council for clarification of his "good offices" mission; clarification was given in Resolution 649, which was passed unanimously on March 13.

The two sides separately indicated satisfaction with the UN resolution. Greek Cypriots emphasized the active role proposed for the UN, including the right to make suggestions, and Turkish Cypriots were pleased with the resolution's references to the separate status of the two communities and to bizonality as an enshrined principle in a prospective settlement.

This eighteen-month round of settlement efforts had begun hopefully. A period of creative tension and groping to create new understandings occurred in mid-1989, when Vassiliou and his advisers privately and informally offered important concessions to the Turkish Cypriot side. That is, none of the Greek Cypriot proposals or suggestions were binding or formally entrenched in official documents, but were offered discreetly as the basis for discussion. These concessions included a willingness to phase in the three freedoms, beginning with freedom of movement and holding freedom of settlement and property in abeyance. New thinking and flexibility on the territorial issue were displayed, with a range of options presented to the Turkish Cypriot side. The options included a smaller but nearly exclusively Turkish Cypriot zone as a substitute for various larger but more demographically mixed zones. Greek Cypriots tried to link the size of the territorial swap with the degree of communal purity. They were more flexible than in the past on the issue of the presidency, offering alternatives such as rotating the position between the two communities or having joint elections, with Turkish Cypriot votes weighted. Turkish Cypriots found themselves challenged by a more flexible interlocutor and reacted with caution, expressing new legal reservations about the proposals. At that point, between October 1989 and February 1990, the Greek Cypriot side seemed to withdraw some of its new ideas, and the president found his freedom of maneuver limited by new domestic resistance to further concessions.

When the talks collapsed in early 1990, both sides appeared to be turning away from the UN process. The two governments seemed able to withstand domestic criticism of the talks; opposition complaints on both sides appeared to focus on tactics and did not challenge the fundamental government positions. Both leaders appeared to be preparing to defend their positions to outside patrons and partners. Greek Cypriots mounted a renewed effort to win international support for their position and stressed the need for international pressure on Turkey if they were to win concessions from the Turkish Cypriots. For Turkish Cypriots, the end of the talks heralded a period of active domestic politics. A push

*Turkish Cypriot leader Rauf Denktaş (left) and Republic of Cyprus
President George Vassiliou (right) meeting at the intercommunal
talks sponsored by the United Nations
Courtesy Embassy of Cyprus, Washington*

for new diplomatic recognition of the "TRNC" was under consideration (see Foreign Policy, this ch.).

Prospects for Creation of a Federal Republic of Cyprus

The second half of 1990 saw little action in Cyprus settlement efforts, in large measure because of the Iraq-Kuwait crisis and the demands it placed on the UN and on much of the world community. Some in Cyprus found parallels between the Gulf situation and Cyprus and hoped that the resolution of the Gulf crisis would renew international interest in a Cyprus settlement. Greek Cypriots saw in the world condemnation of Iraq's invasion of Kuwait possible new interest in pressing for removal of Turkish troops from Cyprus and in using UN resolutions more effectively to resolve outstanding disputes. Greek Cypriots also saw the continued withdrawal of Soviet troops from Eastern Europe as further impetus to bring Cyprus into conformity with these regional and world trends. At the same time, Turkey's pivotal role in the Gulf crisis, including its decision to close Iraq's oil pipeline and its importance as a staging area for Kurdish refugee relief, appeared to deepen some Western countries' support for Turkey, and the prospect for new pressures on Turkey were uncertain. Turkish President Turgut Özal did cite willingness to work on Cyprus among the features of a dynamic Turkish foreign policy he envisioned in the post-Gulf crisis period.

At the end of 1990, the two sides had not disavowed their interest in UN efforts and were aware of Pérez de Cuéllar's strong personal interest in seeing progress on Cyprus before his retirement as secretary general in late 1991. Although no formal meetings between the two Cypriot leaders occurred, there was a slight increase in ministerial and nongovernment contacts between the two communities, which many considered helpful to confidence building. Continued work by the United States Special Cyprus Coordinator, Nelson Ledsky, and by UN officials kept the two communities engaged in thinking about settlement prospects, with the expectation that 1991 would be a more active year.

Politics in the Republic of Cyprus
Political Institutions

In 1990 the Republic of Cyprus operated under the terms of the 1960 constitution as amended in 1964. It consisted of three independent branches: executive, legislative, and judicial. The republic's president, George Vassiliou, was head of state and presided over a council of eleven ministers.

Presidential authority remained as outlined in the constitution. Cabinet portfolios included agriculture and natural resources, commerce and industry, communications and works, defense, education, finance, foreign affairs, health, interior, justice, and labor and social insurance. Policy making was in the hands of administrative directors who were appointed civil servants with lifelong tenure. In an effort to make government more of a meritocracy, Vassiliou reassigned a number of ministerial directors to other positions but encountered resistance from the parties when he tried to replace some of these directors.

The legislative body, the House of Representatives, consisted of fifty-six Greek Cypriot members, with twenty-four seats held for Turkish Cypriots, who had not recognized or participated in the republic's legislative life since the constitutional amendments of 1964. Originally a chamber of fifty, with thirty-five Greek Cypriots and fifteen Turkish Cypriots, the House of Representatives was enlarged in 1985.

The republic's judicial branch largely followed the original structure outlined at independence. The 1964 amalgamation of the Supreme Constitutional Court and the High Court of Justice into the Supreme Court, combining the functions of the two former courts and eliminating the neutral judge, also led to the establishment of the Supreme Council of Judicature. Assigned the judicatory functions of the former high court, it was composed of the attorney general of the republic, the president and two judges of the Supreme Court, the senior president of a district court, a senior district judge, and a practicing advocate elected every six months by a general meeting of the Cyprus Bar Association.

As a result of the withdrawal of Turkish Cypriot public servants from the government, the Public Service Commission could not function as provided for in the constitution. Therefore, the Public Service Law of 1967 established a new commission to exercise the same functions. Its five members were appointed by the president. President Vassiliou's effort to replace the incumbents with members of his choice was thwarted when the parliament would not provide funding to complete the contracts of the replaced members.

At the district level, a district officer coordinated village and government activities and had the right to inspect local village councils. The mayors and councils for municipalities were appointed.

At the village level, there had been since Ottoman times councils, each composed of a village head (*mukhtar*) and elders (*aza*; pl., *azades*). Large villages that prior to 1974 had had sizable mixed populations had separate councils, one for each community. Under the Ottoman Empire, the village head and elders were elected

185

by the villagers. In the British period and after independence, the village heads were appointed by the government and then chose the elders. New legislation in 1979 provided that village and town government officials should be elected rather than appointed, and beginning in 1979 elections for village councils and their presidents have occurred every five years. The cycle for municipal elections was different: elections were held every five years, most recently in 1986. These election results generally followed the national pattern in terms of the relative shares won by each of the parties. In some cases, however, parties were able to cooperate at the village level although competing nationally.

Political Parties

In the early postindependence period, Greek Cypriot political party life centered around a loose coalition of Makarios supporters called the Patriotic Front, plus the communist party, AKEL. The front dissolved in the late 1960s; its major factions broke into discrete parties. The House of Representatives afterwards maintained a fairly stable balance among four parties that ranged from a communist party to one that was right of center. Each of these parties generally received at least 9 percent of the vote, more than the 5 percent being the minimum required to win seats in the legislature (see table 3, Appendix).

Three of the four parties so divided the vote that none ever won a clear majority. The Republic of Cyprus has a modified proportional representation system. There were occasional proposals for a simple proportional system, and the electoral law has been modified five times in the 1980s.

As of 1990, the Democratic Rally (Dimokratikos Synagermos—DISY) was the largest parliamentary party. Created in 1976 and led by Glafkos Clerides, it evolved from the Unified Democratic Party (Eniaion), which was one of the factions that emerged from the Democratic Front in the 1970 parliamentary elections. DISY's platform focused on free-enterprise economic policies and a practical solution to the intercommunal problem. It was the most explicitly pro-Western and pro-NATO of Cyprus's parties and drew its support from middle-class professionals, businessmen, and white-collar employees. Its shares of parliamentary election votes were 24.1 percent in 1976 (but no seats because of the electoral law), 31.9 percent in 1981 (twelve seats), and 33.6 percent in 1985 (nineteen seats).

The Democratic Party (Dimokratiko Komma—DIKO), formed in 1976, was seen as the closest to President Makarios and was headed by his successor, Spyros Kyprianou. The party platform in its first electoral campaign emphasized a nonaligned foreign policy and a long-term struggle over Turkish occupation in the north. Over the years, this party formed uneasy alliances with the two more leftist parties, the communists and socialists. The Democratic Party won twenty-one seats in 1976, eight seats in 1981 (19.5 percent), and sixteen seats in 1985 (27.7 percent). In June 1990, Kyprianou was reelected party leader.

The socialist party, the United Democratic Union of Cyprus (Eniea Dimokratiki Enosis Kyprou—EDEK), often called the Socialist Party EDEK (Socialistiko Komma EDEK), was formed in 1969 by Makarios's personal physician, Vassos Lyssarides. The party advocated socialized medicine and nationalization of banks and foreign-owned mines. It was anti-NATO and pro-Arab and favored a nonaligned foreign policy, although those positions seemed to have softened in the late 1980s. The party supported enosis with a democratic Greece, opposed continued British sovereignty rights on the island, but differed from the communists in keeping its distance from the Soviet Union. Its appeal was strongest among noncommunist leftists, intellectuals, and white-collar workers. Its electoral strength was the weakest of the four parties. In 1976 EDEK won four seats, three in 1981 (8.2 percent), and six in 1985 (11.1 percent).

The communist movement has been a major force on the island since the 1920s, often vying with the Church of Cyprus for the role of dominant political player. The first communist party was formed in 1924 in Limassol, was banned in 1931, and reappeared in 1941 with the creation of the Progressive Party of the Working People (Anorthotikon Komma Ergazomenou Laou—AKEL). Banned in the preindependence emergency from 1955 to 1959, AKEL has been in every parliament since 1960. AKEL won nine seats in 1976, twelve in 1981 (32.8 percent), and fifteen in the enlarged chamber in 1985. The latter number represented a drop to 27.4 percent.

In response to the serious crisis in the communist movement after the collapse of East European regimes in late 1989, AKEL held internal conferences in early 1990, but resisted reform proposals. As a consequence, AKEL dissidents formed a new leftist grouping called the Democratic Socialist Renewal Movement (Ananeotiko Dimokratiko Sosialistiko Kinima—ADISOK) in May 1990. The reformers included five members of parliament elected in 1985 as AKEL leaders. ADISOK selected House Deputy Pavlos Dhinglis as chairman and criticized AKEL for undemocratic behavior and an anachronistic mentality. It petitioned President Vassiliou for representation on the National Council, a forum in which all political groups met to discuss political issues.

The parties had held fairly constant positions on key policy issues since the second half of the 1970s. AKEL and DISY, although at opposite ends of the ideological spectrum, were regarded as most flexible and forthcoming on settlement matters. EDEK and DIKO took a harder line, pushing for a more punitive approach to Turkey. On social and economic policy, the parties' ideological predilections prevailed: EDEK and AKEL advocated greater government support for workers and free public health services; DISY favored free enterprise. Some Cypriot analysts believe that DISY and DIKO have an overlapping constituency and could merge into a single centrist party if DIKO were to drop its far-right support, estimated at 5 percent of its strength.

Media

The press was another major player in Greek Cypriot politics. There were ten Greek-language and one English-language daily papers for a population of 500,000 (see table 22, Appendix). Television broadcasting was government-controlled. In 1989 President Vassiliou proposed a press law, aimed at setting guidelines and a professional code of ethics and at stimulating greater competition by allowing private radio stations (thus ending the monopoly of the Cyprus Broadcasting Corporation). An early version of a comprehensive press bill passed in parliament and in 1990 was under review for further revisions, to address criticisms that in its original form it set too many regulations. In mid-1990, parliament approved and the president signed legislation to make municipalities, companies, and individuals eligible to establish private radio stations. A new relationship with the Greek media, allowing Cypriot television to broadcast Greek programs, was established in 1990, although it was seen as threatening to the financially weak Cyprus Broadcasting Corporation.

Political Dynamics

The politics of Cyprus have gradually evolved from the shadow of the dominant figure of Makarios, who embodied the struggle for independence from Britain and enosis with Greece. After independence was achieved without enosis, Makarios's own thinking changed, and Cypriot politics struggled with its internal ghost—enosis. Makarios became persuaded that true national independence for Cyprus had advantages, and Greek political trends by the mid-1960s convinced him that Cyprus had a destiny distinct from that of Greece. The Greek Cypriot population did not let go of the dream of enosis as quickly, and pro-enosis forces eventually turned on Makarios, leading to the 1974 coup (see Conflict Within the Greek Cypriot Community, 1967–74, ch. 5).

Although the drive for enosis subsided as a mobilizing force, the difficulties of creating a nation out of a bifurcated society took center stage. Makarios failed to draw the Greek and Turkish Cypriot communities together, but, helped by his unusual position and special gifts, he created a consensus among Greek Cypriots. Although the authority of the Church of Cyprus diminished with the rise of new secular institutions, Makarios, as its head, nonetheless embodied the traditional authority of Cypriot Hellenism and, as elected president, had legitimate political authority. In addition, he possessed an extraordinary charisma and a mastery of diplomacy that his adversaries saw as deviousness and duplicity. By the time of the 1974 coup, however, it was clear that Makarios's total domination of Cypriot politics was coming to an end. From July to December 1974, Makarios was out of the country, and the government of the truncated republic was run competently by Glafkos Clerides. Makarios and Clerides then competed as heads of rival political groups, with the differences between them focused on the intercommunal process. Makarios reportedly welcomed this competition as a sign of growing Cypriot political maturity.

After Makarios's death in 1977, Kyprianou succeeded to the presidency, and Clerides continued as the principal opposition leader. The two men differed, among other things, over how to deal with the intercommunal talks.

Sharing the stage with Kyprianou were several other major figures, including Archbishop Chrysostomos, who had succeeded Makarios as head of the Church of Cyprus. Although the archbishop traveled the world meeting with overseas Greeks, Chrysostomos's personal political impact was judged by many to be far less significant than that of Makarios or that of the church as a whole.

Kyprianou was in many ways typical of the centrist, noncontroversial political figures who often follow charismatic leaders. He sought to preserve the Makarios legacy and pursue policies that would further Makarios's goals. But Kyraianou did not have the tactical dexterity or diplomatic skill of Makarios, and he became associated with an approach to the settlement process that preserved the status quo, rather than displaying the openness and initiative that characterized Makarios at the end of his life. By the late 1980s, the Kyprianou presidency was considered weak and passive, unable to break the stalemate in the settlement process and losing respect at home. At the same time, Kyprianou's less authoritative style did allow more competition in Greek Cypriot politics, permitting independents and other party leaders to contest presidential elections with greater prospects for success.

Political Culture in the Vassiliou Era

The election of George Vassiliou in February 1988 was unexpected. Although many Cypriots were increasingly disaffected because of the lack of progress in the intercommunal talks and the incumbent's reputation for passivity and ineffectiveness, the results were an upset. The first round, held on February 14, gave a plurality and 33.3 percent to Glafkos Clerides of DISY. Vassiliou, an independent, came in second, with 30.1 percent, and the incumbent, Spyros Kyprianou of DIKO, came in third with 27.3 percent. Kyprianou was defeated, according to Cypriot press opinion, because of inflexibility in the settlement talks and because of party maneuvering, including an unpopular tactical alliance with the communist party, AKEL.

The runoff between Clerides and Vassiliou was held on February 21, and Vassiliou won by a little over 10,000 votes. He polled 51.6 percent; Clerides, a veteran of Cypriot politics and acting president in 1974, polled 48.4 percent. Ironically, in the final contest the two men were in substantial agreement over the settlement issue; both expressed eagerness to engage in talks with Denktaş, and neither made withdrawal of Turkish troops a precondition for talks. Some observers believe that Clerides narrowly missed victory because of his past associations with right-wing political groups.

Born in Famagusta in 1931, Vassiliou completed secondary school in Cyprus and spent more than a decade studying and working in Europe. He received a doctorate in economics in Hungary. Upon his return to Cyprus in 1962, he founded and became president of the Middle East Marketing Research Bureau, the largest consultancy in the region, with offices in eleven countries.

Vassiliou's campaign emphasized his wish to invigorate the settlement process. He offered to meet directly with both then-Prime Minister Turgut Özal of Turkey and his Turkish Cypriot counterpart, Denktaş. Without a strong party base, Vassiliou also decided to resurrect the National Council, first created by Makarios, with the hope that the political parties meeting together could forge a collective and consensus-based policy toward the settlement process. Vassiliou proceeded to work out new rules with the party leaders, including guidelines on which issues required their unanimous consent. He pledged to put any settlement plan to the people in a referendum. But his seemingly liberal views on a settlement were tempered by his policy commitment to reorganize and reinforce civil defense and increase defense spending.

A number of factors brought Vassiliou to power. The electorate was frustrated by the impasse in the settlement process and welcomed someone who spoke of new ideas and energy. More broadly, the vote may have signaled the end of the Makarios era and the desire for new leaders, rather than Makarios's heir apparent.

Vassiliou brought to the presidential palace skills learned in the private sector, such as prompt decision making, cost-benefit analysis, marketing, and open competition, that promised livelier and more effective policy making. Some Cypriots welcomed his attempt to bring corporate boardroom concepts into politics. Others resented it. In his first two years in office, Vassiliou was constrained by the island's experienced politicians, who had different agendas, and by Turkish Cypriot strategies that did not embrace the spirit of Vassiliou's settlement message.

The new president tried to introduce fresh faces into the executive branch. His first cabinet had only two ministers who had previously held office: George Iacovou continued to serve as foreign minister, ensuring continuity in external relations, and Christodoulos Veniamin took the post of interior minister, which he had held, along with other cabinet posts, between 1975 and 1985. In May 1990, President Vassiliou replaced four of his cabinet ministers and appointed several who had not served in previous cabinets. For the most part, the outside appointees were people who had the approval of one or more of the major parties.

Vassiliou had promised to achieve progress in talks with Turkish Cypriots through intercommunal talks and negotiations with Turkey. However, in his first two years he made no breakthrough toward a settlement.

He achieved more in other areas. In the 1988 election campaign, Vassiliou spoke of his desire to make changes in the civil service, to end the spoils system that had created a large and inefficient public sector. He pledged moves toward a meritocracy and promised to bring into government energetic, talented people from the private sector. During his first two years in office, he was unable to replace the incumbent appointees to the Public Service Commission with his own candidates because the parliament did not approve funds for it. Nor did another campaign promise, to create a government ombudsman as a clearinghouse for complaints, make headway in the first two years of his presidency. He was also unable to wrest from the political parties appointments to quasi-governmental posts such as utilities boards. He failed to pursue vigorously a campaign pledge to investigate charges of corruption in the police force.

Vassiliou's modest gains in these efforts were constrained by the parties' resistance to the businessman-president's ideas. The parliament failed to approve many of his requests for new positions, such as political appointments for ministerial special assistants and even experts to assist the president.

Vassiliou did manage to dilute the parties' power to some extent. Political patronage jobs, formerly the perquisites of the largest party, were shared among the major parties, reflecting Vassiliou's desire for a consensus-based political system. Vassiliou often chose for appointed positions associates whose skills he respected but who were also acceptable to one or more of the major parties. This power sharing with the parties, however, kept the new president from keeping his promise to reduce the size of the public sector.

Yet Vassiliou's intelligence, energy, and worldliness were valued by Cyprus's friends overseas. Vassiliou visited all major European capitals, traveled in the United States, and attended multilateral conferences to explain the Cyprus situation and enlist support for new settlement efforts. He was troubled that the dramatic and triumphant world events of 1989 and 1990 distracted world attention from the Cyprus problem, and he was concerned about the prospects for its neglect. His presidency, nevertheless, although it did not produce dramatic results, won respect and attention from a number of friendly governments.

Politics in the "Turkish Republic of Northern Cyprus"

The Turkish Cypriot government gradually evolved after 1963. In 1975 and again in 1983, major changes were made to develop a national identity and the institutions of statehood, despite the government's dependence on Turkey and lack of recognition by the world community.

The political evolution of the Turkish Cypriot government complicated the search for a settlement. Greek Cypriots held that the institutional changes since 1974 were illegitimate and artificial and could be reversed for the sake of a settlement. Although Turkish Cypriots maintained that these changes need not impede creation of a federal republic and that some of them could be nullified if replaced by acceptable alternatives, it was increasingly clear that the new institutions were becoming rooted in Turkish Cypriot society. In addition, the de facto autonomy that Turkish Cypriots had become accustomed to would be difficult to dismantle.

Thus, the situation on the ground in the north shaped and narrowed the possible outcomes in the talks. Although Turkish Cypriot politics were the politics of a small and fragile entity dependent on an outside patron, the prospects for fundamental change in the

"Turkish Republic of Northern Cyprus" Office of the Prime Minister, Nicosia
Courtesy Office of the "Turkish Republic of Northern Cyprus," Washington

government of Cyprus may depend more on the community in the north than on the better known and more politically stable Greek Cypriot society.

Major Political Institutions in the "TRNC"

The institutional framework for the "TRNC" was set out in the 1985 constitution, drafted by the Constitutional Commission and approved by the Constituent Assembly in March 1985 and by a national referendum in May 1985. The constitution was approved by 70.2 percent of the votes cast; opposition to it centered on its retention of capital punishment and certain other provisions deemed too politically restrictive.

Although based on the 1975 document that established the "Turkish Federated State of Cyprus," the new constitution provided for an unfettered independent republic. It made no reference to a federal republic, but Turkish Cypriot authorities consistently pointed to a March 1985 Constituent Assembly vote declaring that the new constitution would not hinder establishment of a federal republic.

The constitution establishes a secular republic based on principles of democracy, social justice, and the supremacy of law. The balance of powers among the governmental branches is flexible, not fixed; the president and the Legislative Assembly both participate in the Council of Judicature, which names, promotes, and oversees the judicial branch. The president and the legislature also share the power to declare war and commit armed forces overseas.

The president, elected for five years, is required to be of Cypriot parentage and to have resided in Cyprus for five years. He is the head of state and commander in chief, although the security forces are the responsibility of the prime minister. The president may preside over meetings of the cabinet, the Council of Ministers, but does not have a vote. He also names the prime minister from those elected to parliament and appoints, in consultation with the prime minister, other ministers, who need not be elected members. The number of ministries is limited by the constitution to ten. In the event of a vacancy in the office of the president, the president of the Legislative Assembly would become acting president.

The Legislative Assembly is a unicameral body of fifty members elected for five-year terms. It enacts laws, exercises control over the Council of Ministers, approves the budget, has authority to give general and special amnesties, decides whether to carry out death penalties imposed by the courts, and ratifies international agreements. Upon an absolute majority vote, the Legislative Assembly may dissolve itself and call for new elections. Under certain circumstances, the president may also dissolve the body.

The judicial system established by the 1985 constitution roughly corresponds in several features to the provisions of the 1960 constitution of the Republic of Cyprus. The Supreme Court consists of a president and seven judges, and has jurisdiction to sit as the Supreme Constitutional Court, the Court of Appeal, and the High Administrative Court. As the Constitutional Court, it is composed of five justices and as a Court of Appeal, three. The "TRNC," drawing on the 1960 constitution and on the Turkish and United States systems, provides for challenges to the constitutionality of legislation. The Supreme Court, in its role as High Administrative Court, fulfills the same functions as described in article 146 of the 1960 constitution. The Supreme Council of Judicature, consisting of the Supreme Court, the attorney general, and several other officials, is the exclusive authority for appointments, promotions, disciplinary control, and all other matters relating to the judges of the courts.

There are three categories of lower courts. Assize courts, in the capitals of the three districts of the "TRNC," sit three times a year to try persons convicted of indictable offenses. These courts have unlimited jurisdiction in criminal matters. District courts, also located in the district capitals, have jurisdiction in civil and criminal matters. Family courts, each composed of a single judge, hear and determine actions relating to personal status and religious matters.

For administrative purposes, the "TRNC" is divided into three districts, Nicosia (Lefkoşa), Famagusta (Gazimağusa), and Kyrenia (Girne), each headed by a district officer (*kaymakam*), the representative of the central government and subordinate to the minister of interior. There are twenty-six municipalities, consisting of towns and large villages, each governed by a municipal council and its head, the mayor. Council members and the mayor win their posts in municipal elections, usually held every four years. Candidates in these elections may run as independents or be affiliated with a party. Villages, of which there are about 150, are each governed by a village commission consisting of a mayor (*muhtar*) and assistants (*aza*; pl., *azalar*), also elected for four-year terms. Municipalities usually dealt with the relevant ministry when approaching the national government. Villages usually contacted the district *kaymakam* when they wished the services of the central government.

Political Parties

The Turkish Cypriot community had three major political parties. A few smaller parties emerged in the 1980s, and a 1990 alliance among three opposition parties was short-lived.

The ruling party, the National Unity Party (Ulusal Birlik Partisi—UBP), was founded by Denktaş in 1975. Its head in 1990 was Derviş Eroğlu, the prime minister. The UBP was reported to draw on former members of the Turkish Resistance Organization (Türk Mukavemet Teşkilâtı—TMT) and other conservative nationalist forces. The party was also a rallying point for forces that sought close ties to Turkey and identified themselves as Turks more than Cypriots. In the 1980s, the party governed alone or in coalition, but was riven with internal personality conflicts and charges of corruption. Its electoral performance was uneven, but the party implemented electoral law changes that favored its plurality. Its strength was augmented, it was commonly accepted, by support from settlers from the Turkish mainland. In the 1976 elections, the UBP won thirty of the forty parliamentary seats; it dropped to eighteen seats in 1981 but won twenty-four seats in the enlarged parliament of 1985 and thirty-four in the 1990 elections. After March 1990, changes in the electoral law that favored the strongest party, the UBP won nearly 70 percent of the seats with 55 percent of the vote.

As it had in the municipal elections of 1976, 1980, and 1986, the UBP won a majority of the mayoral posts in the elections of

June 1990. The party's victory was not as impressive as in the past, for the other parties boycotted the elections and the UBP had only independent candidates for opponents. Despite the absence of organized opposition, the UBP won only fourteen of the twenty-six mayoral contests, although it was victorious in the three largest municipalities: the capital, Nicosia, and the two ports, Famagusta and Kyrenia.

The second major party in the ''TRNC'' was the Communal Liberation Party (Toplumcu Kurtuluş Partisi—TKP), founded in 1976 by Alpay Durduran. The party has supported a federal solution but has criticized the government for the pace of negotiations, the failure to encourage more contact between the two communities, and the policy of encouraging settlers from Turkey. The party's head, Mustafa Akinci, served three terms as mayor of Nicosia and became known for his bridge-building efforts with his Greek Cypriot counterpart, Lellos Demetriades. In one of the few examples of bicommunal cooperation, the two mayors worked with the UN and other international organizations on joint projects such as restoration of the medieval walls of the capital city and a common sewage system. The TKP was strengthened temporarily in 1990 when İsmet Kotak, former UBP deputy and newspaper publisher, left the small defunct Progressive People's Party and joined the TKP. The TKP backed İsmail Bozkurt, an independent presidential candidate, in the 1990 parliamentary elections. The TKP won six seats in the 1976 elections, thirteen in 1981, ten in the fifty-seat chamber in 1985, and five in the 1990 elections as part of an electoral alliance, the Democratic Struggle Party (Demokratik Mücadele Partisi—DMP). In mid-1990, the strength of the party was weakened when the DMP failed to oust the UBP. The TKP withdrew from the alliance, and most of its members boycotted the parliament to protest what it considered electoral improprieties by the ruling party and by Turkey.

The third of the main parties and the oldest party in the ''TRNC,'' the Republican Turkish Party (Cumhuriyetçi Türk Partisi—CTP), was founded in 1970. Its leader, Özker Özgür, disavowed alleged communist leanings and described his party's ideology as progressive socialist. Much of the CTP's support derived from the small labor movement on the island. The party won two seats in the 1976 elections, six in 1981, twelve in 1985, and seven in 1990, when it joined the TKP and the New Dawn Party (Yeni Doğuş Partisi—YDP) in the DMP electoral alliance. After the elections and the collapse of the alliance, the CTP deputies joined their TKP colleagues in boycotting the parliament.

The YDP emerged with minor electoral strength in the 1985 elections. Founded in 1984 with considerable support from the Turkish Embassy, the YDP consolidated several smaller parties that attracted support from Turkish settlers on the island. Many settlers, however, continued to vote for the UBP. The party's leader for several years was retired Turkish colonel Aytaç Beşeşler, who arrived on Cyprus in 1979. In the 1985 elections, the YDP won four seats in the Legislative Assembly. In 1988 Beşeşler was replaced as party head by Orhan Üçok, reportedly a supporter of Turkish opposition leader Süleyman Demirel and less inclined to provide automatic support for the ruling party and the president. The YDP briefly joined the electoral opposition alliance DMP that stood in the May 1990 elections, presumably because its membership felt the government was not moving quickly enough on some issues of concern to them, one of which was providing legal title to their property. When the DMP failed to defeat the UBP and disbanded, the two YDP candidates took their seats in the Assembly.

Media

The press was an active participant in political life in the "TRNC," and the role of the progovernment press in influencing election outcomes sparked increasing controversy. There was no law regulating media behavior or ethics. The state-controlled radio and television was 80 percent fed from Turkish national television. There were ten daily papers in the north in 1990, three owned by pro-Denktaş business magnate Asil Nadir, three affiliated with parties, and four independents, including one that focused on financial matters.

Rauf Denktaş and Turkish Cypriot Politics

As Makarios was the dominant figure in Greek Cypriot politics for nearly two decades after independence, so Rauf Denktaş overshadowed all other political forces in Turkish Cypriot politics. Born in Paphos in 1924, Denktaş was trained as a lawyer. He was from a prominent family that lived in close proimity to Greek Cypriots, and his biographers have chronicled many grievances and humiliations that he suffered as a youth from intolerant Greek Cypriots. He was politically active from a young age and was exiled to Turkey during the preindependence period. His activity in Turkish Cypriot politics has been continuous; he emerged as a protégé of Vice President Küçük, became intercommunal negotiator in 1968, and was vice president of the republic at the time of the 1974 crisis. He was elected president of the "TSFC" in 1975, was reelected in 1981, became president of the "TRNC" in 1985, and successfully stood for election in that year and again in 1990.

Under Denktaş, constitutional changes have occurred that made the parliament stronger and the president weaker, theoretically, than their counterparts in the republic in the south. Yet Denktaş remained a more powerful figure on the Turkish Cypriot scene than his legal role would suggest. He retained considerable influence over the governing political party by playing personalities against one another and preventing independent leadership of the party, despite his formal claims to being above politics. He used the force of his personal appeals to national security and national interest whenever opposition parties appeared to be gaining in electoral strength.

From one perspective, Denktaş presided over an entity in which the consensus over the core issue—the settlement with Greek Cypriots—remained remarkably strong, and his powerful presence successfully reflected and symbolized national unity. But from another perspective, Turkish Cypriot political culture, with its proclivity toward factiousness and frequent questioning of the rules of the game, seemed to push for more rational and competitive democracy. There also were signs of continued resentment and resistance, in certain quarters, to a domineering father figure.

The three elections of 1990—presidential in April, parliamentary in May, and municipal in June—suggested some new political dynamics in the "TRNC." Denktaş was challenged by two veteran politicians, Alpay Durduran and İsmail Bozkurt. The opposition parties, after considerable debate over strategy, backed Bozkurt's candidacy. Denktaş's two-thirds approval rating thus worked to the disfavor of the opposition parties facing parliamentary elections. In what many considered an alliance of convenience, the TKP and CTP joined with the settler party—the YDP—to form the electoral alliance DMP. The alliance was formed mainly in opposition to UBP domination of the parliament and political patronage. To a lesser degree, its members were united in the view that Denktaş's control of the political system had inhibited democratic competition. The main goal of the alliance was to reduce UBP control of political power; its candidates pledged, if elected, to revise the electoral law and go to new elections within a few months. The alliance did not differ with the ruling establishment on the settlement question and emphasized domestic issues, such as the alleged corruption of the UBP and what it viewed as ineffective economic policies. The parties had worked out a power-sharing arrangement among themselves should they win, including a pledge by the leftist CTP to decline a major post, such as the premiership or speaker of the parliament.

The outcome of the presidential elections hampered the DMP's strategy, and there were reports that many settlers abandoned the YDP, casting their parliamentary votes for Denktaş's party. The alliance's failure at the polls (it won sixteen out of fifty seats) caused considerable internal strain, and the alliance collapsed. The two major opposition parties, the TKP and the CTP, continued to work together after the May vote; they challenged the outcome of the elections and charged Turkish mainland interference and other improprieties. They also continued to complain that the electoral law greatly favored the ruling party. Four of the DMP's fourteen deputies broke from the alliance and joined the parliament; two were from the YDP and two, including İsmet Kotak, had run on the TKP ticket.

Foreign Policy

From the time of independence, Cypriots saw their problem on several levels. First, it was an intercommunal problem that required local, domestic political solutions. Next, and very close to this level, was the relationship of the island to its motherlands, Greece and Turkey; the two Cypriot communities struggled with the question of how much their foreign policies should be determined by the foreign policy interests and resources of the motherlands. At another level, many Cypriots considered their island a pawn in the superpower struggle, often exaggerating its strategic significance. Because the two motherlands, Greece and Turkey, were North Atlantic Treaty Organization (NATO) members, Cyprus was by definition a problem within the Western camp, a circumstance the Soviet Union and its allies, during the Cold War, occasionally sought to exploit. As a response to these constricting relationships, Cypriot foreign policy was nonaligned, and both communities found support among Third World countries for whom the Cyprus problem resonated with their own problems, be it the matter of a larger nearby state occupying territory of a smaller one, or the matter of a religious minority suffering discrimination at the hands of the majority.

Cyprus's relations with the outside world were shaped profoundly by the chronic dilemma of the island's political identity. The two communities conducted narrow foreign policies focused on this single issue. Yet the Republic of Cyprus conducted active and effective diplomatic efforts in many countries to win support for its position in UN settlement talks and in support of sympathetic resolutions in multilateral forums of which Cyprus was a member. The "TRNC" by the mid-1980s tried to break out of its isolation and began to conduct its own foreign policy, in some ways mirroring the efforts of its Greek Cypriot neighbors. Recognition as a state was the primary foreign policy objective of the regime in the north. Foreign policy in general was considerably more important for the republic; the "TRNC" was persuaded that its cause would benefit from "benign neglect" by the world community, allowing the two communities to develop normal relations without external pressure.

The Republic of Cyprus

The founding documents of Cyprus's independence set some requirements for its foreign policy and linked the republic to three NATO members—Turkey, Greece, and Britain—through a Treaty of Alliance and a Treaty of Guarantee. These treaties, calling for the motherlands to garrison troops on the island and for the three NATO countries to guarantee and protect the independence of the republic, seemed to constrain or contradict the commitment to nonalignment enshrined in the constitution. Cypriots complained about these implied limits on their sovereignty, but in time developed foreign policies that were independent of the motherlands.

The Foreign Policy of Internationalization

Greek Cypriots have focused most of their foreign policy energies since 1974 on winning broader international support for a Cyprus settlement providing for a withdrawal of Turkish troops and, to the extent possible, a restoration of the status quo ante of a single government on the island and the free flow of people and goods throughout its territory. The republic continued to enjoy international recognition as the legal government of Cyprus; and membership in the Nonaligned Movement (NAM), the Conference on Security and Cooperation in Europe (CSCE), the United Nations, and the Commonwealth provided opportunities to promote these aims. Resolutions passed by these organizations called for the withdrawal of foreign troops, condemned Turkey's settler policy, urged the immediate implementation of UN resolutions, and called for sanctions against Turkey.

Cyprus placed considerable importance on its membership in the NAM. It hosted a number of NAM meetings and headed an effort in 1989 and 1990 to redefine the NAM's objectives in light of the dramatic changes in East-West relations and the virtual end of superpower rivalry and competition. Support from the nonaligned states was particularly important during UN debates. Greek Cypriots were aware that UN resolutions lacked direct effect on Turkey unless accompanied by substantive sanctions, but they hoped that collective international pressure might yield some results. On occasion, the republic was persuaded by its Western allies to forego the annual UN General Assembly resolution debate, avoiding repetitious and largely ineffective rituals and allowing the UN-sponsored talks to proceed without undue pressure. President Vassiliou adapted the traditional Greek Cypriot strategy to his new thinking by occasionally modifying his language, avoiding punitive measures, and emphasizing positive incentives to engage Turkish Cypriots in negotiations. After the collapse of the 1990 UN talks, however, Greek Cypriot positions in international organizations returned to earlier phases, seeking direct condemnation of Turkish and Turkish Cypriot policies and practices.

The strategy of internationalization became more Europe-oriented in 1990. After the fall of the Berlin wall and the commitment to unification of the two Germanies, the Greek Cypriot republic perceived its situation as increasingly anomalous and unacceptable. It argued that, after Soviet troops completed withdrawing from Eastern Europe, Cyprus would be the only country in Europe with foreign occupying troops. The unification of Germany also underscored the deep Greek Cypriot yearning for reunification, and Greek Cypriots held candlelight processions around the old walls of the capital, Nicosia, calling for an end to the division of the island.

The decline of the relative importance of NATO among European institutions had both advantages and disadvantages for Greek Cypriot foreign policy. On the one hand, it appeared to reduce Turkey's leverage over its Western allies and opened the way for broader pressures on Turkey. On the other hand, the potential loosening of Turkey's ties with Western partners could also weaken those countries' influence on Turkey's policies. In addition, the preoccupation with Germany and the emergence of new violent conflicts in the Balkans made it harder to keep the attention of European powers on Cyprus.

The proposals in mid-1990 to expand the mission and scope of the CSCE appealed to Greek Cypriots. They had found participation in the CSCE, along with six other neutral and nonaligned European states, less satisfactory when the organization's main function was as a forum for East-West confidence-building measures. In a future united Europe, however, Cypriots could envision a greater role for the small states in the CSCE, and some believed that the CSCE's expanded conflict-mediation role might have benefits for Cyprus. The Italian proposal for a southern variant of the CSCE, the CSC-Mediterranean, found tentative support from both Cypriot communities.

Relations with Greece

After the troubles of 1963–64 and the effective separation of the two communities, the Greek Cypriots controlling the republic's institutions did not, ironically, orient their foreign policy more toward Greece. Instead, the growing authority and confidence of President Makarios and divergent trends in Greek and Greek Cypriot politics led to the republic's foreign policy becoming more independent. Greek Cypriots were disappointed that Greece had placed the interests of the Western alliance above those of the island in the preindependence London and Zurich talks. Greek Cypriots also viewed as inadequate the Greek response to the 1963–64 troubles, with Greece again deferring to NATO interests.

Relations deteriorated further when the military seized power in Athens in 1967. Makarios was anathema to the staunchly anti-communist regime in Greece. His flirtation with Eastern Europe and Third World nations, his refusal to stem criticism of the dictatorship, and his charismatic appeal to Greeks everywhere were major concerns of the new Greek leadership. The infiltration of Greek soldiers from the mainland, in excess of levels approved in the Treaty of Alliance, became a threat almost equal to that from the Turkish mainland. By the early 1970s, the rift between the Athens junta and the Makarios government had become open. Athens allegedly financed operations of anti-Makarios organizations and newspapers and was widely thought responsible for attempts on Makarios's life. Pressures mounted, and in July 1974, after Makarios openly challenged the junta's interference, the Cypriot National Guard, led by Greek officers, staged a coup that ultimately resulted in Turkish intervention and the junta's demise.

With the 1974 restoration of civilian government in Athens and the environment of crisis in the Greek-controlled part of the island after the Turkish intervention, relations between the republic and the government in Greece were restored to normal. Closer coordination of foreign policy began, particularly focused on winning support for resolutions in international organizations and from Greeks abroad. Greece gave full public support to policies adopted by the republic and pledged not to interfere in domestic Cypriot politics. The two governments agreed that Greek Cypriot participation in settlement efforts was essential and tried to uncouple the Cyprus issue from other Greek-Turkish disputes, such as those about territorial rights in the Aegean Sea.

Differences remained over the two governments' priorities. Greek prime minister Constantinos Karamanlis was said to favor a more moderate and conciliatory stand on Cyprus than either Makarios or Kyprianou, both of whom advocated a "long struggle" in the face of what they perceived as Turkish intransigence. The Greek government was also eager to return to NATO, which it did in 1981, and to reduce tensions with Turkey. In addition, the tripartite American-British-Canadian plan (the ABC plan) of 1978 won Greece's approval, although it was rejected by Greek Cypriots as a framework for negotiations.

When Greeks elected the socialist government of Andreas Papandreou to office in 1981, the foreign policy of Greece shifted. Less inclined to demonstrate Greece's loyalty to NATO and other Western institutions, Papandreou sought to "internationalize" the Cyprus settlement effort and took a more confrontational approach to bilateral differences with Turkey. This approach led to a new, and sometimes uneasy, division of labor between Greece and the republic, with the latter engaged in intercommunal talks and the former raising the Turkish troop issue in NATO and other international forums. Cyprus was relinked to bilateral Greek-Turkish problems, insofar as Papandreou insisted that relations between the two NATO allies could not improve until the Cyprus problem was solved and Turkish troops withdrawn. This policy was temporarily suspended in early 1988, when Papandreou and Turkish prime minister Özal conducted talks known as the Davos process, aimed at improving ties through Aegean confidence-building measures. The process was stalled in late 1988 by political and health problems of the Greek premier. For most of 1989 and early 1990, Greece was ruled by interim governments that took no new foreign policy initiatives, although the 1988 election of the activist George Vassiliou in Cyprus gave some new vigor and interest to the frequent consultations in Athens between the two governments.

In April 1990, Greeks returned to power the centrist New Democracy Party, and the new prime minister, veteran politician Constantinos Mitsotakis, pledged to renew Greece's efforts to solve the Cyprus problem. The two governments formed a joint committee, administered by their foreign ministries, to share information and coordinate policies and thus avoid the strains that had arisen from divergent approaches to the Cyprus problem.

Relations with the United States and the Soviet Union

Cyprus had ambivalent relations with the superpowers during the Cold War. Despite its nonalignment, the cultural, political, and economic orientation of Cyprus was to the West, and NATO allies played crucial roles in the achievement of Cyprus's independence, the treaties guaranteeing that independence, and the composition of the UN peace-keeping force that was on the island continuously after 1964.

Relations with the United States after the 1974 crisis were shaped by Cypriot convictions that the United States had been too close to the Greek junta, could have prevented its coup against Makarios, supported or acquiesced in the Turkish intervention, and gave insufficient attention to solving the Cyprus problem. Relations between Cyprus and the United States were also haunted by the 1974 assassination of United States Ambassador Roger Davies in Nicosia. Yet, pressed by the United States Congress and the aroused Greek-American community, the Nixon and Ford administrations became involved in refugee resettlement and peace talks during the 1974 crisis and its aftermath.

As the Turkish intervention was consolidated, leading to a long-term division of the island, Greek Cypriots continued to have misgivings about the strategic intentions of United States policy. Cypriots occasionally pressed for new American initiatives, although none was offered after the 1978 ABC plan. A more activist American policy was institutionalized through the establishment in 1981 of a Special Cyprus Coordinator in the Department of State. The position was held by Reginald Bartholemew (1981–82), Christian Chapman (1982–83), Richard Haass (1983–85), James Wilkenson (1985–89), and Nelson Ledsky after 1989. Yet efforts by these diplomats to stimulate discussion about confidence-building measures, intercommunal projects and cooperation, and new directions in the US$15 million annual aid program to Cyprus met resistance from the republic's government. The republic looked to the United States Congress and the Greek-American community to correct what they considered a pro-Turkish bias in United States policy.

Relations with the Soviet Union were more distant and reflected ups and downs in superpower influence in the Mediterranean and in United States-Turkish relations. The Soviets had supported the Greek Cypriot position after 1974 and generally pursued policies that fostered strains in intra-NATO relations. They worked with the island's communist party, but equally well with the centrist governments. In the late 1970s, the Soviets were cooler toward the Greek Cypriot view because of improved relations with Turkey. The Soviets under Mikhail Gorbachev became more interested in Cyprus settlement efforts. In 1986 the Soviets outlined their policy for a Cyprus settlement, calling for a withdrawal of all foreign troops and bases (presumably including the British sovereign base areas), a demilitarization of the island, and a new federal government. Greek Cypriots welcomed the proposal, although in subsequent

President Vassiliou with President George Bush
at the White House, 1991
Courtesy The White House (Susan Biddle)

months it was interpreted by many as part of a broad Third World-Soviet public relations exercise more than a serious diplomatic initiative to which resources would be devoted.

Relations with the European Community

As Europe moved to create a single market by the end of 1992, the European Community (EC—see Glossary) became an increasingly important focus of Cypriot foreign policy. Cyprus became an associate member of the EC in June 1973, motivated largely by a desire to maintain its major trading partnership with Britain. But relations with Brussels were troubled by the uncertainty of the political situation on the island and the EC's preference for avoiding entanglement in political disputes. EC policy throughout the years of the division of the island was to deal with the republic government as the legal authority but at the same time to state that the benefits of association must extend to the entire island and its population. Cypriot efforts to link EC aid to Turkey to progress on a Cyprus settlement were unsuccessful, although the European Parliament passed several supportive but largely symbolic resolutions on Cyprus in the 1980s.

After the 1988 election of George Vassiliou, in an era of revitalized European consciousness, Cyprus's attention to the EC increased dramatically, and its foreign policy became more EC-oriented and focused less on the Third World and the NAM. On July 4, 1990, the republic formally applied for full EC membership. In a public statement, President Vassiliou said that Cyprus had ''declared its European orientation and its desire to participate as actively as possible and on an equal footing with the other EC member states in the historic process of European integration and the building of a Common European House of peace, cooperation and prosperity.''

It was clear that the membership bid, which was not expected to culminate in actual accession until the next century, was strongly driven by the settlement process. The application could be seen as a tactical move intended to give new momentum and new incentives to the Turkish side to achieve progress in talks. For Vassiliou, the EC application and its expected decade-long waiting period were an opportunity. He hoped that the EC accession timetable would parallel a negotiation timetable, so that a new federal government and full membership in the EC could be achieved at the same time. He argued that the benefits of EC membership would be conferred on ''all Cypriots without exception.'' Should settlement talks fail, the EC application would serve a second purpose, giving Cyprus a framework for discussing the lack of progress with its EC trading partners.

It was estimated that by the beginning of the 1990s 85 percent of Greek Cypriots favored full EC membership, with AKEL the notable exception. The Greek Cypriot parliament pressured Vassiliou in the spring of 1990 to move more quickly on the EC issue. Some Cypriots, including DISY leader Clerides and some Vassiliou supporters, floated the proposal to have Turkish Cypriots participate in future negotiations with Brussels, although such proposals, without more formal recognition of Turkish Cypriot separate political rights, appeared doomed to failure.

Other Foreign Policy Concerns

The Republic of Cyprus also participated in foreign policy debates on issues of broader interest to Cyprus as a small, nonaligned country. When approached by its Western friends, including the United States, Cyprus proved a reliable and effective partner in issues of common concern, such as antiterrorism measures and control of illegal narcotics, and it became increasingly interested in environmental causes, particularly in the Mediterranean region.

Cyprus was also compelled because of geographic proximity to address the Arab-Israeli issue and the Lebanon crisis that plagued the Middle East throughout the 1980s. The island was occasionally touched by the violence of these disputes when Israeli and Palestinian commandos carried out missions against each other in Cypriot coastal towns, and even in Nicosia. For the most part, Cyprus remained neutral, allowing the island to be the meeting place for informal diplomatic encounters between Arabs and Israelis. Cyprus had active trade and cultural relations with Israel, and a fully accredited Israeli Embassy functioned in Nicosia. At the same time, Cyprus supported moderate Palestinian positions in international forums and sought more active Arab support of its position, appealing to Arab sentiment over what it saw as analogous situations in the respective Israeli and Turkish occupations of their territories.

The "TRNC"

Turkish Cypriots began developing a rudimentary foreign policy after 1963, focused mainly on public relations efforts to explain the communal perspective on the island's political difficulties. Two factors constrained the development of a Turkish Cypriot foreign policy. First, Turkish Cypriots lacked the personnel and resources to project themselves on the world scene. Second, Turkish Cypriot administrations, in their various forms since 1963, lacked international recognition and were dependent on Turkey's acting as an intermediary to international opinion. The situation changed gradually after 1985, although Turkish Cypriot activism in foreign policy focused on expanding trade and political contact, rather than on the settlement process. The view of the Turkish Cypriot government was that less, not more, international attention would help a Cyprus settlement.

Relations with Turkey

As was the case with Greek Cypriots and their mainland, relations between the Turkish Cypriots and Turkey could be characterized as close and cooperative, although many observers detected strains barely beneath the surface. Turkey usually supported Turkish Cypriot policies in their broadest sense, although tactical differences often occurred. On several key occasions in the UN settlement process, Ankara pressed the Turkish Cypriot government to be more forthcoming. From 1975 until the declaration of the "TRNC" in 1983, for example, it was reported on numerous occasions that Turkey had persuaded Denktaş to delay his unilateral declaration of independence.

The main institutional vehicle for Turkish-Turkish Cypriot cooperation was the Coordination Committee (Koordinasyon Komitesi) formed in the 1960s to administer the extensive economic relationship between the two. The participants in these coordination activities, which became more ad hoc as Turkish Cypriot bureaucratic competence grew, were representatives of the prime minister's office in Turkey and a collection of key decision makers from the Turkish Cypriot executive branch. From 1974 to 1983, coordination was close, including Turkish participation in Turkish Cypriot cabinet meetings. After the establishment of the "TRNC," such contact was replaced with more formal state-to-state relations. Turkey demonstrated in various ways its recognition of the separateness of the Turkish Cypriot political entity, although opposition parties and many observers believed that the Turkish Embassy in the north was engaged in activities beyond the normal purview of a foreign mission.

The economic dimension of bilateral relations also showed its strains. After 1974, the Turkish contribution to the Turkish Cypriot budget was estimated at 80 percent, but by 1990 that subsidy was reported to be in the 30 to 40 percent range. The opposition press in Turkey occasionally complained that aid and assistance to northern Cyprus were an economic burden on Turkey, whose economic performance was uneven in the 1980s. For their part, Turkish Cypriots complained of inadequate aid, the failure as of late 1990 to establish a customs union, and the importation of Turkey's economic problems, most notably rampant inflation in the late 1970s and again in the late 1980s. Relations were also strained by social differences between mainland settlers and the higher levels of education and more urban and secular lifestyles of most Turkish Cypriots.

The Quest for Recognition

Most Turkish Cypriot foreign policy efforts focused on achieving recognition of the "TRNC" and explaining the Turkish Cypriot position on the settlement process. The "TRNC" had one embassy, in Ankara, two consulates, in Istanbul and Mersin, and five representation missions, in London, Washington, New York, Brussels, and Islamabad. These missions did not have diplomatic status. In 1990 there were reports that additional missions might be opened in Abu Dhabi, Canada, Australia, Italy, and Germany.

The Islamic nations were the key target of Turkish Cypriot recognition efforts. In wooing Islamic support, Turkish Cypriot officials emphasized the religious aspect of the Cyprus conflict and stressed the importance of Muslim solidarity. Meetings of the Organization of the Islamic Conference (OIC), in which Turkey played an increasingly active role in the 1980s, were an important focus for the "TRNC." The OIC passed several resolutions urging economic support and cultural contact with the Turkish Cypriots but stopped short of embracing the recognition issue. Many Arab Islamic countries had ambivalent relations with Turkey because of the legacy of the Ottoman Empire, and also because they wished to maintain good relations with the Republic of Cyprus, which served as a financial center and entrepôt for Middle Eastern business activity. These reservations hindered the "TRNC" in its attempt to achieve its goals in the Islamic world. Among these countries, Pakistan, Jordan, and Bangladesh were considered the strongest supporters of the Turkish Cypriot cause.

* * *

The literature on Cyprus in the decade of the 1980s concentrated heavily on the intercommunal talks and UN efforts to settle the island's political dispute. There was little scholarly or journalistic coverage of the politics of the two communities separate from the politics of the settlement question. Nonetheless, elections in the Republic of Cyprus and in the "TRNC" provided opportunities to examine more closely the players and the political dynamics in each community. One particularly useful journalistic account is the 1990 *New Yorker* article by Mary Anne Weaver, reviewing the evolution of views in both communities and describing vividly the political and diplomatic atmosphere on the island. Also of note is Robert McDonald's International Institute for Strategic Studies monograph, *The Problem of Cyprus,* published in 1989. Other major sources of information on settlement positions are official newsletters and fact sheets. The Embassy of the Republic of Cyprus in Washington publishes a monthly bulletin that carefully tracks government positions and occasionally features information on domestic politics. The Washington office of the "TRNC" representative also distributes occasional fact sheets and position papers. Hearings and reports of the United States Congress are informative on the debate between Congress and the executive over United States policy on Cyprus and on United States perceptions of the status of settlement efforts. Such documents can be purchased from the United States Government Printing Office.

Several books, including edited volumes of articles on Cyprus, were published in the 1980s, providing different perspectives on the situation and on prospects for a settlement. *Cyprus in Transition, 1960–1985,* edited by John T.A. Koumoulides, contains several retrospective articles, mostly from the perspectives of outside players in Cypriot affairs: the United Kingdom, the United States, the United Nations, and others. The Canadian Institute for International Peace and Security published in 1991 a volume of articles from a workshop series on conflict resolution on Cyprus. The volume reviews the positions of external players as well as Cypriots and contains several useful chapters by Cypriots discussing confidence-building measures and cultural and sociological factors in settlement efforts. Tozun Bahcheli's *Greek-Turkish Relations since 1955* also contains useful coverage of the Cyprus issue in its foreign policy dimensions.

Because of the importance of legal and constitutional aspects in a settlement, lawyers and legal officials from both communities have published books on these issues. Polyvios G. Polyviou's *Cyprus: In Search of a Constitution* examines the legal and political aspects of the constitution that Greek Cypriots still support. Zaim M. Necatigil, the attorney general of the ''TRNC,'' has published two books that provide the Turkish Cypriot perspective on these matters: *The Cyprus Conflict: A Lawyer's View* (1981), and *The Cyprus Question and the Turkish Position in International Law* (1989). (For further information and complete citations, see Bibliography.)

Chapter 5. National Security

Paphos Castle, partially rebuilt by the Turks in the late sixteenth century after destruction by the Venetians of the original fourteenth-century fortification

THE MANY ANCIENT AND MODERN walled fortresses that dot the landscape of Cyprus attest to the island's long history of armed conflict. Valuable minerals and forest products and the island's strategic location along trade routes between Europe and the Middle East have made Cyprus the object of repeated occupations by the region's dominant military powers since the second millennium B.C. (see The Ancient Period, ch. 1).

The competing interests of Greece and Turkey in Cyprus—freed from British rule in 1960—have deeply affected the country's national security in the modern period. Competition between the two outside powers fueled intercommunal strife between Greek and Turkish Cypriots and subversive acts against President Archbishop Makarios III. Greek military personnel attached to the Cypriot National Guard supported the campaign against Makarios, which culminated in the coup d'état of July 1974 and the subsequent Turkish military intervention and occupation of 37 percent of the island. The events of July–August 1974 further strained relations between the two nations that form the southeastern flank of the North Atlantic Treaty Organization (NATO), endangering Western security in the region.

The Zurich-London agreements, signed in London on February 19, 1959, provided legitimacy to actions taken jointly or individually by Greece and Turkey, as well as by Britain, to uphold the constitution of the new island nation. In the ensuing years, however, the rights spelled out in the constitution were often abused or misapplied. For example, the bicommunal Cyprus Army provided for in the agreements never materialized; rather, each ethnic community created its own military force, trained, armed, and partially staffed by personnel from the mainland. Both Greece and Turkey intervened in Cypriot affairs in a manner that went well beyond their legitimate security roles, and Britain for the most part simply stood aside.

The events of 1974 have resulted in a de facto partition of the island into segregated Greek and Turkish communities with sizable opposing forces in close proximity. More than two Turkish Army divisions in the north alleviated fears of the Turkish Cypriot minority that its physical safety was threatened by intercommunal violence. Although the strong Turkish military presence was a source of insecurity for the Greek Cypriot community, as of 1990 the Turkish forces had shown no further territorial ambitions since

213

the 1974 cease-fire. During the late 1980s, the Greek Cypriot National Guard began to strengthen and modernize its armored units and air defenses to reduce the margin of Turkish superiority. Demonstrations by Greek Cypriot women sometimes crossed into the buffer zone, leading to confrontations with Turkish troops and introducing an element of potential instability.

Greek Cypriots saw the large Turkish Army contingent on Cyprus as an alien force distorting the community's balance. On the other hand, the growing strength of the National Guard was regarded by Turkish Cypriots as a threat justifying the retention of Turkish forces. Nevertheless, as of 1990 the military position seemed a stalemate, furthered by the continued presence (since early 1964) of United Nations (UN) peace-keeping troops. Numerous rounds of bilateral and UN-sponsored talks had failed to reduce the military confrontation, an essential step in any political settlement.

The Cyprus Conflict

The Struggle for Independence

The roots of the Cyprus conflict lie in the striving of the Greek Cypriot majority for unification, or enosis, with Greece, an idea that emerged during the Greek War of Independence in the 1820s and developed under British colonial rule (see British Rule, ch. 1). Popular sentiment for enosis, joined with resentment of British tax policies, ignited in 1931 in a brief but widespread uprising. During the uprising, the British Government House in Nicosia was burned, 6 Cypriots were killed, and 2,000 were arrested by British authorities. From then on, enosis became more popular in the Greek Cypriot community; however, a clampdown on Cypriot political activity and the exigencies of World War II precluded any violent manifestation for twenty-four years.

The barely suppressed desire for enosis erupted on April 1, 1955, when bombs destroyed the transmitter of the Cyprus broadcasting station and exploded at British Army and police installations in Nicosia, Limassol, Famagusta, and Larnaca. The explosions signaled the beginning of a guerrilla war against the British colonial administration that was to continue for four years and claim some 600 lives. The Greek Cypriots fought under the banner of the National Organization of Cypriot Fighters (Ethniki Organosis Kyprion Agoniston—EOKA), led by Colonel (later General) George Grivas. Although EOKA included only a few hundred active guerrillas, it enjoyed wide support in the Greek Cypriot community and was able to keep about 10,000 British soldiers occupied.

However, when EOKA called a cease-fire in March 1959, after the signing in February of the agreements that led to Cypriot independence, it could claim only partial success. The Cypriot tie to Britain was broken sooner than it would have been without the guerrilla struggle, but EOKA's goal of enosis remained unmet.

For members of the Turkish Cypriot minority, who regarded Turkey as their motherland, enosis would have meant becoming a much smaller minority within the Greek nation. In the mid-1950s, Turkish Cypriots responded to the growth of EOKA with the formation of their own paramilitary organization, Volkan (volcano), which later became the Turkish Resistance Organization (Türk Mukavemet Teşkilâtı—TMT). British authorities also armed a paramilitary police force composed entirely of Turkish Cypriots, the Mobile Reserve, to help combat terrorism. The intense intercommunal violence of 1958 implanted a bitterness in both ethnic communities and foreshadowed postindependence strife that would tear the young nation apart.

Three interrelated treaties in February 1959, and the subsequent adoption of a constitution, resulted in Cyprus's gaining its independence on August 19, 1960. Under the Treaty of Establishment, Britain retained sovereign rights over two areas to be used as military bases. The Treaty of Alliance stipulated that contingents of 950 Greek troops and 650 Turkish troops were to provide for the defense of the island and train a new Cypriot army. Under the Treaty of Guarantee, in the event of a threat to the established political arrangements of Cyprus, the treaty's signatories, Greece, Turkey, and Britain, were to consult on appropriate measures to safeguard or restore them; the signatories were granted the right to intervene together or, if concerted action proved impossible, to act unilaterally to uphold the settlement. These elaborate arrangements came to provide the pretexts for repeated foreign intervention that severely undermined Cypriot security and for Turkey's unilateral military action in 1974, which led to the de facto partition of the island.

Intercommunal Violence, 1963–67

Three years of peace followed Cypriot independence in 1960. Beneath the peace, however, lay the resentment of some Greek Cypriots at the prevention of enosis and a growing conflict between Greek and Turkish Cypriots over the bicommunal provisions of the constitution. The Cyprus Army, which was to consist of 1,200 Greek Cypriots and 800 Turkish Cypriots, never materialized because of differences over the six-to-four formula for integrating the force. EOKA had officially disbanded and surrendered its weapons in 1959, and Grivas had returned to Greece. In fact, however, many former EOKA members had retained their weapons, and some joined groups of armed irregulars. The Turkish Cypriot community responded to the growth of these groups by reviving the TMT in early 1962. These forces received arms and assistance from the Greek and Turkish contingents assigned to the island.

In late November 1963, the president, Archbishop Makarios, introduced a thirteen-point proposal to amend the constitution in a way that would ensure the dominance of Greek Cypriots (see Republic of Cyprus, ch. 1). In the tense atmosphere that ensued, a street brawl broke out on December 21 in Nicosia between Turkish Cypriots and Greek Cypriot police. This fight was followed by major attacks by Greek Cypriot irregulars in Nicosia and Larnaca. Looting and destruction of Turkish villages forced many Turkish Cypriots to withdraw into defensible enclaves guarded by the TMT paramilitary. Fearful that Turkey might carry out its threat to invade, Makarios agreed to British intervention from its bases on the island. On December 27, British troops assumed positions between opposing irregular units, and the fighting, which had claimed 100 lives on each side during the previous week, subsided temporarily. The cease-fire held in Nicosia, but by mid-February 1964 Greek Cypriot attacks at Limassol brought a renewed threat of Turkish landings. Britain appealed to the UN Security Council, and on March 4, 1964, the UN approved a resolution to establish an international peace-keeping force for duty in Cyprus. Contingents from Canada, Denmark, Finland, Ireland, and Sweden joined the British soldiers already in place; together they made up the 6,500-member United Nations Peace-keeping Force in Cyprus (UNFICYP). The force was still present on the island, though at much reduced strength, a quarter of a century later (see United Nations Peace-keeping Force in Cyprus, this ch.).

In June 1964, the National Guard was formed by the Greek Cypriot government, which also instituted male conscription. The National Guard absorbed the various private armies into a single national military force loyal to the government and served as a deterrent to a Turkish invasion. Greek Army soldiers were clandestinely transferred to the guard on a large scale; by mid-summer the National Guard consisted of an estimated 24,000 officers and men, about half from the Greek Army. Grivas, thought to be the only man who could enforce discipline over the disparate armed Greek Cypriot factions, returned from Athens to command the National Guard.

Meanwhile, the Turkish Cypriot community, in its newly created enclaves, organized militarily under the TMT, supported by conscription of Turkish Cypriot youths. Turkish Army troops trained the Turkish Cypriot forces, totaling an estimated 10,000 fighters, and directed the defense of the enclaves. Outbreaks of fighting continued, although the presence of UNFICYP prevented them from erupting into major hostilities. In August 1964, the National Guard carried out a coordinated sea and land assault against Kokkina on the northwest coast in an effort to cut off the major Turkish Cypriot supply line to the mainland. Heavy attacks by Turkish jet fighter-bombers, operating beyond the range of the Greek Air Force, halted the Greek Cypriot offensive. Several years of peace followed, while the two communities improved their military readiness.

In November 1967, units of the National Guard, at the instigation of Grivas, launched a massive artillery assault on two Turkish Cypriot villages following a dispute over police patrols. The crisis was defused when United States mediation brought an agreement that endured for the next seven years: all foreign troops in excess of those permitted by the Treaty of Alliance were to be removed from Cyprus, and the National Guard was to be dismantled in exchange for an immediate Turkish demobilization. Grivas was recalled to Athens, along with about 10,000 of the Greek troops assigned to the National Guard. The National Guard, however, was not dissolved.

Conflict Within the Greek Cypriot Community, 1967–74

During the next seven years, events in Cyprus were shaped by the differences over enosis that arose between Makarios and the military government that was installed in Greece after a coup d'état in 1967. Convinced of Turkey's willingness to use its superior force to prevent enosis, Makarios began to seek support among Greek Cypriots—especially those in the communist party—who rejected enosis, at least for the near future, in favor of an independent, nonaligned Cyprus (see Political Dynamics, ch. 4). Because Makarios had decided enosis was no longer possible in the short term, more adamant pro-enosis Cypriot groups and anticommunist Greek officers, both of which infiltrated the National Guard during the late 1960s and early 1970s, would subvert his government increasingly after 1967 and finally overthrow him in 1974.

Makarios failed in his efforts to limit the autonomy of the National Guard, which, under the influence of right-wing Greek officers, remained attached to enosis and bitterly opposed to Makarios's political association with the communist party. Compulsory military service for all Greek Cypriot males—for a period that increased from six months to two years during the 1960s—allowed the arming and training of a great number of men, many of whom subsequently took up arms against the government. Between 1969 and 1971, several groups embarked on a renewed terrorist campaign for enosis. Grivas returned clandestinely to Cyprus sometime in the late summer or early fall of 1971 and set up a new guerrilla organization, the National Organization of Cypriot Fighters B (Ethniki Organosis Kyprion Agoniston B—EOKA B). Most members of the terrorist movement held regular jobs in the Greek Cypriot community; half were police officials and members of the National Guard.

There was also considerable evidence of support of EOKA B activities by the Greek junta, whose hostility to Makarios became increasingly apparent during the early 1970s. The junta was believed to be involved in several attempts on the life of President Makarios. In March 1970, Makarios narrowly escaped death when his helicopter was shot down. Makarios walked away from the crash, but his pilot was killed. Former minister of interior Polykarpos Georkajis, in contact with local right-wing groups and the junta in Athens, was thought to be implicated, and was assassinated shortly afterward. A paramilitary presidential guard loyal to Makarios, called the Tactical Police Reserve, was organized in 1972. Consisting of fewer than 1,000 men, the Tactical Police Reserve succeeded in arresting large numbers of EOKA B guerrillas. In a further attempt to bring subversive forces under control, Makarios dismissed many National Guard and police officers suspected of EOKA B activity.

With the death of Grivas from a heart attack in January 1974, EOKA B came more directly under the control of the military junta in Athens, which, after a change of leadership, was even more hostile to Makarios. The archbishop, however, saw the Greek-officered National Guard as a more serious threat to his government than EOKA B. In a letter to the Greek president in early July, he accused the junta of attempting to subvert the government of Cyprus through the Greek officers of the National Guard, who in turn supported the terrorist activities of EOKA B. Makarios demanded immediate removal of the 650 Greek officers staffing the National Guard and their replacement by 100 instructors who would help reorganize the Greek Cypriot force.

The reply to the Makarios challenge came on July 15 in the form of a coup d'état led by Greek officers in the National Guard, under orders from Athens. The fierce fighting that broke out resulted in casualties estimated at over 500, but the lightly armed Tactical Police Reserve and irregular pro-Makarios units were no match for the heavily armed National Guardsmen and the EOKA B irregulars. Narrowly escaping capture when the presidential palace was bombarded, Makarios was flown to London from the Sovereign Base Area at Akrotiri. Former EOKA gunman and convicted murderer Nicos Sampson, notorious for his brutality in the 1950s and 1960s, was proclaimed president. As Makarios had foreseen, but the Greek military leaders had not, Turkey reacted forcibly to the coup by landing a large number of troops on the northern coast of Cyprus. As a result, both the insurrectionary government in Cyprus and the military dictatorship in Greece fell from power.

The Turkish Military Intervention, July–August 1974

Citing the Treaty of Guarantee as the basis for its action, Turkey launched its seaborne assault west of Kyrenia on July 20, 1974. About 6,000 men participated in the landing force, which was followed shortly afterward by about 1,000 paratroopers dropped north of Nicosia. Turkish Cypriot irregulars joined the Turkish regulars in both areas, but they faced fierce opposition from the National Guard. Kyrenia did not come under Turkish control until heavy sea and air bombardment drove out Greek Cypriot troops on the third day of fighting. Meanwhile, Turkish Cypriot enclaves throughout the southern part of the island fell to Greek Cypriot forces. Only in Nicosia was the Turkish Cypriot enclave successfully defended by TMT irregulars, with the aid of the Turkish Air Force.

When a UN-imposed cease-fire took effect on July 22, Turkish troops held a triangular area in northern Cyprus, with Kyrenia in the center of its base along the coast and northern Nicosia at its apex. Clear Turkish superiority in personnel and equipment deterred Greek leaders from intervening. Nearly half the Turkish Cypriot population lay outside the occupied area, in enclaves now controlled by the National Guard. During the next three weeks, while foreign ministers from Britain, Greece, and Turkey met in Geneva, Turkish troops continued to seize control of areas outside the cease-fire lines, broadening the triangle under their occupation. Their troop strength was augmented through the Kyrenia bridgehead to some 40,000 soldiers and 200 tanks.

On August 14, immediately upon the breakup of the second round of Geneva talks, two divisions of the Turkish Army advanced beyond their cease-fire positions. During the three-day offensive, Greek Cypriot resistance crumpled under heavy air, armor, and artillery bombardment. Civilians, alarmed by reports of atrocities during the first Turkish campaign, fled ahead of the advancing troops, who proceeded unimpeded through much of northern Cyprus. By August 16, the Turkish advance had reached the

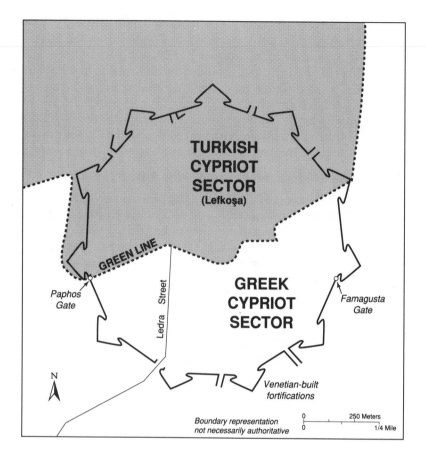

Figure 10. Nicosia and the Green Line

predetermined "Attila Line," behind which troops occupied 37 percent of Cypriot territory, and Turkey ordered a cease-fire (see fig. 1). Although authoritative figures on casualties were not published, it was estimated that Greek Cypriot forces suffered 6,000 casualties, and Turkish-led forces lost 1,500 dead and 2,000 wounded.

De Facto Partition, 1974–

About 180,000 people, an estimated one-third of the population of Cyprus, became refugees during the fighting. The buffer zone between the two cease-fire lines occupied by UNFICYP marked the almost total segregation of the Greek and Turkish ethnic communities. At first, tensions were high along the buffer zone, which extended for 180 kilometers across the island and was in most places 3–7 kilometers wide (although as narrow as 20 meters in the center of Nicosia) (see fig. 10). Sporadic exchanges of gunfire across the lines and infiltrations by Turkish patrols gradually subsided. By the close of 1978, the UN reported that the cease-fire lines were almost completely stabilized. During most of the 1980s, cease-fire violations were confined mostly to occasional incidents of misbehavior by individual soldiers.

All but a few hundred Greek Cypriots fled from the Turkish-occupied area in the north or were induced to leave in the period following the 1974 fighting. As of late 1989, only 611 Greek Cypriots lived under Turkish occupation, almost all of them in the Karpas Peninsula. A further 276 Maronites were in the north. Only about 100 Turkish Cypriots remained in the south. Turkish soldiers who had fought on Cyprus were allowed to settle with their families and given homes. In addition, a significant number of immigrants from Turkey had been allowed to settle in the north. Both the Turkish Cypriot refugees from the south and the settlers from Turkey were granted homes and property abandoned by Greek Cypriots. The presence of Turkish immigrants, the appropriation of property, and the fate of more than 1,600 Greek Cypriots missing since the 1974 fighting complicated the prospects of a settlement to end the division of the island. Beginning in 1976, a succession of low- and high-level meetings, intercommunal talks, and talks initiated by the UN secretary general led to progress on some issues but, as of late 1990, had failed to achieve a political solution (see Search for a New Political Formula, ch. 4).

Problems of Internal Security

There has been little political violence in Cyprus since the Turkish invasion of 1974. Violence on behalf of enosis, which had been prevalent from 1955 until the invasion, was rejected by the vast majority of Greek Cypriots after 1974, although union with Greece continued to command strong emotional appeal in the right wing. Moreover, Turkish troops acted as a deterrent against terrorist operations aimed against the Turkish presence or threatening change in the status quo. Turkish sources have claimed that the Republic of Cyprus supplied arms and possibly even guerrilla-warfare training to Kurdish and Armenian opponents of the Turkish government at secret camps in the Troodos Mountains. Such allegations have been rejected by the Greek Cypriot authorities, however, and most observers thought it unlikely that such activities could be carried out clandestinely. Nonetheless, leaders of the Kurdish rebels had been received officially by members of the Cyprus House of

Representatives, and a former head of the National Guard had reportedly visited training camps for Kurdish guerrillas in Syria.

EOKA B became a factor of diminishing importance after its role in the coup of July 1974, although it continued to be involved in some violence against the Makarios government. Fears that the organization might conduct a terrorist campaign against Turkish occupation in the north never materialized. Many former EOKA B activists accepted an offer of amnesty from Makarios. However, several dozen of the most extreme leaders, including Nicos Sampson, were arrested and imprisoned. A law enacted in 1977 provided the basis for purging EOKA B members from the public service, the police, and the National Guard. In early 1978, the group announced its formal dissolution. During the 1980s, there was no further EOKA B activity, although veterans of the group came together periodically on patriotic occasions, as did other disbanded paramilitary groups. Sampson returned to Cyprus from exile in June 1990, but was immediately arrested by the Greek Cypriot police.

The danger of intercommunal violence was greatly reduced by the buffer provided by UNFICYP. It was feared initially that refugees from the north after the Turkish intervention in 1974 might resort to arms in an effort to regain lost houses and property. The rapid recovery of the economy in southern Cyprus, coupled with large amounts of international aid, enabled the refugees to be accommodated and absorbed by the community. Although permanent housing had by 1990 been provided for all of the refugees, many still wished to return to their homes; this desire was a source of emotion and tension, but not of significant violence.

Beginning in 1987, a series of demonstrations known as the Women's Walk Home were carried out by Greek Cypriot women trying to force their way into Turkish-controlled territory. For the most part, the women were turned back without casualties by UNFICYP and Turkish security personnel after entering the buffer zone and sometimes advancing a few meters into the Turkish-occupied north. The most serious incident occurred in July 1989, when about 1,000 women and religious leaders, some displaying Greek flags and spearheaded by a group of men who pushed aside barriers, crossed the buffer zone without interference from the Greek Cypriot police. More than 100 were arrested by Turkish Cypriot forces, and some women were injured in scuffling. The arrested women were released within a few days, but ten men, including two priests, were detained for ten days. In March 1990, five youths were sentenced to jail terms of up to three months for infiltrating Turkish Cypriot territory and attempting to pull down a Turkish flag. The Women's Walk Home was mainly an effort to bring

*Relatives demonstrating for information about the fate of the 1,600 Greek Cypriots missing in action since the summer of 1974
Courtesy Embassy of Cyprus, Washington*

pressure on the Greek Cypriot government to stand firm on issues of freedom of movement and settlement and compensation for property in the negotiations with the Turkish Cypriots. Nevertheless, it had the potential to provoke a confrontation of forces in the buffer area.

The spillover of terrorism from the Middle East injected additional tensions and violence unconnected to the conflict between the Greek- and Turkish-speaking communities. With its strategic location, Cyprus had increasingly been used as a transit point for the movement of individuals and arms as well as terrorist actions arising out of the fighting in Lebanon and the Arab-Israeli dispute. The presence of missions of Syria, Libya, and Israel and a liaison office of the Palestine Liberation Organization (PLO) all within close proximity in Nicosia complicated the efforts of the Greek Cypriot authorities to counter the security threat. With the curtailment of direct air service to Beirut, a relatively safe way of travel to war-torn Lebanon was by flying to Cyprus and then continuing by ferry. Helicopter flights also connected Cyprus with the beseiged Christian enclaves in Beirut, permitting the movement of personnel and arms. Palestinian terrorist groups regularly transited the island to other destinations, particularly to Eastern Europe. A weekly

223

flight of the Iranian airline linking Tehran with Cyprus also facilitated the movement of terrorists.

A number of international incidents involving Palestinians or Lebanese refugees occurred in the late 1980s. In 1985 three Israelis were murdered aboard their private yacht in Larnaca harbor by gunmen linked to the PLO. This action provoked a damaging raid six days later by the Israeli air force against the PLO headquarters in Tunisia. In 1988 seven PLO officials were killed in two car bombings in Cyprus, and a ship slated to carry Palestinian deportees to Israel was bombed at its dock in Limassol. The Abu Nidal terrorist organization, headquartered in Libya, was suspected in an attempt to bomb the Israeli Embassy; the bomb exploded some distance from the embassy, killing one of the terrorists and two Cypriots. In October 1989, six Lebanese were found guilty of possessing Soviet SAM-7 antiaircraft missiles with the intent of shooting down an airplane carrying the Lebanese dissident Christian leader, General Michel Aoun.

Other violence was linked to protests over the continued existence of British bases on the island and their use by the United States. In 1986 British service personnel and their dependents were targets of attacks by groups believed to be linked with Libya. The attacks were believed to be in retaliation against Britain for making its bases in England available for United States raids against Libya.

The Greek Cypriot communist party, known as the Progressive Party of the Working People (Anorthotikon Komma Ergazomenou Laou—AKEL), has campaigned vigorously against the bases and the use of them for United States intelligence-gathering. AKEL also proclaimed its opposition to what it regarded as the linkage of Cyprus to NATO through the bases, the presence of the United States Sixth Fleet in the Mediterranean, and United States "provocation" against Libya, all of which were perceived as threatening the peace and security of the region. Despite its adamant foreign policy, AKEL has never pursued a violent course in pressing its political demands nor has it been regarded as a security threat.

Armed Forces

By virtue of its strategic situation, Cyprus has been invaded, conquered, and colonized by foreign military powers that successively dominated the region. Since the second millennium B.C., the island has been occupied by the Phoenicians, Assyrians, Egyptians, Persians, Greeks, Romans, crusaders, Genoese, Venetians, and Ottoman Turks. It was employed by the Arabs as a base to launch warfare against Byzantium, and by the crusaders in their efforts to wrest the Holy Land from Muslims. The Turkish Cypriot community on Cyprus originated in the some 50,000 Turkish occupation forces and discharged soldiers who remained on the island after the defeat of the Venetians in 1571. Britain used Cyprus as a base in both world wars and as a staging ground for the attack on Suez in 1956.

Incapable of repelling the many foreign powers that have overrun the island, the Cypriot people have inherited little military tradition of their own. In the twentieth century, some 11,000 Cypriots fought as auxiliaries with the British Army during World War I, and about 30,000 Cypriots served in the Cyprus Regiment and other British units during World War II. But Cyprus itself was not the scene of fighting in either war, and Cypriot recruits were demobilized at the close of hostilities. After independence in 1960, Cyprus remained a neutral country and became a member of the Nonaligned Movement (NAM). It did not join any military alliance.

The intractability of the Cyprus problem nevertheless imposed on the island the presence of six separate military forces. As of the early 1990s, these forces included Turkish troops in the north, the Greek Army contingent in the south, the British in the two Sovereign Base Areas on the southern coast, and UNFICYP manning the buffer zone separating the two Cyprus communities. The indigenous Cypriot armed forces on the island consisted of the Greek Cypriot National Guard in the south and the Turkish Cypriot Security Force (Kıbrıs Türk Emniyet Kuvvetleri) in the north.

In reunification negotiations, the Greek Cypriot government proposed demilitarization as the way to remove both external and internal security threats. Specifically, the government foresaw the withdrawal of all non-Cypriot military forces, the disbanding of Cypriot military forces under a timetable to be drawn up in advance of establishing a new federal government, and a UN-controlled force to assist in internal security.

Turkish Cypriots, on the other hand, called for a "balance" between non-Cypriot and Cypriot forces on both sides of the island. Once a federal government was in place, non-Cypriot forces on both sides would be brought to the level needed for ensuring the fulfillment of guarantees.

Forces in the Government-Controlled Area

Under the provisions of the constitution of 1960, a 2,000-member bicommunal force, the Cyprus Army, composed of 60 percent Greek Cypriots and 40 percent Turkish Cypriots, was to be the primary security arm of the Republic of Cyprus. This force was never brought into being because of disagreement about its organization, and since 1964 the National Guard—composed mainly of Greek Cypriot draftees—had served as the main armed body in the southern part of the island. In addition, a Greek Army regiment of 950 men was present on the island in accordance with the terms of the Treaty of Alliance.

During the decade after its formation by Archbishop Makarios, the National Guard became increasingly oriented toward a pro-Greek junta, anticommunist, and, ironically, ultimately anti-Makarios position that culminated in the 1974 coup. The fall of the military from power in Greece led to the recall of the most avid right-wing Greek officers and their replacement by officers of more moderate views. By the late 1970s, the National Guard was no longer identified with any political faction and exercised no political influence. Although it had not been regarded by Western analysts as a very effective professional military force because of its earlier intense politicization, the National Guard performed credibly in 1974 in resisting the initial landing of overwhelmingly superior Turkish forces.

Although it had undertaken a major strengthening and modernization program in the late 1980s, the National Guard had only a limited ability to deter a major Turkish offensive or to mount counterattacks. According to a statement by Minister of Defense Andreas Aloneftis in 1990, the National Guard buildup was strictly defensive in purpose. Aloneftis acknowledged that the Greek Cypriots would like to ''liberate'' the land in the north but said this was impossible in light of existing realities. He said that he was seeking to build a reliable deterrent force against a Turkish effort to occupy the whole island. The objective, he asserted, was to be able to delay the Turkish advance for two to three weeks until the UN Security Council could intervene.

Personnel and Recruitment

According to *The Military Balance, 1989-90,* published by the International Institute for Strategic Studies in London, the National Guard had a complement of some 13,000 men on active duty in 1989. Scaled back from a peak of 35,000 in 1967, its size had remained fairly constant since the Turkish invasion in 1974. The bulk of its personnel were Greek Cypriot conscripts fulfilling twenty-six months of mandatory service.

The National Guard's officer corps had always consisted mainly of officers detailed to it from the Greek Army. In early 1990, an estimated 1,800 officers and noncommissioned officers (NCOs)

Soldiers of the National Guard
Courtesy Embassy of Cyprus, Washington

from the Greek Army were serving in the National Guard, compared with approximately 800 Greek Cypriot officers and NCOs. Greek officers dominated in senior positions; as of 1990, the National Guard's commander, deputy commander, and chief of staff were all Greek nationals. The senior Greek Cypriot officer was a divisional commander with the rank of brigadier general. Efforts were under way to increase the number of Greek Cypriots in the force. In early 1990, parliament approved the appointment of Greek Cypriots to an additional sixty-five officer and fifty NCO positions.

Young Cypriots wishing to make a career of military service attended the Greek military academy. National Guard officers also obtained their advanced training at Greek military institutions, where a designated number of places were set aside for them. In addition, training was provided in France in the use of the new French equipment being introduced into the National Guard. Some conscripts could become reserve officers after successfully completing a six-month course, then serving as second lieutenants for ten months of active duty. Greek officers assumed the primary responsibility for National Guard training at all levels.

Soldiers completing their active duty continued to serve in the reserves until age fifty, and officers served until age sixty-five. As of 1990, it was estimated that the National Guard could call upon

227

66,000 first-line reserves and more than 30,000 older second-line reserves (over age fifty). Selected reserve units were called up periodically without advance notice to test the mobilization system. A certain percentage of the reserves were mobilized annually to participate in a week of National Guard field exercises.

Uniforms, symbols of rank, and insignia of the National Guard were similar to those of the Greek Army. The color and cut of the uniforms was the same, although the design of the buttons, the device on caps, and the shield on epaulets incorporated an olive branch device corresponding to that found on the Cypriot flag and coat of arms. Fatigue uniforms were of camouflage cloth.

Few exemptions were granted from compulsory service. Exit permits from the island and the opportunity for higher education were not available until the service obligation was fulfilled. The annual call-up was in June, and discharges were granted in August to conform to the academic year. In spite of incentives, it proved difficult to induce qualified individuals to remain in military service, especially at the NCO level. Young men with skilled or semiskilled occupations could easily obtain well-paying jobs in the thriving civilian economy.

Under the influence of an energetic commanding officer, the training regime was intensified in the late 1980s. The morale of the National Guard was considered high, as a result of the more rigorous training program and the introduction of modern weapons systems. Draftee wages were low—about US$15 a month in the late 1980s—and were generally supplemented by help from families to meet personal expenses. Conscripts were often able to arrange postings near their homes. Career personnel were paid on a scale of remuneration that appeared adequate, especially at the officer level.

As of 1990, the first women had been recruited as volunteers into the National Guard, following a decision to accept female applicants for noncombatant positions. The minister of defense said in 1989 that conscription of women was being studied and might be introduced selectively.

In March 1989, Minister of Defense Aloneftis announced that a home guard to provide local defense and protect rear areas would be formed of men from the second-line reserves and other men who had been exempted from military service because of dependents. By late 1990, it was not clear what progress had been made in organizing the home guard, although about 3,000 men, including reservists, living in villages adjacent to the UN buffer zone had been recruited and trained to impede a Turkish attack. They were equipped with small arms and light antitank weapons.

Organization and Equipment

In 1990 the National Guard was commanded by Greek Lieutenant General Panayotis Markopoulos. He was responsible to the minister of defense and ultimately to President George Vassiliou. The National Guard was organized into an army headquarters, two divisional headquarters, and two brigade headquarters that would be filled out with combat units upon mobilization. Its largest active units consisted of two mechanized battalions, one armored battalion, an artillery battalion, and a commando battalion. Reserves were organized into six infantry brigades, each with three infantry battalions, one light artillery battalion, and one armored reconnaissance squadron. These units were maintained only at cadre strength. Greek Army forces were organized into one infantry battalion, one commando battalion, and a support element.

Foreign military observers considered the Greek Cypriot and Greek forces on the southern part of the island to be seriously deficient relative to the Turkish Army contingent in the north, notably with respect to armored strength. They also had little protection against aircraft based on the nearby Turkish mainland. During the 1974 fighting, the 200 Turkish tanks ferried to the island had proven the determining factor in the collapse of the Greek Cypriot defenses. The acquisition of armored equipment, antitank weapons, and antiaircraft systems by the National Guard in the late 1980s addressed the most conspicuous weaknesses in the National Guard's defensive armaments, but they still fell short of matching the Turkish forces in the north.

The National Guard's armor, which had previously consisted of a few Soviet T–34 tanks of World War II vintage and a small number of armored personnel carriers (APCs) and obsolete armored cars, was significantly augmented beginning in 1987, with the delivery of French AMX–30 B–2 tanks mounted with 105mm guns. The total order of fifty-four tanks was due to be in service by the early 1990s. A total of 127 French wheeled APCs had also been acquired; 27 were fitted with 20mm cannons and the rest with turret-mounted machineguns. Also on order were 120 EE–9 Cascavel six-wheeled armored vehicles from Brazil, equipped with 90mm guns, of which 40 had been delivered as of 1989. The EE–11 Urutu, a Brazilian APC, had been purchased and twenty-eight armored reconnaissance vehicles, the EE–3 Jararaca, also manufactured in Brazil, were on order. It was also reported that 500 vehicles, presumably unarmored, would be supplied by Greece as aid in 1990, as part of a longer-term plan to modernize 2,000 vehicles in the National Guard inventory (see table 23, Appendix).

The National Guard's artillery units were equipped with 75mm to 105mm guns and howitzers and truck-mounted 128mm multiple rocket launchers of Yugoslav manufacture. Antitank defenses had been stiffened by the purchase of Milan and HOT (high-subsonic, optically tracked) wire-guided missile systems from France. Some of the HOT missiles were fitted to armored vehicles and to six Gazelle helicopters acquired from France in 1988.

The air defense capability was strengthened in the late 1980s by the acquisition of triple 20mm cannons from Yugoslavia and twin 35mm towed antiaircraft guns from Switzerland, which were to be used in conjunction with the Contraves Skyguard fire-control radar system. The older 40mm and 94mm antiaircraft guns still in the inventory were considered virtually useless against modern fighter aircraft. The National Guard had also acquired from Syria a small number of Soviet SA-7 shoulder-fired surface-to-air missiles.

The National Guard air element as of 1989 included Gazelle helicopters and one Pilatus Maritime Defender suitable for coastal patrol and light transport duties. In mid-1989, the first of two Swiss Pilatus PC-9 turboprop aircraft was delivered. These planes were intended for advanced training but could be modified for combat missions. The National Guard Naval Command, with 330 personnel in 1989, had one coastal patrol craft of 95 tons mounting a 40mm gun.

According to press reports in spring 1990, the Greek Cypriot government had placed orders for additional Gazelle helicopters mounted with HOT missiles, more antiaircraft guns, medium-range antiaircraft missiles, and Leonidas armored vehicles from Greece.

Defense Spending

Defense costs were divided into two categories, budgetary spending and off-budget expenditures. The former were believed to include mainly the ongoing personnel and training expenditures of the National Guard, and the latter included capital expenditures, notably arms purchases. Off-budget expenditures were disbursed from a defense fund, the size of which was not disclosed. The defense fund was financed by a special defense levy on interest, dividends, rents, and company profits. This levy was raised from 2 to 3 percent effective July 1990, and was to be extended for three years until mid-1993. In addition, receipts from increased taxes on gasoline and cigarettes were to be deposited in the defense fund. Private companies and the Church of Cyprus, considered to be the wealthiest institution on the island, also contributed directly to the fund.

According to data published by the United States Arms Control and Disarmament Agency (ACDA), which included only regularly budgeted defense items, military spending had gradually tapered off, from US$42 million in 1981 to US$35 million in 1987. With inflation taken into account, the reduction was even more marked, from US$52 million in 1981 to US$35 million in 1987, in constant 1987 dollars. Budgeted defense spending constituted only 0.9 percent of the gross national product (GNP—see Glossary) in 1987 (down from 2.0 percent in 1981) and 2.9 percent of total central government expenditures (down from 7.0 percent in 1981). Budgeted military expenditures amounted to US$51 per capita annually.

Although total defense outlays were considered classified information, Aloneftis said in a 1990 interview that they would total US$325 million in 1990 and that similar amounts would be spent annually for the following three to five years. This amount was triple 1986 defense spending. According to Aloneftis, the arms buildup was being financed through supplier credits and loans from France, Greece, Italy, Singapore, Yugoslavia, and Switzerland. During the five-year period of 1983–87, total arms imports had been US$320 million, and most of these shipments had occurred in 1987, according to ACDA. France had been the dominant supplier (US$290 million), and most of the rest had come from Brazil.

Forces in the Turkish-Administered Area

In 1990 the dominant military force in the Turkish-administered northern sector of the island remained, as it had been since the Turkish invasion of 1974, the 28th and 39th infantry divisions of the Turkish Army, backed by an independent armored brigade and some artillery support. The 28th division was headquartered at Asha (Paşaköy) to the northeast of Nicosia, and the 39th division near Morphou (Güzelyurt). The corps reserve was at Kythrea (Değirmenlik) to the northeast of Nicosia. The Turkish contingent was referred to officially as the Cyprus Turkish Peace Force. The original force of 40,000 troops was reduced shortly after the 1974 invasion. In early 1990, Turkish defense authorities claimed that the Cyprus contingent amounted to only 17,500, whereas Greek Cypriot authorities placed its strength at 35,000. Independent sources believed that the force numbered about 30,000.

The Turkish detachments on Cyprus were part of the Turkish Aegean Army command structure, with headquarters at İzmir on the Turkish mainland. However, the commander of the Turkish troops reported directly to the Turkish General Staff in the capital, Ankara. The commander on Cyprus as of late 1989 was Lieutenant General Sabahattin Akinci. Although responsible for all security questions, Akinci was not directly involved in political matters of northern Cyprus. The principal missions of the Turkish Army contingent were to maintain the security of the Turkish Cypriot community, defend the borders established in 1974, protect against any Greek Cypriot guerrilla attacks or other cross-border actions, and assist in the training of members of the Turkish Cypriot armed force.

Details on the arms and equipment of the Turkish Army forces were not available, although they were known to include M–47 and M–48 tanks and M–113 APCs of United States origin, as well as 105mm, 155mm, and 203mm guns and howitzers. The forces were supplied with 40mm antiaircraft guns and, according to Greek sources, the Milan antitank missile. Turkey had supplemented its armored inventory in the late 1980s with M–48A5 tanks that had been upgraded and mounted with 105mm guns as part of a major modernization program throughout the Turkish Army. As of 1990, the Turkish forces on Cyprus were believed to have more than 200 converted M–48s and 100 of the original M–48s and M–47s. The Turkish forces were also equipped with light aircraft and Bell UH–1D helicopters, operating from a newly constructed airfield at Lefkoniko (Geçitkale). Small groups of combat jet aircraft of the Turkish Air Force occasionally appeared at the new field, but none were based there.

Even before independence, the Turkish Cypriot community had maintained its own paramilitary force (the TMT), trained and equipped by the Turkish Army contingent on the island. In 1967 this force were named the Mücahit (fighter), and in 1975 the Mücahit was renamed the Turkish Cypriot Security Force. As of 1989, the strength of this force was believed to be about 4,000. It was organized into seven infantry battalions armed with light weapons plus some artillery units equipped with mortars.

The Turkish Cypriot Security Force was commanded in 1989 by an officer of the Turkish Army, Brigadier General Bilgi Buyukunal, who had both operational and administrative responsibilities, as well as control over the police force. The commander was responsible to the prime minister of the self-proclaimed "Turkish Republic of Northern Cyprus" ("TRNC") through the minister of foreign affairs and defense, Kenan Atakol. A unified military-civilian defense staff of the ministry was responsible for defense policy and strategy. Although legally separate from the Turkish Army on the island, the Turkish Cypriot Security Force was believed to remain under the de facto operational control of the Turkish forces. It also depended on Turkey for training and equipment. Most of its officers were regular Turkish Army officers on secondment. Its announced budget for 1990 was US$3.9 million, an unusually small amount, representing only 1.5 percent of the total government budget. Observers believed that many of its expenses were absorbed by the Turkish Army.

Turkish Cypriot males were liable to conscription at age eighteen for a twenty-four-month period of service. Discharged soldiers served in the reserves until the age of fifty. The number of first-line and second-line reserves was estimated at 5,000 and 10,000, respectively, as of 1989.

British Forces on Cyprus

Under the provisions of the Treaty of Establishment, Britain retained perpetual sovereignty over two areas on the southern coast of Cyprus, totaling 256 square kilometers. A further fifteen reserved areas, including water sources and off-base radar sites, remained under British jurisdiction. Since 1960 the British Army and Royal Air Force (RAF) have garrisoned up to 10,000 troops in the Sovereign Base Areas at Akrotiri and Dhekelia. Formerly, two squadrons of bombers and their fighter escorts were based on Cyprus, but since the late 1970s the RAF has no longer stationed combat aircraft on the island.

With the decline of the British military presence in the Middle East, the bases have been used as training sites for RAF and ground force units and staging areas between Britain and southern Asia and the Far East. With permission from the Cyprus government, British troops also carried on extensive training outside the base area in the Troodos Mountains. The bases provided support for UN troops on Cyprus and workshops for maintenance of UN equipment. The most important role of the bases was electronic intelligence gathering and communications relay. Intercepts were made of aircraft, ship, and satellite communications from the eastern Mediterranean through the Middle East to Iran. Information so acquired was shared with the United States. Although the bases had no formal link to NATO, their presence in the primary area of operation of the Soviet naval squadron in the Mediterranean was of material value to the alliance.

The bases provided logistic support for peace-keeping missions by United States forces in the Middle East, including the Multinational Force sent to Lebanon in 1982. U–2 reconnaissance planes were based at Akrotiri beginning in the 1970s, to monitor the cease-fire in the Sinai. The United States also maintained Blackhawk helicopters there, which had flown support missions on behalf of the American Embassy in Beirut prior to its closure.

As of 1990, the British personnel strength of the Sovereign Base Areas was about 4,000, plus approximately the same number of dependents. The army units consisted of one infantry battalion plus two infantry companies and one armored reconnaissance squadron. The only permanent RAF unit was a squadron of five Wessex helicopters. The army had six Gazelle helicopters, which also served to support UNFICYP activities.

The British bases were a long-standing source of contention, although most Greek Cypriots as of 1990 accepted the presence of British forces. Military relations were very good, and British and Greek Cypriot authorities cooperated closely in antiterrorism matters. Almost all Greek Cypriot political parties agreed that Britain should eventually give up its rights on the island. The communist party, AKEL, was the most vocal in attacking the use of the bases for intelligence purposes and in calling for the British to relinquish the territory.

United Nations Peace-keeping Force in Cyprus

United Nations (UN) troops were present on Cyprus beginning with the breakdown of the constitutional arrangements in 1964. The original three-month UNFICYP mandate was extended, initially at three-month intervals and, after 1974, at six-month intervals. Any of the permanent members of the UN Security Council could veto its continuation, but none has ever done so. The Security Council repeatedly affirmed the original mandate and adopted a number of resolutions that required the force to perform additional or modified functions. The basic mandate called on UNFICYP to operate ''in the interest of preserving international peace and security, to use its best efforts to prevent a recurrence of fighting and, as necessary, to contribute to the maintenance and restoration of law and order and a return to normal conditions.''

The UNFICYP force level was maintained at about 4,500 from 1965 to 1968, and 3,500 from 1969 to 1972. Except for a temporary increase to 4,440 for a period after the 1974 fighting, its size gradually declined, reaching about 2,000 as of 1990.

Before 1974 UNFICYP troops were deployed throughout the island between Greek Cypriot and Turkish Cypriot defense positions. Frequently UN soldiers acted as mediators to prevent minor squabbles from leading to armed conflict. Only rarely was force, or even the threat of force, necessary in these efforts. In 1974, however, UNFICYP was unable to prevent either the attack against Makarios or the Turkish intervention (operations that, in any case, exceeded both its mandate and its military preparedness.) During the fighting, however, UN troops took up positions at Nicosia International Airport, preventing either side from capturing this strategic location. UNFICYP also played an essential role in the

234

United Nations troops manning an observation post
looking across the Mesaoria
Courtesy United Nations

exchange of prisoners. After the hostilities, all UN personnel moved back into the buffer zone between the Turkish and Greek Cypriot cease-fire lines.

Through a system of 146 observation posts, 54 of them permanently manned, and mobile and standing patrols, the buffer zone was kept under constant surveillance. A patrol and communications track running the entire length of the buffer zone was used for reconnaissance, monitoring of agricultural activities in the zone, resupply of observation posts, and rapid reaction to any incidents. Regular patrols were generally conducted in Land Rovers or similar vehicles. Armored scout cars formed a reserve, and British helicopters were also available if needed. In 1989 both sides accepted a UNFICYP proposal to dismantle their forward military positions in Nicosia and cease patrolling in three sensitive areas of the city to reduce the risk of incidents.

In April 1989, command of UNFICYP was assumed by Major General Clive Milner of Canada. The head of each national contingent in the UN force was directly responsible to the UNFICYP commander, as was the chief of staff, who oversaw the headquarters staff and the various support units. Each national contingent operated as a unit in prescribed areas in the buffer zone; only at headquarters did personnel from different nations work together on a daily basis. As of 1990, Britain provided 742 soldiers, Canada 575, Austria 410, and Denmark 342. The Irish, Finnish, and Swedish contingents had been reduced to token numbers in 1973, 1977, and 1988, respectively. The main British, Canadian, Austrian, and Danish units were organized as infantry battalions. All seven participating countries supplied military police and headquarters personnel. In addition, Britain furnished a nineteen-member scout car squadron and most of the UNFICYP support units. Austria and Sweden supplied the thirty-five-member civilian police contingent under UNFICYP control.

Each contingent wore the standard uniform of its home country, although UNFICYP personnel wore distinctive blue headgear, blue UN sleeve emblems, and a variety of UN-issued accessories. Each contingent rotated its troops every six months, although a small number of staff personnel undertook longer tours of duty. Salaries were based on those in each contingent's home country and were paid by the home countries. The cost of maintaining UNFICYP came to about US$26 million in 1989, including operational expenses, transport, pay, and allowances above what would have been incurred if contingents were serving at home, and salaries and travel of nonmilitary personnel. Funds for these expenses depended entirely on voluntary contributions by UN member states. These contributions, however, had never been sufficient. Reimbursement claims of troop-contributing countries had been met only to June 1980. The accumulated deficit was nearly US$175 million by the close of 1989.

UNFICYP personnel functioned in several capacities in addition to monitoring the cease-fire lines. They provided security for farmers from both Cypriot communities who lived and worked within the buffer zone. They visited Turkish Cypriots in the south and Greek Cypriots in the north to ensure their safety and welfare, and arranged temporary visits and reunions of relatives. UNFICYP commanders held meetings with commanders of the National Guard and of the Turkish forces as required, and meetings were held with both sides at the chief-of-staff level at regular intervals. The civilian police contingent of UNFICYP functioned as a liaison between the two communities' police forces and maintained law and order in the buffer zone.

Police

The police system, like the armed forces, was split along communal lines. The 1960 constitution called for two police organizations: an urban police force, to be commanded by a Greek Cypriot, and a rural police force, or gendarmerie, to be commanded by a Turkish Cypriot. The constitutional system broke down after the Christmas crisis of 1963, and each community subsequently provided its own police. The Turkish Cypriot police was originally an arm of the paramilitary TMT; after 1974 it operated under the Turkish Cypriot Security Force, within the Ministry of Foreign Affairs and Defense and the Ministry of Interior of the Turkish Cypriot administration in the north. New legislation in 1984 redefined its structure, but it continued to be accountable to the commander of the Turkish Cypriot Security Force.

The Cyprus Police Force, in contrast, was a force organizationally and operationally separate from the National Guard, within the Ministry of Interior of the Republic of Cyprus. After 1963 the police of the government of Cyprus assumed no responsibility for the Turkish Cypriot community (in 1973 the force of over 3,000 contained only one Turkish Cypriot), so that the de facto partition of the island after 1974 meant only a reduction in the amount of territory for which the police were responsible. The Greek Cypriot police force rose in strength from 2,550 in 1969 to 3,500 in 1978, and to 3,700 in 1989.

Organization of the Greek Cypriot Police

The chief of the Cyprus Police Force was responsible to the

minister of interior. He was aided by a deputy chief and, below him, two assistant chiefs, who supervised activities at police headquarters. Headquarters consisted of four departments: administration; traffic; criminal investigation; and planning, training, and public relations. Beneath headquarters in the chain of command stood seven division chiefs, each of whom supervised a police district; beneath them were station chiefs. Directly under the national headquarters were five special units: the Police Training School, the Aliens and Immigration Service, the Fire Service, the Cyprus Information Service, and the Mobile Immediate Action Units. The latter two services, although administratively responsible to the chief of police, were operationally controlled elsewhere. The Cyprus Information Service, a small intelligence unit concerned with both security matters and common crime, received its directions from the president of the republic. The Mobile Immediate Action Units, a reincarnation of the Tactical Police Reserve of the early 1970s, were elite forces trained to protect high-ranking officials and foreign embassies and to provide special weapons assault teams in the event of terrorist attacks. The units' training and operational control were in the hands of the National Guard, and their commander was an officer of the National Guard.

Personnel needs of the police were met through recruitment of career officers from the Greek Cypriot population. Unlike the National Guard, the police force contained no mainland Greeks. New recruits attended a twenty-one-week course at the Police Training School in Athalassa, southeast of Nicosia. A few high-ranking officers received training in Britain, Greece, and other countries.

The police force was armed beyond the requirements of ordinary police work; its arsenal included armored cars and light artillery acquired in the 1960s, when the police played a central role in the intercommunal struggle. In 1989 orders were placed for the purchase of a helicopter with sophisticated surveillance equipment and two coastal patrol boats, as part of stepped-up antinarcotics operations.

Turkish Cypriot Police Organization

Regulations published in 1986 under Law Number 51 of 1984 on Police Organization (Establishment, Functions, and Authorities) of the Turkish Republic of Northern Cyprus defined the area of jurisdiction of the police force of northern Cyprus. The Police Organization was divided into two major components, the central and provincial organizations. The director general of police, the most senior officer of the Police Organization, was responsible to the commander of the Turkish Cypriot Security Force with regard

*Portion of the Green Line,
the line dividing Nicosia
Courtesy Embassy of Cyprus,
Washington*

to planning, coordination, and supervision of police services. Under the immediate control of the director general's deputy were nine central police directorates: administrative; judicial police; political police; air, sea, and ports police; traffic; the fire service; police school; immigration; and indigenous affairs. Two special units, the Mobile Unit for Immediate Action and the narcotics squad, were directly accountable to the director general.

The Judicial Police Directorate assisted provincial police organizations in criminal investigations and carried out its own judicial investigations in matters of special interest to the director general. Its branches included photographic identification and fingerprinting; criminal records; firearms registration; ballistics laboratories; and a bomb squad. The Political Police Directorate included departments of domestic and foreign intelligence. The directorate tried to gain advance knowledge of actions or plans that could affect internal security and carried out measures for dealing with them. Provincial political police departments were directly subordinate to the central directorate, gathering information on threatened offenses or incidents against the security of the state and other duties as assigned by the director of political police. The combined staffing of the central political police organization and the five provincial organizations was set at 107 individuals.

Separate provincial police directorates were established at Nicosia, Famagusta (Gazimağusa), Kyrenia (Girne), Morphou, and the

Karpas Peninsula. Under the supervision of each provincial directorate were three or four regional directorates and six to twelve
police stations. The provincial police directorates also had six service
units: administration, judicial police, traffic, immigration, fire, and
administrative and indigenous affairs.

Crime and Punishment
Incidence of Crime

Somewhat paradoxically, in light of the violence of the nation's
past, statistics of the Republic of Cyprus pointed to a crime rate
that was lower (6.44 crimes per 1,000 inhabitants) than the rate
for most West European countries. The low incidence of crime
among Cypriot nationals was accounted for by the closeness of family ties, the emphasis on upholding the family's honor and reputation, and the social pressures for education and achievement.
According to statistics submitted to the International Criminal
Police Organization (INTERPOL) for the year 1988, various forms
of theft constituted by far the largest number of serious offenses
(2,592). Only fourteen murders, eighteen sex offenses, and seventy-
seven serious assaults were recorded. There were 528 cases of fraud
and 48 drug offenses. Juveniles accounted for 13.6 percent of thefts
and women for 6.7 percent. Corresponding data on crime in the
Turkish Cypriot-administered north were not available.

The domestic use of illegal drugs was low compared with the
situation elsewhere in the eastern Mediterranean and Europe,
although the minister of interior testified in parliament in October
1989 that the problem was growing. Cyprus was not a source of
narcotics but was an important brokering center for narcotics
traffickers, especially those from Lebanon and Turkey. Traffickers met in Cyprus, forwarded shipments of heroin and cannabis
through the island's container transshipment facilities, and used
Cypriot air links to transship currency and bullion to and from
Europe. Narcotics laws were rigidly enforced, and draft legislation to provide stricter penalties for possession and trafficking in
illegal drugs was under discussion in early 1990. Cypriot police
cooperated closely with law enforcement authorities in neighboring countries, resulting in significant seizures and arrests. There
were, however, no direct working relations with Turkish Cypriot
enforcement authorities or with Turkey. According to Turkish
sources, northern Cyprus had also become a transit point for drugs,
and there were indications of major drug-processing activities.

In 1989 a total of 134 arrests were recorded by the Republic of
Cyprus for drug offenses; 72 were of Cypriot nationals and 62 of

foreigners. The number of arrests had mounted steadily since 1986, when 26 Cypriots and 29 foreigners were arrested.

The Criminal Justice System

The courts exercising criminal jurisdiction in the Republic of Cyprus were district courts, assize courts, and the Supreme Court in its appellate functions. District courts served as the courts of first instance for all but the most serious crimes; their jurisdiction was over any crime with a penalty of up to three years' imprisonment, a fine of up to C£500 (Cyprus pound—for value, see Glossary), or both. Assize courts had unlimited jurisdiction in the first instance but in practice heard only a small percentage of the cases coming before the district courts. The Supreme Court heard all criminal appeals but had no original jurisdiction in criminal matters. There were no special courts to deal with security or political offenses, and civilians were not subject to trial by military courts.

The court system in the Turkish-administered area was similar to that of the Republic of Cyprus. In district courts, a judge sitting alone had jurisdiction to try summarily all offenses punishable by imprisonment not exceeding three years. Assize courts, composed of three judges, had jurisdiction to try offenses punishable with more than three years imprisonment. The Supreme Court dealt with criminal appeals from assize courts and district courts, but did not exercise initial jurisdiction in criminal matters except when, sitting as the Supreme Council of Judicature, it might try the president for treason or the prime minister and other ministers for charges preferred by the Legislative Assembly.

District courts of the Republic of Cyprus sat permanently, consisted of one judge each, and conducted exclusively summary trials held immediately after preliminary inquiries. Assize courts met three times a year in each judicial district and were each composed of three judges chosen from the district court. Assize courts heard preliminary inquiries, or trials of information, after which the accused could be discharged or bound over for trial. Trial procedure was based on English common law and was identical in both courts: the charge was read, the accused entered a plea, the prosecution presented witnesses and evidence, the defense presented its case, closing statements were made, and the verdict and sentence were handed down. Cases were generally tried before judges, although a request for a jury trial was usually granted.

Within ten days of the pronouncement of sentence, the accused could appeal any case involving a sentence of imprisonment or a fine over C£20. The accused could appeal either a conviction or a sentence; the prosecutor could also appeal a sentence or, from a district court, a judgment. All appeals went to the Supreme Court and had to be heard by at least three of its seven members. The Supreme Court had wide latitude in its appeal findings: it could increase, decrease, or modify a sentence; it could acquit or convict in overruling a lower court; or it could remand a case to the lower court for retrial.

Defendants had the right to be present at their trials, to be represented by counsel, to be provided with a public defender if unable to afford a lawyer, to confront witnesses, and to present evidence in their own defense. According to the *Country Reports on Human Rights Practices* published annually by the United States Department of State, freedom from arbitrary arrest and detention was provided by law and respected in practice by both the Government of Cyprus and the Turkish Cypriot authorities. Preventive detention was not legally authorized and was not reported in practice. Under the Greek Cypriot system, no one could be held for more than one day for investigation of a crime without referral of the case to the courts for extension. Most periods of investigative detention did not exceed eight or ten days before formal charges were filed. Attorneys had free access to detainees.

Punishments allowed by law included death by hanging, imprisonment up to life, whipping, and fines. Criminal punishments as actually implemented were light. The death penalty, which could be handed down for premeditated murder, high treason, piracy, and certain capital offenses under military law, was in practice commuted by the president of the republic. The punishment of whipping was not imposed in practice. The few long prison sentences handed down by Greek Cypriot courts were usually shortened by pardons or parole actions. The vast majority of punishments for criminal convictions were in the form of fines.

Prisoners in the Republic of Cyprus were housed in the Nicosia Central Prison. The prison population was very low. In 1990, of 260 inmates, 65 were aliens. Thus, although foreigners constituted only 1 percent of the population, they accounted for 25 percent of the prisoners. Most of these were Middle Easterners convicted of drug trafficking.

Both the Cyprus constitution and the basic document governing the Turkish Cypriot community specifically prohibited torture. In both communities, freedom from cruel, unhuman, or degrading treatment was provided by law and respected in practice. Adequate health care was provided in detention facilities, and diets were considered normal. Family members were permitted monthly visits after conviction, and attorneys could visit at any time.

*   *   *

The Republic of Cyprus and the Turkish Cypriot authorities release few details on the size, equipment, organization, and deployment of troops at their disposal. Their public statements tend to minimize the strength of their own forces and to exaggerate the strength of the other side. Estimates in the foregoing section rely primarily on data found in *The Military Balance, 1989-1990* published by the International Institute for Strategic Studies, supplemented by reports in *Jane's Defence Weekly*. The article on Cyprus by Gwynne Dyer in *World Armies* (1983 edition) provides additional particulars on the National Guard and other military contingents, although its information on Turkish and Turkish Cypriot forces is limited. An interview with Defense Minister Aloneftis, reported by Mary Anne Weaver in the *New Yorker*, reveals numerous details on the defense preparations of the Greek Cypriot forces as of 1990. A study by Keith Kyle on Cyprus, published by the Minority Rights Group in London, is a concise but balanced review of politico-military events through 1984. The international strategic dimensions of the Cyprus dispute are analyzed by Robert McDonald in *The Problem of Cyprus* in the Adelphi Papers series. The role of the United Nations Peace-keeping Force in Cyprus (UNFICYP) during its quarter century of peace-keeping is treated by Alan James in ''The UN Force in Cyprus'' in the journal *International Affairs*. (For further information and complete citations, see Bibliography.)

Appendix

Table 1. Metric Conversion Coefficients and Factors

When you know	Multiply by	To find
Millimeters	0.04	inches
Centimeters	0.39	inches
Meters	3.3	feet
Kilometers	0.62	miles
Hectares (10,000 m²)	2.47	acres
Square kilometers	0.39	square miles
Cubic meters	35.3	cubic feet
Liters	0.26	gallons
Kilograms	2.2	pounds
Metric tons	0.98	long tons
....	1.1	short tons
....	2,204	pounds
Degrees Celsius	9	degrees Fahrenheit
(Centigrade)	divide by 5 and add 32	

Table 2. Selected Turkish Cypriot Place-Names

Turkish Form	International Standard Form
Boğaz	Boghaz
Değirmenlik	Kythrea
Gazimağusa	Famagusta
Geçitkale	Lefkoniko
Girne	Kyrenia
Güzelyurt	Morphou
Koruçam	Kormakiti
Lapta	Lapithos
Lefke	Lefka
Lefkoşa	Nicosia
Paşaköy	Asha

Table 3. *Republic of Cyprus: Parliamentary Election Results, 1976–85*

Party	1976 Seats	1976 Percentages of Votes	1981 Seats	1981 Percentages of Votes	1985 Seats	1985 Percentages of Votes
AKEL [1]	9	69.5 [2]	12	32.8	15	27.4
DIKO [3]	21	— [2]	8	19.5	16	27.7
DISY [4]	0	24.1	12	31.9	19	33.6
EDEK [5]	4	— [2]	3	8.2	6	11.1
Other	1	n.a.	0	n.a.	0	n.a.

n.a.—not available

[1] Anorthotikon Komma Ergazomenou Laou (Progressive Party of the Working People).
[2] AKEL, DIKO, and EDEK formed an electoral coalition in 1976 against DISY.
[3] Dimokratiko Komma (Democratic Party).
[4] Dimokratikos Synagermos (Democratic Rally).
[5] Eniea Dimokratiki Enosis Kyprou (United Democratic Union of Cyprus).

Table 4. *"Turkish Republic of Northern Cyprus": Parliamentary Election Results, 1976–90*

Party	1976 Seats	1976 Percentages of Votes	1981 Seats	1981 Percentages of Votes	1985 Seats	1985 Percentages of Votes	1990 Seats	1990 Percentages of Votes
CTP [1]	2	5	6	15	12	21	7	44 [2]
TKP [3]	6	15	13	29	10	16	5	— [2]
UBP [4]	30	75	18	43	24	37	34	55
YDP [5]	— [6]	— [6]	— [6]	— [6]	4	9	2	— [2]
Other	2	5	3	14	0	7	0	1
TOTAL [7] .	40	100	40	100	50	100	5	100

[1] Cumhuriyetçi Türk Partisi (Republican Turkish Party).
[2] CTP, TKP, and YDP formed an electoral alliance in 1990 against UBP.
[3] Toplumcu Kurtuluş Partisi (Communal Liberation Party).
[4] Ulusal Birlik Partisi (National Unity Party).
[5] Yeni Doğuş Partisi (New Dawn Party).
[6] YDP was not established until 1984.
[7] Figures may not add to total because of rounding.

Table 5. Population of Cyprus, Selected Years, 1491–1973

Year	Population
1491	168,000
1575	180,000
1881	186,200
1891	209,300
1901	237,000
1911	274,100
1921	310,700
1931	348,000
1946	450,100
1960	573,600
1973 *	631,800

* De Jure census.

Source: Based on information from L.W. St. John-Jones, *The Population of Cyprus,* Hounslow, Middlesex, United Kingdom, 1983, 33; and Republic of Cyprus, Ministry
of Finance, Department of Statistics and Research, *Statistical Abstract, 1987 and 1988,*
Nos. 33–34, Nicosia, 1989, 33.

Table 6. Population of Cyprus, Selected Years, 1975–88

Year	Entire Island	Area Controlled by Republic of Cyprus
1975	618,000	498,300
1978	616,000	501,300
1980	627,000	513,300
1982	640,000	524,600
1984	657,000	538,400
1986	673,000	550,900
1988	688,000	562,700

Source: Based on information from Republic of Cyprus, Ministry of Finance, Department
of Statistics and Research, *Statistical Abstract, 1987 and 1988,* Nos. 33–34, Nicosia,
1989, 41, 45.

Table 7. Turkish Cypriot Population, Selected Dates,
Sixteenth Century to 1988

Date	Population *
Sixteenth century	40,000 to 60,000
Eighteenth century	60,000
1881	45,458
1911	56,428
1921	61,339
1931	64,245
1946	80,548
1960	104,333
1963	120,000
1972	78,000
1978	146,740
1982	152,239
1986	162,676
1988	167,256

* Figures through 1960 are based on Ottoman and British estimates and censuses. Figures thereafter are provided by Turkish Cypriot authorities.

Table 8. Republic of Cyprus: Schools, Teachers, and
Enrollments, Selected School Years, 1975–76 to 1988–89

	1975–76	1980–81	1984–85	1988–89
Preprimary schools				
Schools	96	259	374	497
Teachers	222	418	592	826
Enrollment	4,229	10,397	15,607	20,280
Primary schools				
Schools	400	443	396	382
Teachers	2,093	2,183	2,193	2,689
Enrollment	56,554	48,701	47,381	58,706
Secondary schools				
Schools	80	91	105	105
Teachers	2,364	2,910	3,126	3,439
Enrollment	49,373	47,599	48,752	42,613
Vocational and technical schools				
Schools	8	13	15	24
Teachers	78	191	250	430
Enrollment	769	1,940	2,580	5,065

Source: Based on information from Republic of Cyprus, Ministry of Finance, Department of Statistics and Research, *Statistical Abstract, 1987 and 1988,* Nos. 33–34, Nicosia, 1989, 87.

Table 9. "Turkish Republic of Northern Cyprus": Schools, Teachers, and Enrollments, 1976–77 and 1988–89

	1976–77	1988–89
Preprimary schools		
Schools	24	82
Teachers	37	100
Enrollment	1,095	2,658
Elementary schools		
Schools	120	158
Teachers	608	770
Enrollment	18,220	17,963
Junior high schools		
Schools	22	24
Teachers	344	545
Enrollment	6,895	11,898
Senior high schools		
Schools	10	13
Teachers	183	303
Enrollment	3,667	3,965
Vocational and technical schools		
Schools	9	10
Teachers	246	235
Enrollment	1,160	1,788
Higher education		
Schools	1	4
Teachers	7	n.a.
Enrollment	120	3,885

n.a.—not available.

Table 10. *Republic of Cyprus: Distribution of Gross Domestic Product by Sector (GDP), Selected Years, 1979–88* (in percentages at current market prices)

Sector	1979	1982	1985	1986	1987	1988 *
Agriculture, forestry, and fishing	10.7	9.6	7.8	7.6	7.8	7.7
Mining and quarrying	1.6	0.9	0.5	0.5	0.4	0.4
Manufacturing	18.3	17.6	16.4	15.7	16.0	16.3
Electricity, gas, and water ...	1.3	1.7	2.3	2.3	2.2	2.2
Construction	13.4	11.7	10.5	10.1	10.0	9.9
Wholesale and retail trade, restaurants, and hotels	16.0	16.7	19.6	19.8	20.3	20.8
Transportation, storage, and telecommunications ...	8.1	8.6	9.8	10.2	9.8	9.4
Finance, insurance, real estate, and business services	15.2	15.5	14.7	15.0	14.8	14.5
Community, social, and personal services	3.4	3.8	4.8	5.1	5.3	5.5
Public administration and defense	6.7	7.9	7.7	7.8	7.6	7.5
Public services	4.9	5.6	5.3	5.3	5.2	5.2
Other	0.4	0.4	0.6	0.6	0.6	0.6
TOTAL	100.0	100.0	100.0	100.0	100.0	100.0

* Provisional.

Source: Based on information from Republic of Cyprus, Ministry of Finance, *Economic Report, 1987,* Nicosia, May 1989, 60.

Table 11. *Republic of Cyprus: Gainfully Employed Population by Sector, Selected Years, 1976–87*
(in percentages)

Sector	1976	1979	1982	1985	1986	1987
Agriculture, forestry, and fishing	25.2	20.7	18.4	16.7	16.1	15.8
Mining and quarrying	1.6	1.0	0.6	0.5	0.5	0.4
Manufacturing (including cottage industries)	19.4	21.1	21.5	20.6	19.9	20.1
Electricity, gas, and water ...	0.9	0.8	0.8	0.7	0.6	0.6
Construction	7.3	11.5	10.3	9.8	9.9	9.8
Wholesale and retail trade, restaurants, and hotels	16.7	17.4	19.6	21.7	22.1	22.3
Transportation, storage, and telecommunications	5.7	5.0	5.4	5.8	5.8	6.0
Finance, insurance, real estate, and business services	4.2	4.3	4.6	5.1	5.4	5.5
Community, social, and personal services	3.3	4.7	5.8	6.9	7.2	7.2
Public administration and defense	7.6	6.6	6.4	5.9	6.1	6.0
Public services	7.2	6.0	5.6	5.4	5.4	5.3
Other	0.9	0.9	1.0	0.9	1.0	1.0
TOTAL	100.0	100.0	100.0	100.0	100.0	100.0

Source: Based on information from Republic of Cyprus, Ministry of Finance, *Economic Report, 1987,* Nicosia, May 1989, 126.

Table 12. *Republic of Cyprus: Production and Value of Principal Agricultural Products, Selected Years, 1979–87*

Products	1979 Quantity [1]	1979 Value [2]	1982 Quantity [1]	1982 Value [2]	1985 Quantity [1]	1985 Value [2]	1986 Quantity [1]	1986 Value [2]	1987 Quantity [1]	1987 Value [2]
Cereals										
Wheat	13.2	1,082	10.2	1,120	9.0	1,089	6.5	787	13.5	1,688
Barley	64.0	4,788	81.3	7,808	102.8	10,907	61.0	6,466	112.0	12,320
Vegetables										
Potatoes	172.7	12,648	171.7	20,821	128.0	10,074	172.0	16,512	150.0	22,500
Carrots	8.8	713	9.6	541	5.7	551	6.3	517	5.0	500
Tomatoes	21.8	2,475	22.9	3,420	23.0	4,478	25.0	4,750	28.0	6,692
Cucumbers	13.0	1,541	9.7	1,900	10.5	2,156	10.0	2,240	12.0	2,916
Fruits and tree crops										
Grapes	203.2	11,840	201.2	15,466	210.0	16,687	151.0	12,657	173.0	14,796
Oranges	36.0	2,542	43.2	3,264	45.5	4,778	40.0	3,360	51.0	4,437
Lemons	16.7	1,519	24.9	2,332	28.5	3,420	32.0	2,912	30.0	2,640
Melons	30.0	1,532	26.2	2,100	39.4	5,661	36.5	4,280	34.8	4,034
Grapefruit	47.0	2,067	56.0	2,909	51.8	4,040	55.0	3,740	64.2	4,301
Apples	9.3	1,197	8.6	1,462	7.0	2,993	6.5	2,828	7.5	3,135
Pears	1.8	289	2.1	445	1.5	596	1.4	605	0.8	467
Peaches	2.0	364	1.6	486	1.2	544	1.0	547	0.6	478
Cherries	1.6	385	1.5	498	1.0	671	1.2	588	0.8	756
Bananas	4.4	732	6.6	1,274	9.0	1,678	10.0	1,720	11.0	1,793
Almonds	2.4	864	1.9	570	1.6	731	3.0	1,650	1.4	882
Olives	10.7	3,780	13.2	5,720	11.5	7,845	12.0	8,60	48.0	6,000
Carobs	18.5	888	12.8	1,038	7.6	931	25.0	3,275	7.0	861
Livestock products										
Beef	1.8	1,800	2.0	2,916	2.8	3,575	3.6	4,248	4.1	4,879
Sheep and goat meat	5.5	6,325	5.6	10,178	7.4	12,613	7.8	13,725	9.0	14,999

Table 12. Continued

Products	1979 Quantity [1]	1979 Value [2]	1982 Quantity [1]	1982 Value [2]	1985 Quantity [1]	1985 Value [2]	1986 Quantity [1]	1986 Value [2]	1987 Quantity [1]	1987 Value [2]
Livestock products—*Continued*										
Pork	15.6	6,930	19.6	11,001	23.6	12,036	23.2	13,108	25.3	13,409
Poultry	10.0	5,410	11.3	7,548	12.6	9,036	14.2	10,224	13.5	9,788
Milk	66.0	8,152	83.9	12,691	107.4	16,585	112.5	16,345	118.2	17,001

[1] In thousands of tons.
[2] In thousands of Cyprus pounds (for value of the Cyprus pound—see Glossary).

Source: Based on information from Republic of Cyprus, Ministry of Finance, *Economic Report, 1987*, Nicosia, May 1989, 142.

Table 13. *Republic of Cyprus: Exports, 1985–88*
(in millions of Cyprus pounds)[1]

Product	1985	1986	1987	1988
Agricultural products				
Citrus	18.3	14.1	15.5	13.8
Carobs	1.3	1.7	1.5	1.9
Potatoes	10.4	20.2	22.2	16.2
Vegetables	4.3	3.4	3.6	3.2
Grapes	5.9	5.5	4.8	4.9
Other	9.1	7.0	10.0	7.5
Total agricultural products	49.3	51.9	57.6	47.5
Manufactured products				
Wine and alcoholic beverages	9.0	4.8	4.3	5.2
Paper products	7.4	3.2	4.0	3.4
Clothing	49.7	41.0	68.6	74.6
Footwear	16.7	14.4	16.0	16.4
Cement	1.3	3.5	4.7	5.9
Cigarettes	4.8	2.3	6.2	7.7
Chemicals and toiletries	9.5	7.7	8.1	18.1
Machinery and transportation equipment	13.0	7.5	7.8	11.3
Leather and travel goods	5.0	4.1	4.5	5.0
Processed fruit	4.5	8.9	9.3	9.1
Wood and metal manufactures	5.4	3.8	5.8	5.6
Other	16.6	18.2	18.8	17.4
Total manufactured products	142.9	119.4	158.1	179.7
Minerals [2]	6.6	5.2	5.8	4.8
Other	0.5	0.6	0.8	n.a.
TOTAL	199.3	177.1	222.3	232.0

n.a.—not available.

[1] For value of the Cyprus pound—see Glossary.

[2] Includes quarrying materials.

Source: Based on information from Republic of Cyprus, Central Bank of Cyprus, *Annual Report, 1988,* Nicosia, May 1989, 39.

Table 14. Republic of Cyprus: Value of Gross
Domestic Product (GDP) by Sector, Selected Years, 1979–88
(in millions of Cyprus pounds at current market prices) [1]

Sector	1979	1982	1985	1986	1987	1988 [2]
Agriculture, forestry, and						
fishing	64.5	95.0	111.0	117.3	132.3	144.2
Mining and quarrying ...	9.5	8.8	7.1	7.5	6.7	6.9
Manufacturing	110.8	174.5	231.9	240.5	273.9	306.5
Electricity, gas, and						
water	7.8	17.5	33.3	35.2	37.0	41.1
Construction	81.1	115.5	148.6	156.5	170.0	186.8
Wholesale and retail						
trade, restaurants, and						
hotels	96.4	165.8	277.0	303.9	346.4	391.9
Transportation, storage,						
and telecommuni-						
cations	48.7	84.6	138.3	155.9	168.0	178.0
Finance, insurance, real						
estate, and business						
services	92.0	153.5	207.7	229.7	252.0	272.3
Community, social, and						
personal services	21.0	37.7	68.4	78.9	90.1	103.3
Public administration and						
defense	40.4	77.9	108.8	119.4	129.8	141.6
Public services	29.5	55.9	74.9	81.8	89.2	97.6
Other	2.4	4.2	8.1	9.1	9.8	11.3
TOTAL	604.1	990.9	1,415.1	1,535.7	1,705.2	1,881.5

[1] For value of the Cyprus pound—see Glossary.
[2] Provisional.

Source: Based on information from Republic of Cyprus, Ministry of Finance, *Economic Report,*
    1987, Nicosia, May 1989, 57.

Table 15. Republic of Cyprus: Annual Increase of Gross
Domestic Product (GDP) by Sector, Selected Years, 1979–88
(in percentages)

Sector	1979	1982	1985	1986	1987	1988 *
Agriculture, forestry, and fishing ..	16.6	17.1	-7.2	5.7	12.8	9.0
Mining and quarrying	9.2	-10.2	-11.3	5.6	-10.7	3.0
Manufacturing	19.7	13.2	7.8	3.7	13.9	11.9
Electricity, gas, and water	9.9	19.0	18.9	5.7	5.1	11.1
Construction	36.3	9.8	8.5	5.3	8.6	9.9
Wholesale and retail trade, restaurants, and hotels	29.7	20.6	19.6	9.7	14.0	13.1
Transportation, storage, and telecommunications	16.8	17.5	14.7	12.7	7.8	6.0
Finance, insurance, real estate, and business services	23.5	14.5	10.0	10.6	9.7	8.1
Community, social, and personal services	25.7	16.0	20.4	15.4	14.2	14.7
Public administration and defense .	27.8	19.8	10.3	9.7	8.7	9.1
Public services	26.6	27.9	10.1	9.2	9.0	9.4
Other	26.3	13.5	5.2	12.3	7.7	15.3
GDP	24.0	16.1	10.6	8.5	11.0	10.3

* Provisional.

Source: Based on information from Republic of Cyprus, Ministry of Finance, *Economic Report, 1987*, Nicosia, May 1989, 59.

Table 16. Republic of Cyprus: Balance of Payments, 1985–88
(in millions of Cyprus pounds) [1]

	1985	1986	1987	1988 [2]
Exports (f.o.b.) [3]	255.4	234.0	272.5	301.2
Imports (f.o.b.)	687.2 [4]	-591.5 [5]	-638.3 [6]	-777.8
Trade balance	-431.8	-357.5	-365.8	-476.6
Invisibles receipts	583.8	601.6	689.2	790.2
Invisibles payments	-249.2	-245.6	-274.2	-307.4
Invisibles balance	334.6	356.0	415.0	482.8
Current account balance	-97.2	-1.5	49.2	6.2
Short-term capital	-3.0	-3.2	-4.0	5.0
Long-term loans	30.1	64.8	-6.5	-5.6 [7]
Other private long-term capital	35.5	24.0	25.0	29.0
Capital account balance	62.6	85.6	14.5	28.4
Errors and omissions	17.5	-18.1	-53.9	-38.9
Overall balance	-17.1	66.0	9.8	-4.3

[1] For value of the Cyprus pound—see Glossary.
[2] Provisional.
[3] f.o.b.—free on board.
[4] Includes aircraft valued at C£228.6 million.
[5] Includes pipes for Southern Conveyor Project valued at C£218.8 million.
[6] Includes pipes for Southern Conveyor Project valued at C£21.8 million.
[7] Includes loan prepayments by government amounting to C£244.0 million.

Source: Based on information from Central Bank of Cyprus, *Annual Report, 1988*, Nicosia, May 1989, 46.

Table 17. "Turkish Republic of Northern Cyprus": Value of Gross Domestic Product (GDP) by Sector, Selected Years, 1977–90 (in millions of Turkish lira at 1977 value) *

Sector	1977	1980	1985	1988	1989	1990
Agriculture, forestry, and fishing	619.3	779.3	801.0	726.7	709.1	639.7
Manufacturing, mining, electricity, and water	365.1	612.7	510.8	700.1	912.2	947.3
Construction	153.0	135.7	263.8	465.6	501.3	506.5
Wholesale and retail trade, restaurants, and hotels	801.0	770.9	957.3	1,087.4	1,207.0	1,334.1
Transportation and telecommunications .	257.4	285.0	474.5	694.6	753.8	791.8
Financial institutions .	115.4	150.1	217.5	266.3	287.5	310.0
Ownership of dwellings	355.3	324.9	337.5	360.3	369.4	377.3
Business and personal services	128.1	152.3	169.4	214.2	235.7	259.3
Government services .	752.7	894.6	1,115.0	1,197.8	1,227.7	1,278.1
Import duties	228.2	87.6	151.5	286.1	312.1	491.7
TOTAL	3,775.5	4,193.1	4,998.3	5,999.1	6,515.9	6,935.8

* For value of the Turkish lira—see Glossary.

Source: Based on information from "Turkish Republic of Northern Cyprus," State Planning Organisation.

Table 18. "Turkish Republic of Northern Cyprus": Distribution of Gross Domestic Product (GDP) by Sector, Selected Years, 1977–90 (in percentages)

Sector	1977	1980	1985	1988	1989	1990
Agriculture, forestry, and fishing	16.4	18.6	16.0	12.1	10.9	9.2
Manufacturing, mining, electricity, and water	9.7	14.6	10.2	11.7	14.0	13.7
Construction	4.1	3.2	5.3	7.8	7.7	7.3
Wholesale and retail trade, restaurants, and hotels	21.2	18.4	19.2	18.1	18.5	19.2
Transportation and telecommunications	6.8	6.8	9.5	11.6	11.6	11.4
Financial institutions	3.1	3.6	4.4	4.4	4.4	4.4
Ownership of dwellings	9.4	7.7	6.8	6.0	5.6	5.4
Business and personal services ..	3.4	3.6	3.4	3.5	3.6	3.7
Government services	19.9	21.3	22.3	19.9	18.8	18.4
Import duties	6.0	2.1	3.0	4.8	4.8	7.1
TOTAL *	100.0	100.0	100.0	100.0	100.0	100.0

* Figures may not add to total because of rounding.

Source: Based on information from "Turkish Republic of Northern Cyprus," State Planning Organisation.

Table 19. *"Turkish Republic of Northern Cyprus":*
Gainfully Employed Population by Sector, 1986–89
(in percentages)

Sector	1986	1987	1988	1989 *
Agriculture, forestry, and fishing	31.4	29.9	28.9	27.8
Manufacturing, mining, electricity, and water	10.3	10.4	10.5	11.4
Construction	9.0	10.2	10.4	10.4
Wholesale and retail trade, restaurants, and hotels .	8.9	9.1	9.2	9.4
Transportation and telecommunications	7.2	7.2	7.7	7.9
Financial institutions	2.5	2.5	2.6	2.6
Business and personal services	7.8	7.9	8.1	8.5
Government services (including state economic enterprises)	22.9	22.8	22.6	22.0
TOTAL	100.0	100.0	100.0	100.0

* Provisional.

Source: Based on information from Center for Business and Economic Research of the
Eastern Mediterranean University and Cyprus Turkish-German Cultural Association, *Structural Changes in the Economy of North Cyprus,* Famagusta, Cyprus, 1990.

Table 20. *"Turkish Republic of Northern Cyprus": Balance of*
Payments, 1987–90
(in millons of United States dollars)

	1987	1988	1989	1990
Exports	55.1	52.4	55.2	65.5
Imports	221.0	–218.1	–262.5	–381.5
Trade balance	–165.9	–165.7	–207.3	–316.0
Tourism (net)	103.5	118.0	154.9	224.8
Other invisibles (net)	41.7	38.9	47.9	74.8
Invisibles balance	145.2	156.9	202.8	299.6
Current account balance	–20.7	–8.8	–4.5	–16.4
Turkish aid and credit	35.5	10.9	15.6	22.5
Other foreign aid	8.3	5.8	4.3	2.1
Financing of imports by waiver as against official allocation	63.9	61.9	103.9	169.9
Other short-term capital	–63.9	–40.4	–87.7	–169.3
Net capital movements	43.8	38.2	36.1	25.2
Overall balance	23.1	29.4	31.6	8.8

Source: Based on information from "Turkish Republic of Northern Cyprus," State Planning Organisation.

Table 21. *"Turkish Republic of Northern Cyprus": Major Trading Partners, Selected Years, 1982–90* (in millions of United States dollars)

Country or Region	1982		1985		1987		1989		1990	
	Imports	Exports	Imports	Exports	Imports	Exports	Imports	Exports	Imports	Exports
Turkey	49.5	7.3	65.1	5.4	94.3	7.9	112.5	9.2	153.5	7.9
Britain	25.9	25.9	27.5	31.2	31.4	36.7	49.6	35.2	67.1	44.0
Other members of European Community ...	24.6	0.5	25.4	3.9	40.3	4.7	45.1	5.0	64.0	7.0
Middle East	0.1	5.4	0.8	4.5	3.2	3.6	4.2	3.4	6.4	1.6
Other	19.8	0.4	24.2	1.3	51.8	2.2	51.1	2.4	90.5	5.0
TOTAL	119.9	39.5	143.0	46.3	221.0	55.1	262.5	55.2	381.5	65.5

Source: Based on information from "Turkish Republic of North Cyprus," State Planning Organisation.

Table 22. Selected Newspapers, 1990

Newspaper	Political Stance	Circulation
Greek Cypriot		
Agon	center-right	9,000
Apogevmatini	centrist	10,000
Cyprus Mail	center-right	4,000
Eleftheria Tis Gnomis	–do–	2,000
Eleftherotypia	DIKO party organ [1]	6,500
Haravghi	AKEL party organ [2]	13,000
Phileleftheros	centrist	20,000
Proina Nea	EDEK party organ [3]	1,200
Simerini	supports DISY [4]	13,000
Turkish Cypriot		
Birlik	UBP party organ [5]	4,500
Cyprus Times	centrist	n.a.
Halkın Sesi	–do–	6,000
Kıbrıs	center-right	4,000
Kıbrıs Postası	center-left	4,500
Ortam	TKP party organ [6]	1,250
Yenidüzen	CTP party organ [7]	1,000

n.a.—not available.

[1] DIKO—Dimokratiko Komma (Democratic Party).
[2] AKEL—Anorthotikon Komma Ergazomenou Laou (Progressive Party of the Working People).
[3] EDEK—Eniea Dimokratiki Enosis Kyprou (United Democratic Union of Cyprus).
[4] DISY—Dimokratikos Synagermos (Democratic Rally).
[5] UBP—Ulusal Birlik Partisi (National Unity Party).
[6] TKP—Toplumcu Kurtuluş Partisi (Communal Liberation Party).
[7] CTP—Cumhuriyetçi Türk Partisi (Republican Turkish Party).

Source: Based on information from *Europa World Year Book, 1991,* 1, London, 1991, 848–49; and *Political Handbook of the World, 1991,* Binghamton, New York, 1991, 169, 171.

Table 23. Republic of Cyprus: Major National Guard Equipment, 1990

Type and Description	Country of Origin	Inventory
Tanks		
AMX-30 B-2	France	30 of 54 ordered
Armored reconnaissance vehicles		
EE-9 Cascavel	Brazil	40
Marmon-Harrington armored cars	Britain	24
Armored infantry fighting vehicles		
VAB-VCI, 20mm cannon	France	27
Armored personnel carriers		
Leonidas	Greece	16
VAB-VTT	France	100
EE-11 Urutu	Brazil	15
BTR-50P	Soviet Union	17
Towed artillery		
M-116A1, 75mm	United States	4
M-42, 76mm	Soviet Union	18
25 pounder	Britain	52
M-1944, 100mm	Soviet Union	18
M-101, 105mm	United States	18
M-56, 105mm	Soviet Union	18
Mortars		
81mm, some self-propelled	n.a.	71
M-41/43, 82mm, some self-propelled	Soviet Union	n.a.
M-2, 107mm	United States	12
Multiple rocket launchers		
Yug M-77, 128mm	Yugoslavia	8
Recoilless rifles		
M-18, 57mm	United States	189
M-40, 106mm	–do–	126
Antitank guided weapons		
Milan	France	n.a.
HOT	–do–	n.a.
Air defense weapons		
M-55, 20mm gun	Yugoslavia	100
Oerlikon GDF-003 35mm gun	Switzerland	8
40mm, 94mm gun	n.a.	n.a.
SA-7 surface-to-air missile	Soviet Union	20
Aircraft		
SA-342 Gazelle helicopters	France	6
Pilatus PC-9 trainer	Switzerland	1
Pilatus BN-2A Maritime Defender	Britain	1
Ships		
Coastal patrol boat, 95 tons, 40mm gun	–do–	1

n.a.—not available.

Source: Based on information from *The Military Balance, 1989–1990,* London, 1989, 85; and Christopher F. Foss, "Cypriot Rearmament Completed," *Jane's Defence Weekly* [London], March 12, 1988, 445.

Bibliography

Chapter 1

Adams, T.W. *AKEL: The Communist Party of Cyprus.* (Hoover Institution Studies, No. 27.) Stanford: Hoover Institution Press, 1971.

Adams, Thomas W., and Alvin J. Cottrell. *Cyprus Between East and West.* (Studies in International Affairs, No. 7.) Baltimore: Johns Hopkins Press, 1968.

Alastos, Doros. *Cyprus in History, 2.* London: Zeno, 1976.

Attalides, Michael A. *Cyprus: Nationalism and International Politics.* New York: St. Martin's Press, 1979.

Bahcheli, Tozun. *Greek-Turkish Relations since 1955.* Boulder, Colorado: Westview Press, 1990.

Ball, George W. *The Past Has Another Pattern.* New York: Norton, 1982.

Battle, Lucius D., and Dennis P. Williams. *Cyprus: Two Decades of Crisis.* (Middle East Problem Paper No. 16.) Washington: Middle East Institute, 1976.

Birand, Mehmet Ali. *30 Hot Days.* London: K. Rüstem and Brother, 1985.

Bitsios, Dimitri S. *Cyprus: The Vulnerable Republic.* Salonika: Institute for Balkan Studies, 1975.

Clerides, Glafkos. *Cyprus: My Deposition.* (3 vols.) Nicosia: Alithia, 1989–90.

Coufoudakis, Van (ed.). *Essays on the Cyprus Conflict.* New York: Pella, 1976.

Crawshaw, Nancy. *The Cyprus Revolt.* London: George Allen and Unwin, 1978.

Crouzet, François. *Le Conflit de Chypre, 1946–1959.* (2 vols.) Brussels: Etablissements Émile Bruylant, 1973.

Denktash [Denktaş], Rauf R. *The Cyprus Triangle.* London: K. Rüstem and Brother, 1982.

Durrell, Lawrence. *Bitter Lemons.* New York: Dutton, 1957.

Edbury, Peter W. *The Kingdom of Cyprus and the Crusades, 1191–1374.* Cambridge: Cambridge University Press, 1991.

Eden, Anthony. *Full Circle.* London: Cassel, 1960.

Ehrlich, Thomas. *Cyprus, 1958–1967.* (International Crises and the Role of Law.) London: Oxford University Press, 1974.

Ertekün, N.M. *The Cyprus Dispute and the Birth of the Turkish Republic of Northern Cyprus.* Oxford: K. Rüstem and Brother, 1984.

265

Foley, Charles. *Legacy of Strife.* Baltimore: Penguin Books, 1964.

Foley, Charles, and W.I. Scobie. *The Struggle for Cyprus.* Stanford: Hoover Institution Press, 1975.

Foot, Hugh. *A Start in Freedom.* London: Hodder and Stoughton, 1964.

Hart, Parker T. *Two NATO Allies at the Threshold of War: Cyprus— A Firsthand Account of Crisis Management, 1965-1968.* (Duke Press Policy Studies.) Durham, North Carolina: Duke University Press, 1990.

Hill, George. *History of Cyprus.* (4 vols.) London: Cambridge University Press, 1940-1952.

Hitchens, Christopher. *Cyprus.* London: Quartet Books, 1984.

Hunt, David (ed.). *Footprints in Cyprus: An Illustrated History.* London: Trigraph, 1982.

Joseph, Joseph S. *Cyprus: Ethnic Conflict and International Concern.* (American University Studies, Series X; Political Science, No. 6.) New York: Peter Land, 1985.

Karageorghis, Vassos. *The Ancient Civilization of Cyprus.* New York: Cowles Education, 1969.

Kelling, George Horton. *Countdown to Rebellion: British Policy in Cyprus, 1939-1955.* (Contributions in Comparative Colonial Studies, No. 27.) New York: Greenwood Press, 1990.

Koumoulides, John T.A. (ed.). *Greece and Cyprus in History.* Amsterdam: Adolf M. Hakkert, 1985.

Maier, Franz Georg. *Cyprus: From the Earliest Times to the Present Day.* London: Elek Books, 1968.

Markides, Kyriacos C. *The Rise and Fall of the Cyprus Republic.* New Haven: Yale University Press, 1977.

Mayes, Stanley. *Makarios: A Biography.* New York: St. Martin's Press, 1981.

Necatigil, Zaim M. *The Cyprus Question and the Turkish Position in International Law.* Oxford: Oxford University Press, 1989.

Oberling, Pierre. *The Road to Bellapais: The Turkish Cypriot Exodus to Northern Cyprus.* (East European Monographs, No. 125.) Boulder, Colorado: Social Science Monographs, 1982.

Panteli, Stavros. *A New History of Cyprus: From the Earliest Times to the Present Day.* London: East-West, 1984.

Patrick, Richard A. *Political Geography and the Cyprus Conflict: 1963-1971.* (Department of Geography Publication Series, No. 4.) Waterloo, Canada: Department of Geography, University of Waterloo, 1976.

Peltenburg, Edgar (ed.). *Early Society in Cyprus.* Edinburgh: Edinburgh University Press, 1989.

Polyviou, Polyvios G. *Cyprus: Conflict and Negotiation, 1960–1980.* New York: Holmes and Meier, 1980.

———. *Cyprus: The Tragedy and the Challenge.* Washington: American Hellenic Institute, 1975.

Purcell, H.D. *Cyprus.* New York: Praeger, 1969.

Reddaway, John. *Burdened with Cyprus: The British Connection.* London: Weidenfeld and Nicolson, 1986.

Salih, Halil Ibrahim. *Cyprus: An Analysis of Cypriot Political Discord.* Brooklyn: T. Gaus' Sons, 1968.

Stavrinides, Zenon. *The Cyprus Conflict: National Identity and Statehood.* Nicosia: Stavrinides, 1976.

Stern, Laurence. *The Wrong Horse: The Politics of Intervention and the Failure of American Diplomacy.* New York: New York Times Books, 1977.

Tzermias, Pavlos. *Geschichte der Republik Zypern: Mit Berücksichtigung der historischen Entwicklung der Insel während der Jahrtausende.* Tübingen, Germany: Franke Verlag, 1991.

Urquhart, Brian. *A Life in Peace and War.* New York: Harper and Row, 1987.

Vanezis, P.N. *Makarios: Pragmatism versus Idealism.* London: Abelard-Schuman, 1974.

Woodhouse, Christopher Montague. *The Rise and Fall of the Greek Colonels.* London: Granada, 1985.

Xydis, Stephen G. *Cyprus: Reluctant Republic.* The Hague: Mouton, 1973.

Chapter 2

Anthias, Floya. "Cyprus." Pages 184–200 in Colin Clarke and Tony Payne (eds.), *Politics, Security and Development in Small States.* London: Allen and Unwin, 1987.

———. "Women and Nationalism in Cyprus." Pages 150–67 in Nira Yuval-Davis and Floya Anthias (eds.), *Woman—Nation—State.* New York: St. Martin's Press, 1989.

Anthias, Floya, and Ron Ayres. "Ethnicity and Class in Cyprus," *Race and Class* [London], 25, No. 1, 1983, 59–76.

Attalides, Michael A. *Cyprus: Nationalism and International Politics.* New York: St. Martin's Press, 1979.

———. *Social Change and Urbanization in Cyprus: A Study of Nicosia.* (Publications of the Social Research Center, No. 2.) Nicosia: Zavallis Press, 1981.

———. "The Turkish Cypriots: Their Relations to the Greek Cypriots in Perspective." Pages 71–100 in Michael A. Attalides (ed.), *Cyprus Reviewed.* Nicosia: Jus Cypri Association, 1977.

Beckingham, Charles Fraser. "The Cypriot Turks," *Journal of the Royal Central Asian Society* [London], 43, No. 2, 1956, 126-30.

Christodoulides, Andreas D. "Family and Youth in Cyprus," *Cyprus Review* [Nicosia], 2, No. 1, Spring 1990, 61-96.

Coufoudakis, Van. "The Dynamics of Political Partition and Division in Multiethnic and Multireligious Societies—The Cyprus Case." Pages 27-49 in Van Coufoudakis (ed.), *Essays on the Cyprus Conflict.* New York: Pella, 1976.

Cyprus. Ministry of Finance. Department of Statistics and Research. *Demographic Report, 1988.* (Population Statistics: Series No. 2, Report No. 26.) Nicosia: Printing Office of the Republic of Cyprus, 1989.

_____. Ministry of Finance. Department of Statistics and Research. *Statistical Abstract, 1987 and 1988.* (General Statistics: Series No. 1, Report Nos. 33-34.) Nicosia: Printing Office of the Republic of Cyprus, 1989.

Demetriades, E.I. "Cyprus." Pages 217-23 in T. Neville Postlethwaite (ed.), *The Encyclopedia of Comparative Education and National Systems of Education.* Oxford: Pergamon Press, 1988.

_____. "Cyprus: A System of Education." Pages 1275-81 in T. Neville Postlethwaite and Torsten Husen (eds.), *The International Encyclopedia of Education,* 2. Oxford: Pergamon Press, 1985.

Deveci, Hasan. *Cyprus, Yesterday, and Today—What Next?* London: Cyprus Turkish Association, 1976.

Diamantides, N. D., and S. T. Constantinou. "Modeling the Macrodynamics of International Migration: Determinants of Emigration from Cyprus, 1946-85," *Environment and Planning* [London], 21, No. 7, July 1989, 927-50.

Doob, Leonard. "Cypriot Patriotism and Nationalism," *Journal of Conflict Resolution,* 30, No. 2, June 1986, 383-96.

Durrell, Lawrence. *Bitter Lemons.* New York: Dutton, 1957.

Hadjipavlou-Trigeorgis, Maria. "Cyprus and Lebanon: A Historical Comparative Study in Ethnic Conflict and Outside Interference," *Cyprus Review* [Nicosia], 2, No. 1, Spring 1990, 97-129.

House, William J. *Cypriot Women in the Labor Market.* (Women, Work and Development, No. 10.) Geneva: International Labor Office, 1985.

_____. *Population, Employment Planning, and Labour Force Mobility in Cyprus.* Nicosia: Cyprus, Ministry of Finance, Department of Statistics and Research, Printing Office of the Republic of Cyprus, 1982.

_____. *Present Status and Future Prospects of Older Workers in Cyprus.* Nicosia: Cyprus, Ministry of Finance, Department of Statistics and Research, Printing Office of the Republic of Cyprus, 1987.

House, William J., Dora Kyriakides, and Olympia Stylianou. *The Changing Status of Female Workers in Cyprus*. Nicosia: Cyprus, Ministry of Finance, Department of Statistics and Research, Printing Office of the Republic of Cyprus, 1987.

Ioannou, Yiannis E. "Language, Politics, and Identity: An Analysis of the Cypriot Dilemma," *Cyprus Review* [Nicosia], 3, No. 1, Spring 1991, 15–41.

Ismail, Sabahattin. *1974 Öncesi–1974 Sonras* (Before 1974–After 1974). Istanbul: Kaştaş Press, 1989.

Karoulla-Vrikkis, Dimitra. "The Language of the Greek Cypriots Today: A Revelation of an Identity Crisis?" *Cyprus Review* [Nicosia], 3, No. 1, Spring 1991, 42–58.

King, Russell, and Sarah Ladbury. "The Cultural Reconstruction of Political Reality: Greek and Turkish Cyprus since 1974," *Anthropological Quarterly*, 55, No. 1, January 1982, 1–16.

Kitromilides, Paschalis M. "From Coexistence to Confrontation: The Dynamics of Ethnic Conflict in Cyprus." Pages 35–70 in Michael A. Attalides (ed.), *Cyprus Reviewed*. Nicosia: Jus Cypri Association, 1977.

Kourvetaris, George A. "Greek and Turkish Interethnic Conflict and Polarization in Cyprus," *Journal of Political and Military Sociology*, 16, No. 2, Fall 1988, 185–99.

Loizos, Peter. *The Greek Gift: Politics in a Cypriot Village*. Oxford: Blackwell, 1975.

_____. *The Heart Grown Bitter: A Chronicle of War Refugees*. Cambridge: Cambridge University Press, 1981.

_____. "Intercommunal Killing in Cyprus," *Man* [London], New Series, 23, No. 4, December 1988, 639–65.

_____. "The Progress of Greek Nationalism in Cyprus, 1878–1970." Pages 114–33 in J. Davis (ed.), *Choice and Change: Essays in Honour of Lucy Mair*. (London School of Economics, Monographs on Social Anthropology, No. 50.) London: Athlone Press, 1974.

_____. "Violence and the Family: Some Mediterranean Examples." Pages 183–96 in J.P. Martin (ed.), *Violence and the Family*. Chichester, West Sussex, Britain: Wiley and Sons, 1978.

Manizade, Derviş. *Kıbrıs: Dün Bugün Yarın* (Cyprus: Yesterday, Today, Tomorrow). Istanbul: Yaylacık Matbaası, 1975.

Markides, Kyriacos C. *The Rise and Fall of the Cyprus Republic*. New Haven: Yale University Press, 1977.

Markides, Kyriacos C., and Steven F. Cohn. "External Conflict/Internal Cohesion: A Reevaluation of an Old Theory," *American Sociological Review*, 47, No. 1, February 1982, 88–98.

Markides, Kyriacos C., Eleni S. Nikita, and Elengo N. Rangou. *Lysi: Social Change in a Cypriot Village*. (Publications of the Social Research Center, No. 1.) Nicosia: Zavallis Press, 1978.

Massialas, Byron G. "Cyprus." Pages 275–90 in George Thomas Kurian (ed.), *World Education Encyclopedia,* 1. New York: Facts on File, 1988.

Moseley, L.G. (ed.). *Research for Social Welfare: Six Case Studies in Cyprus.* London: Bedford Square Press of the National Council of Social Service, 1979.

Mumcu, Uğur. *Rabıta* (Connections). Istanbul: Tekin Yayınevi, 1987.

Necatigil, Zaim M. *Our Republic in Perspective.* Nicosia: Tezel Offset and Printing, 1985.

Oberling, Pierre. *The Road to Bellapais: The Turkish Cypriot Exodus to Northern Cyprus.* (East European Monographs, No. 125.) Boulder, Colorado: Social Science Monographs, 1982.

Pollis, Adamantia. "International Factors and the Failure of Political Integration in Cyprus." Pages 44–83 in Stephanie G. Neuman (ed.), *Small States and Segmented Societies: National Political Integration in a Global Environment.* New York: Praeger, 1976.

Roussou, Maria. "War in Cyprus: Patriarchy and the Penelope Myth." Pages 25–44 in Rosemary Ridd and Helen Callaway (eds.), *Women and Political Conflict.* New York: New York University Press, 1987.

Rüstem, K. (ed.). "Turkish Republic of North Cyprus." *North Cyprus Almanack.* London: K. Rüstem and Brother, 1987.

St. John-Jones, L. W. *The Population of Cyprus: Demographic Trends and Socioeconomic Influences.* Hounslow, Middlesex: Publishers for the Institute of Commonwealth Studies by M. Templeton Smith, 1983.

Salih, Halil Ibrahim. *Cyprus: The Impact of Diverse Nationalism on a State.* University, Alabama: University of Alabama Press, 1978.

Sant Cassia, Paul. "Patterns of Covert Politics in Post-Independence Cyprus," *Archives Européennes de Sociologie* [Paris], 24, No. 1, 1983, 115–35.

_____. "Religion, Politics and Ethnicity in Cyprus During the Turkocratia (1571–1878)," *Archives Européennes de Sociologie* [Paris], 27, No. 1, 1986, 3–28.

Sparsis, Mikis. *Attila in Cyprus.* Nicosia: "Proodos," 1986.

Stamatakis, Nikos A. "History and Nationalism: The Cultural Reconstruction of Modern Greek Cypriot Identity," *Cyprus Review* [Nicosia], 3, No. 1, Spring 1991, 59–87.

Tenzel, James H., and Marvin Gerst. "The Psychology of Cross-Cultural Conflict: A Case Study. (The Psychocultural Aspects of a Conflict.)" (Paper prepared for the 125th Annual Meeting of the American Psychiatric Association, Dallas, May 1, 1972.)

"Turkish Republic of Northern Cyprus." State Planning Organisation. *Economic and Social Developments in the Turkish Republic of Northern Cyprus.* Nicosia: 1987.

_____. State Planning Organisation. Statistics and Research Department. *Statistical Yearbook, 1986.* Nicosia: 1987.

_____. State Planning Organisation. Statistics and Research Department. *Statistical Yearbook, 1987.* Nicosia: 1988.

_____. State Planning Organisation. Statistics and Research Department. *Statistical Yearbook, 1988.* Nicosia: 1989.

United Nations. Secretariat. *Report of the Secretary General on Voluntary Movement of Populations.* (S/11789.) New York: September 13, 1975.

Volkan, Vamik. "The Birds of Cyprus: A Psychopolitical Observation," *American Journal of Psychotherapy,* 26, No. 3, 1972, 378–83.

_____. "Cyprus: Ethnic Conflicts and Tensions," *International Journal of Group Tensions,* 19, No. 4, Winter 1989, 297–316.

_____. "Externalization among Cypriot Turks," *World Journal of Psychosynthesis,* 5, No. 3, March 1973, 24–30.

_____. *The Need to Have Enemies and Allies.* Northvale, New Jersey: Aronson, 1988.

_____. *War and Adaptation: A Psychoanalytic History of Two Ethnic Groups in Conflict.* Charlottesville: University Press of Virginia, 1979.

Walker, Anita M. "Enosis in Cyprus: Dhali, A Case Study," *Middle East Journal,* 38, No. 3, Summer 1984, 474–94.

Worsley, Peter. "Communalism and Nationalism in Small Countries: The Case of Cyprus." Pages 9–24 in Peter Worsley (ed.), *Small States in the Modern World: Conditions of Survival.* Manchester: University of Manchester, 1976.

Yesilada, Birol. "Social Progress and Political Development in the Turkish Republic of Northern Cyprus." *Cyprus Review* [Nicosia], 1, No. 2, Fall 1989, 90–113.

Zetter, Roger. "Rehousing the Greek-Cypriot Refugees from 1974: Dependency, Assimilation, Politicisation." Pages 106–25 in John T.A. Koumoulides (ed.), *Cyprus in Transition: 1960–1985.* London: Trigraph, 1986.

(Various issues of the following publication were also used in the preparation of this chapter: *Kuzey Kibris* [Nicosia].)

Chapter 3

Andronikou, Antonios. *Development of Tourism in Cyprus, Harmonization of Tourism with the Environment.* Nicosia: Cosmos, 1987.

"Bakanlar Kurulu Kararlarve 1990 Yılı Program" (The Decision of the Cabinet Ministers and the 1990 Program), *Resmi Gazete* [Nicosia], October 1, 1989.

Center for Business and Economic Research of the Eastern Mediterranean University and Cyprus Turkish-German Cultural Association. *Structural Changes in the Economy of North Cyprus.* Famagusta, Cyprus: 1990.

Central Bank of Cyprus. *Annual Report, 1988.* Nicosia: 1989.

_____. *Annual Report, 1989.* Nicosia: 1990.

_____. *Bulletin,* 103. Nicosia: 1989.

_____. *A Centre for International Business.* Nicosia: 1989.

_____. "Developments in the Cyprus Economy During 1988 and Prospects for 1989." (Research paper.) Nicosia: 1989.

_____. *Eight Speeches on Business Opportunities.* Nicosia: 1989.

_____. *A Guide for Foreign Investors.* Nicosia: 1989.

_____. *A Guide to Shipping.* Nicosia: 1990.

_____. *The Republic of Cyprus.* Nicosia: 1989.

Christodoulou, C.A. "Optimizing Limited Resources: Cyprus' Southern Conveyor Water Development Project." Pages 27–44 in Adel Salman (ed.), *Agriculture in the Middle East: Challenges and Possibilities.* New York: Paragon House, 1990.

Coufoudakis, Van (ed.). *Essays on the Cyprus Conflict.* New York: Pella, 1976.

Cyprus. Electricity Authority. *Annual Report, 1988.* Nicosia: 1989.

_____. Ministry of Finance. *Economic Report, 1970.* Nicosia: Printing Office of the Republic of Cyprus, 1971.

_____. Ministry of Finance. *Economic Report* (Annuals 1977 through 1987). Nicosia: Printing Office of the Republic of Cyprus, 1979 through 1989.

_____. Official Gazette of the Republic. *Main Provisions of the Cyprus—E.E.C. Customs Union Agreement.* Nicosia: Press and Information Office, 1987.

_____. Press and Information Office. *Cyprus: EC Relations.* Nicosia: 1989.

_____. Press and Information Office. *Cyprus: Republic of Cyprus— 30 Years, 1960–1990.* Nicosia: 1990.

_____. Press and Information Office. *The Cyprus Economy in 1988 and Prospects for the Immediate Future.* Nicosia: 1989.

_____. Press and Information Office. *Offshore Enterprise.* Nicosia: 1989.

_____. Press and Information Office. *President George Vassiliou on Fiscal Policy.* Nicosia: November 3, 1988.

_____. Telecommunications Authority. *Annual Report, 1988.* Nicosia: 1989.

_____. Tourism Organisation. *Annual Report, 1986.* Nicosia: 1987.

Cyprus Development Bank. *Consumption Expenditures in Cyprus: An Empirical Analysis.* Nicosia: 1988.

_____. *The Cyprus Economy: Forecasts for 1988–1990.* Nicosia: September 1988.

_____. *Economic and Business Profile of Cyprus.* Nicosia: April 1989.

Economist Intelligence Unit. *Country Profile: Lebanon, Cyprus, 1986–87.* London: 1986.

_____. *Country Profile: Lebanon, Cyprus, 1987–88.* London: 1987.

_____. *Country Profile: Lebanon, Cyprus, 1988–89.* London: 1988.

_____. *Country Profile: Lebanon, Cyprus, 1989–90.* London: 1989.

_____. *Country Profile: Lebanon, Cyprus, 1990–91.* London: 1990.

_____. *Country Profile: Lebanon, Cyprus, 1991–92.* London: 1991.

The Europa World Year Book, 1989, 1. London: Europa, 1989.

The Europa World Year Book, 1990, 1. London: Europa, 1990.

The Europa World Year Book, 1991, 1. London: Europa, 1991.

Fadil, Magda Abu. "A Bit of Britain in the Med," *Middle East* [London], No. 182, December 1989, 18–19.

Federal Republic of Germany. Statistisches Bundesamt. *Länderbericht Zypern, 1986.* Wiesbaden, 1986.

"Focus on Cyprus," *World Development* [Oxford], 1, No. 9, September 1973, 69–79.

Henderson, Celia. *Cyprus: The Country and Its People.* London: Queen Ann, 1968.

Hudson, John, and Marina Dymiotou-Jensen. *Modelling a Developing Country: A Case Study of Cyprus.* Aldershot, Hampshire, United Kingdom: Avebury, 1989.

Ismail, Sabahattin. *1974 Öncesi–1974 Sonras* (Before 1974–After 1974). Istanbul: Kaştaş, 1989.

Kamanardies, John S. *The Cyprus Economy: A Case in the Industrialization Process.* Nicosia: Socrates, 1973.

Karouzis, George. *Land Ownership in Cyprus, Past, and Present, with Special Reference to Greek and Turkish Ownerships.* Nicosia: Strabo, 1977.

Kondonassis, Alex J. "The European Economic Community in the Mediterranean: Developments and Prospects on a Mediterranean Policy." (Research Papers, No. 4.) Athens: Center of Planning and Economic Research, 1976.

Lavender, David. *The Story of Cyprus Mines Corporation.* Huntington Library: San Marino, California, 1962.

Leontiades, Leontios. "Developing Forestry under Middle East Conditions: The Cyprus Experience." Pages 335–50 in Adel Salman (ed.), *Agriculture in the Middle East: Challenges and Possibilities.* New York: Paragon House, 1990.

The Middle East and North Africa, 1990. London: Europa, 1991.

The Middle East and North Africa, 1991. London: Europa, 1991.

Rüstem, K. (ed.). "Turkish Republic of North Cyprus." *North Cyprus Almanack.* London: K. Rüstem and Brother, 1987.

The Stateman's Yearbook, 1989-90. (Ed., John Paxton.) New York: St. Martin's Press, 1989.

The Stateman's Yearbook, 1990-91. (Ed., John Paxton.) New York: St. Martin's Press, 1990.

The Stateman's Yearbook, 1991-92. (Ed., Brian Hunter.) New York: St. Martin's Press, 1991.

Syrimis, G. "Address Before the House of Representatives on the Occasion of the Debate on the Budgets for 1989." Nicosia: Press and Information Office, December 8, 1988.

_____. "Address Before the House of Representatives on the Occasion of the Debate on the Budgets for 1990." Nicosia: Press and Information Office, November 16, 1989.

Thirgood, J.V. *Cyprus: A Chronicle of Its Forests, Land, and People.* Vancouver: University of British Columbia, 1987.

"Turkish Federated State of Cyprus." State Planning Organisation. *Statistical Yearbook, 1978.* Nicosia: 1979.

"Turkish Republic of Northern Cyprus." *North Cyprus Almanack.* London: K. Rüstem and Brother, 1987.

_____. State Planning Organisation. *Economic and Social Developments in the Turkish Republic of Northern Cyprus.* Nicosia, 1987.

_____. State Planning Organisation. Statistics and Research Department. *Statistical Yearbook, 1986.* Nicosia: 1987.

_____. State Planning Organisation. Statistics and Research Department. *Statistical Yearbook, 1987.* Nicosia: 1988.

United States. Department of Commerce, International Trade Administration. *Foreign Economic Trends and Their Implications for the United States: Cyprus.* Washington: GPO, October 1989.

Uras, Güngör. "Notes on the Economy of Cyprus." Pages 120-32 in SISAV (ed.), *The Political and Economic Problems of the Turkish Community of Cyprus in the International Field.* Istanbul: Fatih Gençlik Vaktı Matbaa İşletmesi, 1986.

Weaver, Mary Anne. "Report From Cyprus," *New Yorker,* 66, August 6, 1990, 65-66, 68-72, 74-81.

Yesilada, Birol. "Social Progress and Political Development in the Turkish Republic of Northern Cyprus," *Cyprus Review* [Nicosia], 1, No. 2, Fall 1989, 90-113.

(Various issues of the following publications were also used in the preparation of this chapter: *Economist* [London]; Economist Intelligence Unit, *Country Report: Lebanon, Cyprus* [London]; *Guardian*

[London]; *Neue Zürcher Zeitung* [Zurich]; *Sunday Times* [London]; *Times* [London].)

Chapter 4

Adams, Thomas W. *AKEL: The Communist Party of Cyprus.* (Hoover Institution Studies, No. 27.) Stanford: Hoover Institution Press, 1971.

Bahcheli, Tozun. *Greek-Turkish Relations since 1955.* Boulder, Colorado: Westview Press, 1990.

Bendahmane, Diane, and John W. McDonald, Jr. (eds.). *Perspectives on Negotiation: Four Case Studies and Interpretations.* Washington: GPO, 1986.

Birand, Mehmet Ali. "A Turkish View of Greek-Turkish Relations," *Journal of Political and Military Sociology,* 16, No. 2, Fall 1988, 173-83.

Crawshaw, Nancy. "Cyprus: A Failure in Western Diplomacy." *World Today* [London], 40, No. 2, February 1984, 73-78.

_____. "A New President for Cyprus." *World Today* [London], 44, No. 5, May 1988, 74-76.

Cyprus: International Law and the Prospects for Settlement. (Proceedings, 78th Annual Meeting of the American Society of International Law, Washington, April 12-14, 1984.)

Denktash [Denktaş], Rauf R. *The Cyprus Triangle.* London: K. Rüstem and Brother, 1982.

The Europa World Year Book, 1991, 1. London: Europa, 1991.

Groom, A.J.R. "Cyprus, Greece and Turkey: A Treadmill for Diplomacy." Pages 126-56 in John T.A. Koumoulides (ed.), *Cyprus in Transition, 1960-85.* London: Trigraph, 1986.

Haass, Richard N. "Cyprus: Moving Beyond Solution," *Washington Quarterly,* 10, No. 2, Spring 1987, 183-90.

Hitchens, Christopher. *Cyprus.* London: Quartet Books, 1984.

Jacobs, Francis (ed.). "Cyprus." Pages 500-19 in Francis Jacobs (ed.), *Western European Political Parties: A Comprehensive Guide.* Harlow, Essex, United Kingdom: Longman, 1989.

Kemp, Peter. "MEED Special Report: Cyprus." *Middle East Economic Digest* [London], 33, September 21, 1989, 9-10, 13-14.

Koumoulides, John T.A. (ed.). *Cyprus in Transition, 1960-1985.* London: Trigraph, 1986.

Kyle, Keith. *Cyprus.* (Report No. 30.) London: Minority Rights Group, 1984.

Kyriakides, Stanley. *Cyprus: Constitutionalism and Crisis Government.* Philadelphia: University of Pennsylvania Press, 1968.

Lafrenière, François, and Robert Mitchell. "Cyprus: Visions for the Future." (A Summary of Conference and Workshop Proceedings, November 1988 to June 1989.) (Working Paper No. 21.) Ottawa: Canadian Institute for International Peace and Security, 1991.

Laipson, Ellen B. "Cyprus: A Quarter Century of US Policy." Pages 54–81 in John T.A. Koumoulides (ed.), *Cyprus in Transition, 1960–1985*. London: Trigraph, 1986.

McCaskill, Charles. "U.S.-Greek Relations and the Problems of the Aegean and Cyprus," *Journal of Political and Military Sociology*, 16, No. 2, Fall 1988, 215–31.

McDonald, Robert. "International Implications of Ethnic Conflict in Cyprus." (Paper presented at ICES workshop on Internationalization of Ethnic Conflict, Colombo, Sri Lanka, August 1989.)

_____. *The Problem of Cyprus*. (Adelphi Papers, No. 234.) London: Brassey's for the International Institute for Strategic Studies, 1989.

Markides, Kyriacos C. *The Rise and Fall of the Cyprus Republic*. New Haven: Yale University Press, 1977.

The Middle East and North Africa, 1991. London: Europa, 1990.

Necatigil, Zaim M. *The Cyprus Conflict: A Lawyer's View*. Nicosia: K. Rüstem and Brother, 1981.

_____. *The Cyprus Question and the Turkish Position in International Law*. Oxford: Oxford University Press, 1989.

_____. "The Judicial System of the Turkish Republic of Northern Cyprus." *Northern Cyprus Monthly* [Nicosia], November 15, 1989, 13–15.

Oberling, Pierre. *The Cyprus Tragedy*. London: K. Rüstem and Brother, 1989.

Political Handbook of the World, 1991 (Ed., Arthur S. Banks). Binghamton, New York: CSA, 1991.

Polyviou, Polyvios G. *Cyprus—In Search of a Constitution*. Nicosia: Chr. Nicoaou and Sons, 1976.

Rüstem, K. (ed.). *North Cyprus Almanack*. London: K. Rüstem and Brother, 1987.

Sophocleous, Andreas C., and Panayiotis Papademetris. *Mass Media in Cyprus*. Nicosia: Republic of Cyprus, Press and Information Office, 1991.

Souter, David. "The Cyprus Conundrum." *Third World Quarterly* [London], 11, No. 2, April 1989, 76–91.

_____. "An Island Apart: A Review of the Cyprus Problem." *Third World Quarterly* [London], 6, No. 3, July 1984, 657–74.

The Statesman's Yearbook, 1990-91 (Ed., John Paxton). New York: St. Martin's Press, 1990.

Tsardanidis, Charalambos. "The EC-Cyprus Association Agreement: Ten Years of a Troubled Relationship, 1973-1983," *Journal of Common Market Studies* [Oxford], 22, No. 4, June 1984, 351-76.

_____. "The European Community and the Cyprus Problem since 1974." *Journal of Political and Military Sociology*, 16, No. 2, Fall 1988, 155-71.

United States. Central Intelligence Agency. *The World Factbook, 1991.* Washington: GPO, 1991.

_____. Congress. 98th, 1st Session. House of Representatives. Committee on Foreign Affairs. *Status of Negotiations on the Cyprus Dispute and Recent Developments in Cyprus.* Washington: GPO, 1984.

_____. Congress. 100th, 2d Session. House of Representatives. Committee on Foreign Affairs. *Greek-Turkish Relations: Beginning of a New Era?* Washington: GPO, 1988.

_____. Congress. 101st, 1st Session. Senate. Committee on Foreign Relations. *New Opportunities for U.S. Policy in the Eastern Mediterranean: A Staff Report to the Committee on Foreign Relations.* Washington: GPO, 1989.

Weaver, Mary Anne. "Report from Cyprus," *New Yorker*, 66, August 6, 1990, 65-66, 68-72, 74-81.

Chapter 5

Adams, T.W. "Cyprus." Pages 459-61 in Richard F. Staar (ed.), *1988 Yearbook on International Communist Affairs.* Stanford: Hoover Institution Press, 1988.

"Cyprus." Pages 268-74 in Gregory R. Copley (ed.), *Defense and Foreign Affairs Handbook.* Alexandria, Virginia: International Media, 1989.

"Defense Ministry on New Armed Civil Guard," Foreign Broadcast Information Service, *Western Europe.* (FBIS-WEU-89-057.) March 27, 1989, 34-35.

Dyer, Gwynne. "Cyprus." Pages 135-40 in John Keegan (ed.), *World Armies.* Detroit, Michigan: Gale Research, 1983.

Foss, Christopher F. "Cypriot Rearmament Completed," *Jane's Defence Weekly* [London], 10, No. 9, March 12, 1988, 445.

Fursdon, Edward. "UNFICYP," *Defense and Diplomacy* [United States], 7, No. 12, December 1989, 46-51.

James, Alan. "The UN force in Cyprus," *International Affairs* [London], 65, No. 3, Summer 1989, 481-500.

Kyle, Keith. *Cyprus.* (Report No. 30.) London: Minority Rights Group, 1984.

Laipson, Ellen B. *Cyprus: Status of U.N. Negotiations.* Library of Congress, Congressional Research Service. Washington: 1990.

"Law on Internal Organization of Police Department," *Resmi Gazete* [Nicosia], August 25, 1986. Foreign Broadcast Information Service, *West Europe Report.* (FBIS-WER-87-035.) April 27, 1987, 28-97.

McDonald, Robert. *The Problem of Cyprus.* (Adelphi Papers, No. 234.) London: Brassey's for the International Institute for Strategic Studies, 1989.

MacInnis, J.A. "Cyprus—Canada's Perpetual Vigil," *Canadian Defence Quarterly* [Toronto], 19, No. 1, August 1989, 21-26.

The Military Balance, 1989-90. London: International Institute for Strategic Studies, 1989.

Mitchell, Robert. *Peacekeeping and Peacemaking in Cyprus.* (Background Paper No. 23.) Ottowa: Canadian Institute for International Peace and Security, 1988.

Rüstem, K. (ed.). *North Cyprus Almanack.* London: K. Rüstem and Brother, 1987.

Tyler, Patrick E. "Smugglers, Gun Runners, Spies Cross Paths in Cyprus," *Washington Post,* March 12, 1987, A29, A36.

United Nations Security Council. *Report of the Secretary-General on the United Nations Operation in Cyprus* (for the period June 1–December 4, 1989). New York: 1989.

United States. Arms Control and Disarmament Agency. *World Military Expenditures and Armed Transfers 1988.* Washington: GPO, 1989.

———. Department of State. Bureau of Public Affairs. Office of Public Communication. *Background Notes: Cyprus.* (Department of State Publication No. 7932.) Washington: GPO, 1988.

———. Department of State. *Country Reports on Human Rights Practices for 1989.* (Report submitted to United States Congress, 101st, 2d Session, House of Representatives, Committee on Foreign Affairs, and Senate, Committee on Foreign Relations.) Washington: GPO, February 1990.

———. Department of State. *International Narcotics Control Strategy Report.* Washington: 1990.

———. Department of State. *Patterns of Global Terrorism, 1988.* Washington: 1989.

Weaver, Mary Anne. "Report from Cyprus," *New Yorker,* 66, August 6, 1990, 65-66, 68-72, 74-81.

(Various issues of the following publications were also used in the preparation of this chapter: Foreign Broadcast Information Service,

Daily Report: Western Europe; Jane's Defence Weekly [London]; Joint Publications Research Service, *Translations on Western Europe; Keesing's Record of World Events* [London]; *New York Times;* and *Washington Post.*

Glossary

Cyprus pound—(C£)—Republic of Cyprus monetary unit consisting of 100 cents. At independence C£1 was worth US$2.80. The average annual exchange rate for C£1 in 1979 was US$2.82; in 1982, US$2.11; in 1985, US$1.64; in 1986, US$1.94; in 1987, US$2.08; in 1988, US$2.14; in 1989, US$2.03; and in 1990, US$2.19.

European Community (EC—also commonly called the Community)—The EC comprises three communities: the European Coal and Steel Community (ECSC), the European Economic Community (EEC, also known as the Common Market), and the European Atomic Energy Community (EURATOM). Each community is a legally distinct body, but since 1967 they have shared common governing institutions. The EC forms more than a framework for free trade and economic cooperation: the signatories to the treaties governing the communities have agreed in principle to integrate their economies and ultimately to form a political union. Belgium, France, Italy, Luxembourg, the Netherlands, and the Federal Republic of Germany (West Germany) are charter members of the EC. Britain, Denmark, and Ireland joined on January 1, 1973; Greece became a member on January 1, 1981; and Portugal and Spain entered on January 1, 1986. Cyprus became an associate member in June 1973.

European Economic Community (EEC)—*See* European Community.

gross domestic product (GDP)—The total value of goods and services produced by the domestic economy during a given period, usually one year. Obtained by adding the value contributed by each sector of the economy in the form of profits, compensation to employees, and depreciation (consumption of capital). Most GDP usage in this book was based on GDP at factor cost. Real GDP is the value of GDP when inflation has been taken into account.

gross national product (GNP)—Obtained by adding GDP (*q.v.*) and the income received from abroad by residents less payments remitted abroad to nonresidents. Real GNP is the value of GNP when inflation has been taken into account.

International Monetary Fund (IMF)—Established along with the World Bank (*q.v.*) in 1945, the IMF is a specialized agency affiliated with the United Nations that takes responsibility for stabilizing international exchange rates and payments. The main business of the IMF is the provision of loans to its members when they experience balance of payment difficulties. These loans often carry conditions that require substantial internal economic adjustments by the recipients.

Latin—*See* Roman Catholic.

Roman Catholic—In historical use, the Latin Church refers to the western wing of Christianity using Latin as its liturgical language, jurisdictionally related to the bishop of Rome (the pope) rather than one of the other patriarchs, and generally corresponding to the area of the Western Roman Empire rather than the Eastern Roman or Byzantine section. After the Great Schism of 1054, those churches accepting papal authority became known as Catholic in contrast to the Orthodox; the vast majority of these were Latin rite or Roman Catholic. Since the religious conflict in Lusignan and Venetian Cyprus was as much cultural as one of hierarchical structure, Roman Catholics have continued to be known in Cyprus as Latins; the term also is used to distinguish the descendants of the former Lusignan and Venetian elites from Greek Cypriots.

Turkish lira (TL)—Monetary unit used in "Turkish Republic of Northern Cyprus." Also known as Turkish pound. Consists of 100 kurus. In terms of the United States dollar, the annual average exchange rate was TL19.3 in 1977, TL76.0 in 1980, TL522.0 in 1985, TL674.5 in 1986, TL857.2 in 1987, TL1,422.3 in 1988, TL2,121.7 in 1980, and TL2,608.6 in 1990.

Value-added tax (VAT)—A tax applied to the additional value created at a given stage of production and calculated as a percentage of the difference between the product value at that stage and the cost of all materials and services purchased as inputs. The VAT is the primary form of indirect taxation applied in the EEC (*q.v.*), and it is the basis of each country's contribution to the community budget.

World Bank—Informal name used to designate a group of three affiliated international institutions: the International Bank of Reconstruction and Development (IBRD), the International Development Association (IDA), and the International Finance Corporation (IFC). The IBRD, established in 1945, has the primary purpose of providing loans to developing countries for productive projects. The IDA, a legally separate loan fund administered by the staff of the IBRD, was set up in 1960 to furnish credits to the poorest developing countries on much easier terms than those of conventional IBRD loans. The IFC, founded in 1956, supplements the activities of the IBRD through loans and assistance designed specifically to encourage the growth of productive private enterprises in less developed countries. The president and certain senior officers of the IBRD hold the same positions in the IFC. The three institutions are owned by the governments of the countries that subscribe their capital. To participate in the World Bank group, member states must first belong to the International Monetary Fund (*q.v.*).

Index

285

social welfare, 79–80, 102–3; under British rule, 103; child and family, 79–80; economic assistance under, 80; objectives of, 82; services, 79; social defense services, 79

Society of Worldwide Interbank Financial Telecommunications (SWIFT), 137

Soli: as city-kingdom, 8

Southern Conveyor Project, 114, 119

Sovereign Base Areas, xxii, 32, 225, 233; Cypriot attitude toward, 234; intelligence gathering in, 233; personnel strength in, 233–34; as training sites, 233

Soviet Union, xxxii, 24; matériel from, 229, 230; policy of, toward settlement, 204–5; relations with, 203–5

Special Cyprus Coordinator, 204

Special Service for the Care and Rehabilitation of Displaced persons, 80–82; emergency relief, 80–81

SPO. *See* State Planning Organisation

standard of living, xxvi, 65; of Greek Cypriots, 57, 64; improvements in, 59, 65, 107; of Turkish Cypriots, 44, 145

State Laboratories Directorate, 102

State Planning Organisation (SPO), 143

state-sponsored entities, 143–44

storage, 134

Storrs, Ronald, 20

strategic importance, 109, 224–25, 199; to Crusaders, 13, 14; economic, 132; in World War II, 24

strikes: general, 30; outlawed, 31

subsidies: for agriculture, 113, 117, 123; for health care, 76; for livestock production, 124; from Turkey, 208

Suez Canal zone, 29

suffrage: male, 25–26; universal, 33; women's, 26

Supreme Constitutional Court, 33, 166–67, 170, 185, 194

Supreme Council of Judicature, 185

Supreme Court, 170, 185, 194

Sweden: in United Nations Peace-keeping Force in Cyprus (UNFICYP), 216, 236

SWIFT. *See* Society of Worldwide Interbank Financial Telecommunications

Switzerland: loans from, 231; matériel from, 229

symferon, 67

Synomospondia Ergaton Kyprou (SEK). *See* Cyprus Workers' Confederation

Syria, 12, 223

Tactical Police Reserve, 238; organized, 218

taksim, 4, 49, 57, 168

Taliotis, Yiannakis,

Tamassos: as city-kingdom, 8

tariffs: instituted, 127; reduced, 113; removed, 127, 129, 141

Tarım Sigortası, 147

Taurus Mountains, 50

taxes: and agriculture, 117; under British, 22; income, 114, 170; proposed, 114; remissions of, 127; revenue from, 114, 115; used for defense, 230

teachers, 73; training, 100; women as, 70

telecommunications, 109, 111, 134, 135, 156–57

telephones, 135, 157

television, 135, 157, 188, 197

Tenzel, James H., 87

terrain, 50–53

terrorism, 223–24

tertiary sector. *See* service sector

Thutmose III, 5

TKP. *See* Communal Liberation Party

TMT. *See* Turkish Resistance Organization

Toplumcu Kurtuluş Partisi (TKP). *See* Communal Liberation Party

tourist industry, xxvi, xxxiii, 54, 110, 132, 144, 157; construction for, 130, 131, 154; effect of Turkish invasion on, 132; employment in, 115, 132, 145; expansion of, 43–44, 65, 107, 108, 132–34, 154, 157; foreign exchange from, 157; as percentage of GDP, 109; receipts, 110, 138; as source of foreign exchange, 108, 109; upgrading of, 107, 113, 133–34

tourists, 117; demographics of, 133; number of, 109, 132, 157

trade, 109, 132, 157–58; in ancient period, 5; deficit, 110, 112, 138, 140–41, 158; exhibitions, 128; in medieval period, 14; as percentage of GDP, 132; value added by, 132

trade unions. *See* labor unions

Trade Unions Law, 146

Published Country Studies

(Area Handbook Series)

550-65	Afghanistan		550-87	Greece
550-98	Albania		550-78	Guatemala
550-44	Algeria		550-174	Guinea
550-59	Angola		550-82	Guyana and Belize
550-73	Argentina		550-151	Honduras
550-169	Australia		550-165	Hungary
550-176	Austria		550-21	India
550-175	Bangladesh		550-154	Indian Ocean
550-170	Belgium		550-39	Indonesia
550-66	Bolivia		550-68	Iran
550-20	Brazil		550-31	Iraq
550-168	Bulgaria		550-25	Israel
550-61	Burma		550-182	Italy
550-50	Cambodia		550-30	Japan
550-166	Cameroon		550-34	Jordan
550-159	Chad		550-56	Kenya
550-77	Chile		550-81	Korea, North
550-60	China		550-41	Korea, South
550-26	Colombia		550-58	Laos
550-33	Commonwealth Caribbean, Islands of the		550-24	Lebanon
550-91	Congo		550-38	Liberia
550-90	Costa Rica		550-85	Libya
550-69	Côte d'Ivoire (Ivory Coast)		550-172	Malawi
550-152	Cuba		550-45	Malaysia
550-22	Cyprus		550-161	Mauritania
550-158	Czechoslovakia		550-79	Mexico
550-36	Dominican Republic and Haiti		550-76	Mongolia
550-52	Ecuador		550-49	Morocco
550-43	Egypt		550-64	Mozambique
550-150	El Salvador		550-35	Nepal and Bhutan
550-28	Ethiopia		550-88	Nicaragua
550-167	Finland		550-157	Nigeria
550-155	Germany, East		550-94	Oceania
550-173	Germany, Fed. Rep. of		550-48	Pakistan
550-153	Ghana		550-46	Panama